THE SOCIAL AND ETHNIC DIMENSIONS OF MATTHEAN SALVATION HISTORY

"Go nowhere among the Gentiles . . ." (Matt. 10:5b)

Amy-Jill Levine

THE SOCIAL AND ETHNIC DIMENSIONS OF MATTHEAN SALVATION HISTORY

"Go nowhere among the Gentiles . . ." (Matt. 10:5b)

Amy-Jill Levine

Studies in the Bible and Early Christianity
Volume 14

The Edwin Mellen Press
Lewiston•Queenston
Lampeter

Library of Congress Cataloging-in-Publication Data

Levine, Amy-Jill, 1956-
The social and ethnic dimensions of Matthean salvation history/
Amy-Jill Levine.
p. cm. -- (Studies in the Bible and early Christianity; v.
14)
Bibliography: p.
Includes index.
ISBN 0-88946-614-9
1. Bible. N.T. Matthew--Criticism, interpretation, etc.
2. Sociology, Biblical. 3. Jews in the New Testament. 4. Gentiles
in the New Testament. 5. Great Commission (Bible) I. Title.
II. Series.
BS2575.2.L48 1988
226' .2067--dc19
88-12701
CIP

This is volume 14 in the continuing series
Studies in Bible & Early Christianity
Volume 14 ISBN 0-88946-614-9
SBEC Series ISBN 0-88946-913-X

The Edwin Mellen Press

Box 450
Lewiston, New York
USA 14092

Box 67
Queenston, Ontario
L0S 1L0 CANADA

Mellen House
Lampeter, Dyfed, Wales
UNITED KINGDOM SA48 7DY

Printed in the United States of America

For

Anne H. Levine

Table of Contents

ACKNOWLEDGMENTS

My deepest gratitude is due to the following individuals who have, in various ways, contributed to the research and writing of this work. Frank H. Ellis and Nora Crow Jaffe of Smith College stimulated my interest in literature and taught me that humor need not be exorcised from the educational process; Karl Donfried both inspired me to pursue advanced work in biblical studies and gave me the training in order to accomplish that goal. To Dr. W. D. Davies I am particularly grateful. The present study springs directly from his Duke University graduate seminar on the Gospel of Matthew. The insights of both Dr. Davies and my colleagues in the class, particularly Dale C. Allison, Jr. and Randall D. Chesnutt, have contributed subtantially to my understanding of the first gospel. Also at Duke, both D. Moody Smith and Elizabeth Clark selflessly spent time discussing the various ideas contained in this work. Their dedication to their students is equalled only by the example their excellent scholarship sets. To Kalman Bland, Wesley Kort, James H. Charlesworth, James Rolleston, Conrad Levesque, and Arthur H. Bennett, Jr. I also express my thanks. Appreciation is due as well to the Swarthmore College Faculty Research Fund and to Kristen Johnson, Lee Mercone, Lori Kenschaft, Edward Hsu, and especially Bill Ryan, who have undertaken the mechanics of preparing the text for publication.

Finally, mention must be made of the three people who inspire and guide in very special ways. Saul Levine, whose bedtime stories to me were often articles in the old *Jewish Encyclopedia,* would have been proud that his daughter followed his interest in Jewish history. Anne H. Levine, who still wonders what this nice Jewish girl is doing in the field of New Testament studies, nevertheless continues to encourage me as only a parent can. Jay Geller shared his knowledge of method, his critical insights, and his editing expertise; further, without his understanding, his support, his love, and his willingness to spend those needed extra hours with our daughter, Sarah Elizabeth, this study never would have materialized.

Abbreviations

Ant	Josephus *Antiquities of the Jews*
ATR	*Anglican Theological Review*
BAG	W. Bauer, *A Greek-English Lexicon of the New Testament and Other Early Christian Writings*, 4th rev. ed., trans. and adapted by W. F. Arndt and F. W. Gingrich
CBQ	*Catholic Biblical Quarterly*
ET	*Expository Times*
Int	*Interpretation*
JBL	*Journal of Biblical Literature*
HTR	*Harvard Theological Review*
HUCA	*Hebrew Union College Annual*
JB	*Jerusalem Bible*
JJS	*Journal of Judaic Studies*
JSNT	*Journal for the Study of the New Testament*
LXX	Septuagint
MT	Masoretic Text
NEB	*New English Bible*
NTS	*New Testament Studies*
NovTest	*Novum Testamentum*
RSV	*Revised Standard Version*
ScottJT	*Scottish Journal of Theology*
SNTSB	*Studiorum Novi Testamenti Societas Bulletin*
Stanton	Stanton, G. (ed.). *The Interpretation of Matthew*, Issues in Religion and Theology 3
StEv	*Studia Evangelica*
StTh	*Studia Theologica*
TDNT	*Theological Dictionary of the New Testament*
TLZ	*Theologische Literaturzeitung*

TS	*Theological Studies*
TU	*Texte und Untersuchungen zur Geschichte der altchristlichen Literatur*
TZ	*Theologische Zeitschrift*
VT	*Vetus Testamentum*
ZNW	*Zeitschrift für die neutestamentliche Wissenschaft*
ZTK	*Zeitschrift für Theologie und Kirche*
ZWT	*Zeitschrift für wissenschaftliche Theologie*

Introduction

Jesus' command in Matt 10:5b that his disciples "go nowhere among the gentiles" has long been a focus of critical debate. From the Patristic writers who adopted allegorical explanations of the logion to the modern tendency to assign the statement to a Jewish-Christian source, the exclusivistic restriction of the mission has been viewed as antithetical both to Jesus' and to Matthew's universalistic outlook. The true expression of Christian soteriology, this interpretation claims, is revealed in a passage viewed as inconsistent with the verse's thrust: the Great Commission with which the gospel concludes. Even when the creative capacities of the evangelists to omit, modify, and invent material are acknowledged, Matt 10:5b-6 and its companion verse 15:24 remain classified as un-Christian in the abstract and inconsistent within the specific context of the gospel. For example, J. P. Meier concludes: "by constructing...a schema of difference-within-continuity...Matthew is able to accept the Jewish-Christian traditions of his church and insert them into a higher synthesis, a higher viewpoint."[1]

The claim that the evangelist depicts a Jewish-Christian exclusivism superseded by a higher, more "purely Christian" program is problematic. Literary-critical and sociological

---

[1] *The Vision of Matthew: Christ, Church and Morality in the First Gospel* (New York: Paulist, 1979), p. 30; cf. R. Brown and J. P. Meier, *Antioch and Rome* (New York and Ramsay, NJ: Paulist, 1983), p. 59.

analyseś both call into question the traditional interpretations of the gospel and provide an alternative: the Matthean program of salvation history revolves around two axes. The evangelist has constructed a temporal axis, along which falls the distinction between the time of Jesus and the time of the church, and a social axis, which transcends the religious as well as the ethnic implications of this temporal distinction.

This study seeks to redress the methodologically questionable and often implicitly anti-Jewish technique of negatively valuing the exclusivity logia and then assigning them to a narrow "Jewish-Christian" source incompatible with Matthew's own outlook. It, further, attempts to avoid the implication that the evangelist is either an incompetent author who presents contradictory material or a redactor constrained to repeat received material that conflicts with an overall vision. Therefore, I begin with the premise that the exclusivity logia and the Great Commission are complementary statements explicable without recourse to apologetic, hypothetical sources, or an unflattering assessment of the evangelist's ability.

Matthew 10:5b-6 signals for the gospel one end of the temporal axis that begins in the Hebrew scriptures.[2] By

---

[2]Since Tertullian (*De Fuga in Persecutione* 6; cf. *De Praescriptione Haereticorum* 8) biblical scholars have entertained the theory that Matt 10:5b-6 was applicable only to the time of Jesus' ministry. See, among others, M. Hooker, "Uncomfortable Words X: The Prohibition of Foreign Missions (Matt 10[5-6]," *ET* 82 (1971): 363; N. A. Dahl, "The Passion Narrative in Matthew," in Stanton, p. 52; G. Strecker, "The Concept of History in Matthew," in Stanton, p. 72; J. S. Kennard, Jr., "The Place of Origin of Matthew's Gospel," *ATR* 31 (1949): 244 (following B. H. Streeter, *The Four Gospels* [London: Macmillan, 1956], p. 502); M. H. Franzmann, *Follow Me: Discipleship According to St. Matthew* (St. Louis: Concordia,

restricting the mission of Jesus and of his disciples to the Jewish community, the evangelist offers twin points usually associated with Paul, another Jew struggling with the problems of the gentiles flooding a church founded by Jews. First, Matthew reinforces the fulfillment of the promises made to the Jews -- to them belong the sonship, the covenants, and the Christ (cf. Rom 9:4-5); second, the exclusivity statements recapitulate the progress of Jesus' career itself -- "Christ became a servant to the circumcised to show God's truthfulness, in order to confirm the promises given to the patriarchs" (Rom 15:8).

At the other end of the axis, marked by the resurrection and the concomitant shift in Jesus' christological status, the mission is extended to the gentiles. But the Great Commission (Matt 28:16-20) does not entail a loss of privilege for the Jewish community; instead it indicates that the gentiles now stand on an equal level with the Jews. Because the Great Commission is both structurally and thematically a rewriting of the mission discourse of chapter 10 in light of the resurrection, continuity with the first era -- including the mission to the Jews and the promises granted to them -- is maintained rather than abolished.

1961), p. 222; Stephen G. Wilson, *The Gentiles and the Gentile Mission in Luke-Acts* (Cambridge: University Press, 1973), pp. 14-15; J. P. Meier, "Salvation-History in Matthew: In Search of a Starting Point," *CBQ* 37 (1975): 204-5 and n. 4 ("There is here no sloppy, eclectic, or schizophrenic juxtaposition of contradictory material...Matthew is quite consciously ordering an 'economy of salvation': To the Jew first, and then to the Gentiles"); and T. W. Manson, *Jesus and the Non-Jews* (London: Athlone, 1955), p. 3 and n. 6. See also W. G. Thompson, "An Historical Perspective in the Gospel of Matthew," *JBL* 93 (1974): 252-53; and J. Blauw, *Missionary Nature of the Church* (New York: McGraw-Hill, 1962), p. 71.

Matthew's soteriological program conforms to a second axis which transcends these ethnic and religious distinctions between Jew and gentile. The social axis delineates its own criterion for salvation: faith manifested in action. Although the temporal axis indicates that until the resurrection the Jews retain their privileged position in salvation history, the social axis reveals this ethnic division is ultimately subsumed under and, in the era of the church, made irrelevant by the more general categories of authority and oppression, of elites and marginals. While lepers, sinners, tax collectors, and even gentiles who manifest faith in Jesus are rewarded, the leaders of both the Jewish and gentile societies who exclude others from equal participation in those societies and who set their own power against that of heaven are the true sons who are cast into the outer darkness.

Most modern scholarship remains content with the conclusion that Matthean soteriology is based on the thematic division between recalcitrant Jews and faithful gentiles, and several instances in the gospel can be invoked to support this viewpoint. For example, the eschatological pronouncement in Matt 8:11-12 is usually interpreted as creating a correspondence on the one hand between the Jews and the "sons of the *Basileia*" and, on the other, between the gentiles and the many who dine with the patriarchs. Or, Herod and "all Jerusalem" are seen to represent faithless Judaism while the Magi symbolize the faithful gentiles who inherit the new covenant community. But such interpretations of both passages ignore the implications of the contextual placement of the relevant verses, and each is occasioned by the limitations of the historical-critical method.

While not discounting historical criticism and its attendent methods (e.g., text, source, form, and redaction criticisms), this book employs textual strategies shared by deconstruction and feminist analysis. First, rather than locate Matt 10:5b-6 and 15:24 on the periphery of the gospel, I have placed them at the center of Matthew's program of salvation history. If this procedure leads to a consistent, plausible reading of the gospel -- and I believe that it does -- then both the interpretation of the verses themselves and the interpretation of the entire gospel need to be reformulated from the traditional scholarly understanding. Second, one methodological principle associated particularly with feminist criticism emphasizes the search for and advocacy of relationships and continuities rather than divisions and oppositional categories. Indeed, the premise of this study involves placing the restriction of the mission in continuity with the design of the narrative whole and not in opposition to it. Third, my approach adopts the premise, succinctly expressed by William Thompson, that "Matthew's editorial activity...was so thoroughgoing and proceeded out of such a unique vision that it transformed all that he [*sic*] touched."[3] The evangelist's ability to manipulate numerical patterns, to emphasize through recapitulation and repetition, and to redact sources for purposes of updating, reinforcing, or correcting has long been recognized.

Contextual analysis indicates that faithful gentiles are not only contrasted with perfidious Jews determined to kill Jesus or otherwise prevent the birth of the church, they are also compared to faithful Jews equally interested in hearing the gospel message. Thus the gentile supplicant of 8:5-13 has more in common with the marginal or disenfranchised members of the local Jewish society -- the leper, Peter's

---

[3]"Historical Perspective," p. 244 n. 2; and on "composition criticism," idem, *Matthew's Advice to a Divided Community: Mt. 17,22-18,35* (Rome: Biblical Institute, 1970), pp. 7-10, 166-67.

mother-in-law, the sinners and the tax collectors, the deaf, and even the truly marginal, the dead -- than he does with either the Jewish leadership or with his own military superior, Pontius Pilate. And while the gentile Magi are contrasted with the Jewish-identified Herod, they find a parallel in the explicitly Jewish Holy Family who remain faithful to the tradition of their past and in conformity to the fulfillment quotations that describe their actions.

The appropriation of analytic categories such as elite and marginal sharpens the outline of the social axis. The cross-ethnic association of faithlessness with the leaders of the community and its inverse, the equation of the marginal with the faithful, are first indicated in the genealogy, continue in the infancy material, are epitomized in the narrative section between the Sermon on the Mount and the second discourse (chapter 10), reappear in the condemnation of the disciples' desire for power (20:20-28) and the similar complaint against the Pharisees (23:10-12), and receive subtle repetition in the failures of the disciples during the passion.

Matthew's depiction of the disciples offers a further indication of the gospel's cross-ethnic focus. Marginal individuals of both Jewish and gentile background are contrasted not only with the Jewish elite but also with others who might claim privileged status: the disciples of both Jesus and John. Chapters 8-9 provide another example of this motif: while the soldier's faith is lauded and the woman who stopped Jesus in the crowd is "saved" because of her faith, the twelve are of "little faith" (ὀλιγόπιστος), and the disciples of the Baptist align themselves thematically not with the sinners and the suffering members of the Jewish community, but with the Pharisees and scribes. Throughout the gospel Jesus continually insists that discipleship is based on egalitarian principles rather than on the privileged positions of the few. The many unnamed individuals who follow Jesus during his mission heed this message; the Pharisees and, surprisingly, the disciples frequently ignore it.

The position of the faithful on the periphery of official society also questions the legitimacy of the generally acknowledged religious and social centers. Urban areas compare unfavorably with the open road; the two missions begin not from Jerusalem but from an unnamed mountain in Galilee; even the focus of the church shifts from the Temple to the continuing but unlocalized presence of Jesus within the community. Rather than establish a new center -- which always presupposes a periphery -- Matthew reinforces the egalitarian structure of the church by refusing to locate it spatially. By shifting from both an institutionalized, centralized, and geographically fixed cult and a synagogue system directed by a self-appointed elite to a church lacking a physical center and based on the activities of the divinely commissioned eleven, the evangelist both reinforces the egalitarian character of the Christian community and distinguishes the church from all previous institutions, both Jewish and gentile.

Confirming the importance of the categories of center and periphery is Matthew's consistent association between faithfulness and mobility, faithlessness and stasis. While Jesus, the disciples, the Holy Family, the Magi, the women from Galilee, and even the crowds who follow Jesus are all characterized by mobility, Herod, the Pharisees, Pilate, and the chief priests are well positioned in every sense of the term. Mobility and stasis are not simply arbitrary descriptive devices geared to provide a handy distinction between the faithful and the faithless, they are heuristics utilized by the evangelist to indicate the radical shift created by the church's social focus. Matthew opposes centrally oriented systems in which everything and everyone has a particular function, status is determined by position rather than action, and a prevailing patriarchal system structures modes of relationships. In the gospel's purview, action or mobility denies the eternal validity of these established positions and threatens the existence of the system: change is afoot. For Matthew, the only valid position, a seat at the heavenly banquet, is determined by faith manifested in action, and not by descent, relation to the center, or position in a hierarchy.

These conclusions have substantial implications for both exegesis and hermeneutics. For example, because Matt 10:5b-6 is usually viewed as antithetic to the evangelist's interests, it is almost invariably classified as traditional and so usually assigned to that proverbial, narrow, Jewish-Christian [M] source. More rarely it is considered authentic Jesus material. Scholars in part have hesitated to view the logion as authentic because its interpretation conflicts with preconceived notions of how the messiah is to act. As Morna Hooker observes, "what offends the Christian in the suggestion that Mt 10:5-6 is a true report of Jesus' attitude...is the idea that he might have shared the notion that privilege was confined to the chosen people."[4] The recognition of the temporal axis calls both assignations into question and provides a helpful framework within which the possible redactional origins of the logion can be discussed.

Any exegesis of the first gospel's program of salvation history in general and of such verses as 10:5b-6, 15:24, 23:15, and 28:19 also necessarily leads to a discussion of the relationship between Matthew's church and the synagogue. Since Papias first indicated that "Matthew compiled the reports in the Hebrew language" and Eusebius added that the evangelist "preached among the Hebrews" the question of the

---

[4]"Uncomfortable Words," p. 364.

relationship between the gospel and the Jewish community has been a mainstay of Matthean exegesis. Some commentators emphasize the intimate courtship between Jesus and the adoring Jewish crowds and the marriage of traditions signaled by the fulfillment quotations and the restriction of Jesus' mission to the "lost sheep of the house of Israel." Yet pointing to such vituperative attacks as the polemic against the Pharisees in Matthew 23, they all acknowledge that there was trouble in the marriage.[5] Others suggest a divorce has occurred: the church has separated from the synagogue and gone to court the gentiles.[6] And a third party identifies the relationship as a fiction, suggesting instead that the evangelist or a later redactor has remained faithful to one spouse: the gentile community.[7] Each position can be

---

[5]On the *intra muros* conflict see in particular: G. Bornkamm, "End-Expectation and Church in Matthew," in G. Bornkamm et al., *Tradition and Interpretation in Matthew* (Philadelphia: Westminster, 1963), pp. 22, 39; A. W. Argyle, *The Gospel According to Matthew* (Cambridge: University Press, 1963), pp. 4-7; W. D. Davies, *The Setting of the Sermon on the Mount* (Cambridge: University Press, 1964), pp. 290-91; and cf. R. Hummel, *Die Auseinandersetzung zwischen Kirche und Judentum im Matthäusevangelium* (Munich: Kaiser, 1966), pp. 28-33.

[6]D. R. A. Hare, *The Theme of Jewish Persecution of Christians in the Gospel According to St. Matthew* (Cambridge: University Press, 1967), p. 5 (but classifying the evangelist as a "moderately conservative" Jewish-Christian); R. P. Martin, "St. Matthew's Gospel in Recent Study," *ET* 80 (1969): 136; S. van Tilborg, *The Jewish Leaders in Matthew* (Leiden: Brill, 1972), pp. 26, 66; D. Hill, *The Gospel of Matthew* (London: Oliphants, 1972), pp. 41, 50.

[7]K. W. Clark, "The Gentile Bias in Matthew," *JBL* 66 (1947): 165-72; G. Strecker, *Der Weg der Gerechtigkeit* (Göttingen: Vandenhoeck and Ruprecht, 1966), pp. 34-35 (final redactor a

supported with quotations from the text, and each can be countered with alternative citations. As Meier states: "If there is one area of Matthean Studies in which consensus does not reign, it is in the question of a Jewish-Christian vs. Gentile-Christian redactor."[8]

The dual axes of the gospel's salvation history offer a solution to this crux. The temporal axis indicates that the church's mission has extended to the gentiles: therefore it is likely that some members of the community were of non-Jewish ancestry. And the gospel's stress on continuity with Jewish tradition as well as the obvious struggle with the Jewish leadership signaled by the social axis indicates that ethnic Jews too belonged to Matthew's community.[9] But members of this church would classify themselves as neither "Jew" nor "gentile"; in the new era of the ἐκκλησία, the terms are no longer operative. The "gentile" or, perhaps more accurately translated "pagan," is that person who refuses to

---

gentile Christian); L. Gaston, "The Messiah of Israel as Teacher of the Gentiles: The Setting of Matthew's Christology," *Int* 29 (1975): 34. See also the summaries of all three positions in Thompson, *Matthew's Advice* , p. 11; and especially J. P. Meier, *Law and History in Matthew's Gospel. A Redactional Study of Mt. 5:17-48* (Rome: Biblical Institute, 1976), pp. 7-20. S. Brown, "The Matthean Community and the Gentile Mission," *NovTest* 22 (1980): 215-18, identifies the evangelist as a gentile presiding over a church split over engaging in a gentile mission because "orthodox Judaism's hostility to Jewish Christianity...dried up the source of Jewish conversions."

[8] *Law and History*, p. 163.

[9] Although the evangelist's ethnic background is still a matter of debate, "Matthew" is best viewed as an ethnic Jew writing to a predominantly Jewish church. Whether the gospel's authorship is individual or collective, female or male, is even more debatable.

heed the Christian message: the ἐθνικός of 6:7 and 18:17 epitomizes the gentile world set apart from the church. And the Jews, the Ἰουδαίοι, are those who continue to assert that the resurrection was a fraud: these are the people mentioned in 28:15. Consequently, the church is neither the new Israel nor the true Israel. The time of Israel, the time when the Jews retain their privileged position in salvation history, ends with the crucifixion and resurrection. The new era belongs not to Israel at all, but to the ἐκκλησία. And in the era of the church, the mission remains open to the "lost sheep of the house of Israel" and to "all the gentiles" (πάντα τὰ ἔθνη) who must hear the word before the final judgment.

The hermeneutical implications of these conclusions affect both Jewish-Christian relations in the modern world and feminist analysis of Western religious traditions. For the former, Jews and Christians can find common ground in the gospel's supersession of ethnic and religious differences by an appeal to moral behavior. And for the latter, the gospel provides an excellent example of the breakdown of patriarchal viewpoints. For example, not only does Matthew restructure the family into one in which mothers and children rather than fathers are the norm (cf. 12:50), the evangelist dismantles all forms of hierarchies. The text does more than ultimately dispense with ethnic categorizations: it depicts an ideal of egalitarianism guided by the paradigm of service to all. For this text, neither Jews nor gentiles can claim ontological superiority; disciples are not superior to sinners; and men are not superior to women. All are under the protection of the deity who, by the Christ event interpreted through the various lenses of Jewish tradition, shows solidarity with rather than distance from the new covenant community.

I

The Exclusivity Logion and Matthean Salvation History

According to most of the critical literature, the limitation of the disciples' mission to the "lost sheep of the house of Israel" in Matt 10:5b-6 is traditional material inconsistent with the gospel's universalism. Those commentaries arguing that the words are from the historical Jesus explain the verse in one of two ways. Some see the restriction as an example of representative universalism: through the Jews the nations of the world will be redeemed. Others view 10:5b-6 as an anticipation of the eschatological pilgrimage of the nations: the Jews will achieve redemption in the present, and at the end of time the deity will bring about the salvation of the gentiles. The majority of studies, however, locate the logion in a Jewish-Christian community antithetic to the gentile mission. Regardless of where these commentaries find the source of 10:5b-6, they conclude that the evangelist is either inconsistent or is constrained to preserve earlier material whose content has been supplanted. Even in those few studies which pronounce 10:5b-6 (and, by implication, 15:24) harmonious with Matthew's soteriological program, the restriction is seen as contradictory to the final universalistic thrust of the text. In such cases, the restriction is most often seen as evidence of Israel's last chance; the mission is limited to the Jews *in order that* their guilt might be completed. Thus, if the statement is assigned to Jesus it is most often viewed as positively privileging the Jews, and no negative evaluation of the gentiles is emphasized; if it is assigned to a Jewish-Christian source, the implication is that it stems from ethnic prejudice against gentiles; and if it is assigned to the evangelist, then Matthew is implicitly categorized as anti-Jewish.

The following pages suggest that assigning the exclusivity statement to a source is methodologically problematic and that labeling it inconsistent with Matthean universalism misinterprets the narrative as a whole. Rather than antithetical to the evangelist's universalism, Matt 10:5b-6 is a central part of the gospel's soteriological pattern. Along the temporal axis, Jesus' mission and message are continuous with the era of Abraham and David, of the prophets and John the Baptist -- in other words, of Israel. Consequently, during his ministry the Jews still possess their privileged position in salvation history. In the new era inaugurated by the Great Commission, the exclusivity pronouncement is abrogated, the privileges of the Jews are extended to all the gentiles, and a third group -- the ἐκκλησία -- joins the pagans and the Jews in the historical process. Matthew 10:5b-6 can also be plotted along the social axis: the expression "lost sheep of the house of Israel" does not primarily refer to the entire Jewish community which is in a lost state; the phrase emphasizes the people betrayed by and distanced from their leaders and the structures of patriarchy these leaders uphold. It is to such marginal participants in society that Jesus' message is particularly directed. Instead of signaling the guilt of the corporate community, Matt 10:5b-6 therefore both reinforces the temporal privileges of Israel and anticipates the ultimate cross-ethnic distinction of elites characterized by exploitation and stasis from the marginal and disenfranchised characterized by faith and mobility.

The Argument for Authenticity

According to the classical formulation, the case for the "authenticity" of a particular logion -- that is, for claiming the statement was pronounced by the historical Jesus -- should be supported by the criteria of *dissimilarity* (distinction from the proclamations of both the early church and first-century Judaism), *multiple attestation* (appearance in independent sources), *coherence* (consistency with material determined to be authentic on the basis of the first two criteria), and *consonance* (consistency with linguistic, cultural, and environmental factors of the period).[1] The difficulties with these criteria are almost as well known as their formulation. Is present knowledge of either first-century Judaisms or early Christianities sufficient to satisfy the criterion of dissimilarity? Does this criterion produce an unbalanced portrait of Jesus by eliminating his principal concerns -- which may have been similar to many Pharisaic claims, for example -- and emphasizing details peripheral to his preaching? Or, does it overemphasize Jesus' perceived uniqueness so that the creative artistry of his followers goes unnoticed? The criterion of multiple attestation has its own stumbling blocks: how is the independence of sources to be established since scholars still debate the connections among the synoptics, the relationship between the first three gospels and John has yet to be settled, and the familiarity of the

[1]Helpful summaries include Norman Perrin, *What is Redaction Criticism?* (Philadelphia: Fortress, 1969); E. Käsemann, "The Problem of the Historical Jesus," *Essays on New Testament Themes* (Napierville, IL: Allenson, 1964). For criticisms, see esp. M. Hooker, "Christology and Methodology," *NTS* 17 (1971): 481-85. On the limitations of applying form criticism to the first gospel, see Thompson, *Matthew's Advice*, pp. 7-10; Krister Stendahl, *The School of Saint Matthew*, 2d ed. (Philadelphia: Fortress, 1968), pp. 13-19.

evangelists with Pauline material remains disputed? The criterion of coherence faces not only the caveats applied to the first two steps, it has a comparatively greater dependence on the viewpoint of the interpreter which, while in itself not a bad thing, can lead to "leap of faith" arguments to which questions or challenges cannot be applied. And apart from obvious anachronisms or cultural accommodations the criterion of consonance offers little in the way of a check on the other steps. Conversely, even if a statement can be shown to be consonant with life in first-century Palestine through the use of "translations" into Aramaic, this is still no guarantee that the material represents Jesus' own outlook or opinion.

The rise of redaction criticism and its literary-critical offspring has also weakened the principles upon which both the search for the historical Jesus and the reconstruction of the early church are based. As the creative talents of the evangelists are unearthed, the separation of tradition (either authentic material or material preserved by the early church) from redaction becomes increasingly difficult. The composers of the gospels may have fully agreed with their received materials; they may have created new sayings and stories by elaborating upon their sources; they may have modified their writings to reinforce old values, to inculcate new ones, to emphasize theological fervor, or even to display literary artistry. These observations are particularly applicable to Matthew, whose narrative art is well known. As O. L. Cope states, "a major cause of the current confusion [over the first evangelist's background] has been the lack of any definite, critically defensible way of separating tradition from Matthean redaction."[2] Finally, the categories of authentic,

---

[2] *Matthew, A Scribe Trained for the Kingdom of Heaven* (Washington, D.C.: Catholic Biblical Association, 1976), pp. 2-

traditional, and redactional are themselves flawed: all the extant material has undergone at least one stage of editing. The eyewitnesses and ministers of the first Christian generation not only preserved what they heard, they supplemented it, interpreted it, and placed it in various contexts depending upon their particular ecclesiological needs or aesthetic tastes.

Such difficulties need not, however, lead to the extreme position of those within biblical studies who assert the futility of "doing history" and whose literary, philosophical, and aesthetic analyses divorce the text from its historical and cultural contexts. Instead, they caution against allowing one approach -- source or composition criticism, the historical-critical method, or narratology -- to dominate the analysis to such an extent that the insights of the others are ignored or declared worthless. Therefore, a complete analysis of Matt 10:5b-6 requires an investigation both of its literary function and of its historical background. The first approach responds to the claim that the statement is received material antithetic to the gospel's agenda of universalism; the second is mandatory if the gospel is to be appreciated as a literary whole.

The investigation of Matt 10:5b-6 according to the

3; but see W. O. Walker, Jr., "A Method for Identifying Redactional Passages in Matthew on Functional and Linguistic Grounds," *CBQ* 39 (1977): 76-93. On the evangelist's literary art, see e.g., N. Perrin, "The Evangelist as Author: Reflections on Method in the Study and Interpretation of the Synoptic Gospels and Acts," *Biblical Research* 17 (1972): 10; Thompson, *Matthew's Advice*, pp. 7-10, 266-67; S. V. McCasland, "Matthew Twists the Scriptures," *JBL* 80 (1961): 146; J. Rohde, *Rediscovering the Teachings of the Evangelists* (Philadelphia: Westminster, 1968), pp. 14, 37-38; E. von Dobschütz, "Matthäus als Rabbi und Katechet," *ZNW* 27 (1928): 338-40.

criteria of authenticity is inconclusive. The claim of dissimilarity is countered by the diversity of early Christianity. While one scholar cites Acts 11:20ff. to indicate that "the church which since pre-Pauline times had been engaged on mission...would not have created such a particularistic saying,"[3] it is not clear that Luke is reflecting the same church of which Matthew is a member; nor is it clear that Luke is historically trustworthy. Indeed, if Jesus had been so explicit about the universal mission of his disciples, then passages depicting the hesitancy of various early Christians toward approaching the gentiles become difficult to explain. Acts 11:19, for example, states that "those who were scattered because of the persecution that arose over Stephen" engaged in mission work to Phoenicia, Cyprus, and Antioch, *speaking the word to none except Jews* " (μηδενὶ λαλοῦντες τὸν λόγον εἰ μὴ μόνον Ἰουδαίοις). This group -- likely comprised of Diaspora Jews [Hellenists] -- could have invented a logion such as Matt 10:5b-6 to support its limited focus. Although this evidence from Acts makes the historicity of the exclusivity statement plausible, it does not clinch the argument.

The uniqueness of the logion eliminates the criterion of multiple attestation. While Luke's pre-resurrected Jesus does not inaugurate the formal mission to the gentiles, he is depicted as willingly healing non-Jews: the centurion's son in 7:1-10 (cf. Matt 8:5-13) as well as the Samaritan in 17:16.[4] He

---

[3]Hill, *The Gospel*, p. 70, cf. J. Jeremias, *Jesus' Promise to the Nations* (London: SCM, 1967), p. 24.

[4]Jeremias, *Jesus' Promise*, pp. 24, 34; Rohde, *Rediscovering*, pp. 158, 163-64, 189-90; John Gager, *The Origins of Anti-Semitism: Attitudes toward Judaism in Pagan and Christian Antiquity* (New York and Oxford: Oxford University, 1983), p. 149 (following Jervell); and T. W. Manson, *The Sayings of Jesus* (London: SCM, 1971) p. 257. A. Feuillet, "Les Origines et la signification de Mt 10,23b," *CBQ 23* (1961): 186, proposes that

even participates in a brief, unsuccessful mission to a Samaritan village (Lk 9:51-56). According to John, Jesus engages in an extended discussion with a Samaritan (Jn 4:1-38) and converts many of her neighbors to his cause (4:39-42). While Jn 12:20-21 mentions that some "Greeks" (Ἕλληνές) wish to see Jesus, they are never presented as becoming his disciples. Nor is multiple attestation supported by Rom 15:8 -- "Christ became a servant to the circumcised" (διάκονον περιτομῆς). While Jesus' mission concentrated on the Jews, the literary evidence does not indicate that he deliberately limited both his own mission and that of his disciples to Israel; that he was the messenger to the circumcised does not preclude his welcoming gentiles sympathetic to his message. Behind Jesus' historical focus may lie more an accident of geographical limitation than a soteriological program. Thus there is not enough evidence, either literary or historical, on which the claim of multiple attestation can rest.

Because the appeals to the criteria of both dissimilarity and multiple attestation are at best inconclusive, the criterion of coherence is difficult to apply. If one concludes that Jesus willingly heals gentiles (e.g., Mk 5:1-20) and Samaritans (e.g., Lk 17:11-19), the exclusivity logion is not consistent with Jesus' behavior. But if one accepts Paul's implicit limitation of Jesus to Israel or reads Mark 7 as depicting Jesus' hesitance in fulfilling the request of the Syro-Phoenician woman, then the logion fits the criterion. The appeal to consonance is also weak: the historical and cultural situations of the early religious movements neither support nor disprove the impetus

---

the verses 5b-6, placed at the beginning of the discourse, "aient fait partie primitivement de ce discours, il n'est guere possible d'en doubter. On concoit fort bien que Marc et Luc aient omis ces paroles," but the argument from silence is weak.

for or application of the restriction. Although it is unlikely it would have occurred to the disciples to take their message beyond the borders of Judaism -- first-century Jews were not for the most part engaged in an active proselytizing program similar to that of the early church -- and thus Jesus would have had no reason to issue a restriction, it is nevertheless conceivable that the new message would have created a new impetus for missionary activity. Hooker approaches the question of authenticity along similar lines, but frames her argument according to Jesus' personal mission rather than according to Jewish practices. She correctly notes that prohibitions are usually given when a particular occasion for them arises, "and it seems very unlikely that it would have occured to the disciples to announce the coming of the Kingdom to Gentiles." Since Jesus "had not come to found a new religion," there would be no need for him to evangelize among the gentiles.[5] While Hooker is probably correct, the argument itself is not without problems. Debates on Jesus' personal agenda continue, and even less is known about the concerns of the twelve; perhaps they required instruction in dealing with non-Jews they encountered during their journeys. To answer the question of whether Jesus would have needed to restrict the mission of his disciples one needs to inquire whether the Galilean disciples would have thought to evangelize among those not of Jewish background. While individual Jews did encourage gentiles to join the Jewish community, missionary activity was neither undertaken by the majority of Jews in

---

[5]"Uncomfortable Words," pp. 364-65; cf. S. Brown, "Matthean Community," p. 194. H. Stoevesandt, "Jesus und die Heidenmission," diss., Göttingen, summarized in *TLZ* 74 (1949): 242, concludes that Jesus expected the gentiles to enter the new community, and the church began the mission to them because it believed the new age had arrived.

Palestine or in the Diaspora, nor was it encouraged by an evangelistic mandate such as the church's Great Commission. Proselytes to Judaism were in many cases heartily welcomed, but their affiliation was not actively sought. Consequently, it is not likely that either Jesus or his disciples would have thought to restrict the mission: the outreach to the gentiles was not part of Jesus' plan, and the question of a mission beyond the people Israel would consequently not have arisen. Conversely, the universal evangelistic enterprise, the program of missionaries journeying from town to town to preach the truth of their position, is more of a Christian rather than Jewish technique. Thus it is most likely within a Christian context that the idea of an exclusivity pronouncement would have arisen.

Finally, J. Munck takes these observations to the other extreme. Since "Judaism was no evangelizing religion, it is remarkable that Jesus needed to say, 'Not to the Gentiles, not to the Samaritans.'... The view must therefore have existed from the first that the gospel concerned everyone; and so it had to be laid down that the sending of the twelve disciples concerned no one but the Jews."[6] To bring the arguments full circle, one need merely observe that Munck's conclusion is undercut by his own wording: who else but Jews were there "from the first" to decide that "the gospel concerned everyone?" Similarly, while Munck is correct that the majority of Jesus' Jewish contemporaries did not have a missionary outreach program to the gentiles -- the reference to Jewish proselytizing efforts as "evangelizing" is an unfortunate choice of words -- this same observation may not hold for Matthew's Jewish community in which scribes and Pharisees "traverse sea and land to make a single proselyte" (23:15).

---

[6] *Paul and the Salvation of Mankind* (Richmond, VA: John Knox, 1959), p. 259.

Arguments based on the language of the logion fare poorly as well. Hill states Matt 10:5b-6 has "a strongly Semitic character," and Jeremias not only offers the Aramaic original but describes it as a Palestinian tristich containing two lines of three beats each in synthetic parallelism followed by a final line in antithetic parallelism,[7] but neither an Aramaic nor a Hebrew version underlying the Greek proves authenticity. Such linguistic exercises can equally well support the claim that the saying arose in the primitive church. Further, the statement makes sense in Greek: it does not demand a retrotranslation for greater comprehensibility. Finally, an argument based on linguistic criteria alone is insufficient: the critic must also explain what the words mean.

The two theologically based arguments for the authenticity of the logion are equally problematic. Representative universalism, the first explanation, is best expressed by Munck: "Jesus did not turn to others besides the Jews, and he forbad his disciples to go to Samaritans and Gentiles. This apparent particularism is an expression of his universalism -- it is because his mission concerns the whole world that he comes to Israel.... Only in Israel, God's chosen people, can Jesus speak and act for the whole world."[8] Thus the

---

[7]Hill, *The Gospel*, p. 70; Jeremias, *Jesus' Promise*, p. 20 and n. 3. Conversely, H. B. Green, *The Gospel According to Matthew* (London: Oxford University, 1975), p. 109, suggests that the saying "accurately represents Jesus' view of his own mission, but the wording is probably Matthew's own."

[8]*Paul and the Salvation of Mankind*, pp. 271-72, cf. pp. 276-79. See also Jeremias, *Jesus' Promise*, p. 73 (citing Munck); R. R. De Ridder, *The Dispersion of the People of God: The Covenant Basis of Matthew 28:18-20 against the Background of Jewish, pre-Christian Proselytizing and Diaspora, and the Apostleship of Jesus Christ* (Kampen, Neth.: J. H. Kok, 1971), p. 153 ("the universal goal would be reached by way of a restoration of the

apparently particularist connotations of the exclusivity pronouncements have universalistic import. This argument is logically flawed: Matt 10:5b-6 and Matt 15:24 are by no means "an expression of his universalism"; indeed, the context of 15:24 explicitly denies a universalistic focus. Nor does representative universalism provide an explanation for the gentiles' entry -- either as converts to Judaism or through divine fiat -- into the *Basileia*. Finally, while this theory initially sounds quite congenial -- what was initially perceived to be a problematic and prejudicial statement is now the epitome of biblically faithful universalism -- it ultimately leads to an unsupportable theory of Jewish guilt. Because Israel -- or the Jewish community as a whole -- is neither transformed by Jesus nor does it become a future agent of transformation, the standard theological explanation for the failure of representative universalism is not that Jesus was mistaken but that the Jews failed in their mission. Thus, for example, Hooker states that "salvation did indeed come to the Gentiles through Israel -- but it was not through her witness, but through her rejection of the Messiah."[9] Therefore, the claim

---

servant nation"); Manson, *Jesus and the Non-Jews*, pp. 23-24; L. Baeck, *The Essence of Judaism* (New York: Schocken, 1961), p. 79; Gaston, "Messiah of Israel," p. 38; A. Plummer, *An Exegetical Commentary on the Gospel According to St. Matthew*, 3d ed. (London: Robert Scott, 1911), p. 216; Franzmann, *Discipleship*, pp. 84, 98-99. C. H. Giblin, "Theological Perspective and Matthew 10:23b," *TS* 29 (1968): 657, offers a confusing variant of this theory; Wilson, *Gentiles*, pp. 18, 22-23, has a helpful discussion.

[9]"Uncomfortable Words," p. 365; cf. Franzmann, *Discipleship*, pp. 113-14; K. Barth, "An Exegetical Study of Matthew 28:16-20," in *The Theology of the Christian Mission* (New York: McGraw-Hill, 1961), p. 65; and F. W. Beare, "The Mission of the Disciples and the Mission Charge: Matthew 10 and Parallels," *JBL* 89 (1970): 9 (but arguing that the statement is Matthew's

of authenticity becomes less a depiction of Israel, whether as representing the world or as being the agent of its transformation, than a confirmation of Israel's guilt.

Eschatological univeralism, the theory that Jesus did not evangelize among the gentiles because he expected God to bring them into the *Basileia* at the end of time (cf. Zech 8:23), finds its most eloquent exponent in Jeremias.[10] This argument for authenticity rests on several weak planks. First are the methodological difficulties of confirming Jesus' own opinion; second the inconclusive nature of the gospel evidence; and third the evidence from history: the early Christians did begin the mission to the gentiles. To explain this third inconsistency Jeremias states that although the eschatological pilgrimage of the nations is divinely inaugurated, "*the missionary task is a part of the final fulfillment...an eschatology in process of realization.*"[11] On the positive side, this observation permits divine-human cooperation;[12] but from the critical viewpoint, distinguishing between earthly and heavenly initiative becomes impossible. The final argument against Jeremias's program of eschatological universalism is his own evaluation of Matt 15:24. While he concludes that Matthew preserved the exclusivity logion "in spite of its repellent implication" only because "it bore the stamp of the Lord's authority,"[13] the

---

"literary device").

[10]*Jesus' Promise*; and "The Gentile World in the Thought of Jesus," *SNTSB* 3 (1952): 18-28. See the review by J. A. T. Robinson, *JBL* 68 (1959): 101-4; W. G. Kümmel, *Promise and Fulfillment*, 2d Eng. ed. (London: SCM, 1961), pp. 85-86; and Wilson, *Gentiles*, pp. 25-28.

[11]*Jesus' Promise*, p. 75; cf. De Ridder, *Dispersion*, pp. 147-48.

[12]See here N. Perrin's review of *Die Heidenmission in der Zukunftsschau Jesus* by D. Bosch, *JBL* 79 (1960): 188.

[13]*Jesus' Promise*, p. 27; cf. Hill, *The Gospel*, pp. 70, 185; and

statement cannot be repellent because it is part of God's soteriological program. That Jeremias adopts such a negative view of the restriction is surprising since he too suggests Jesus limited the mission because the scriptural promises made to the Jews had to be completed (cf. Rom 1:16; 2:9, 10; Acts 3:21; 13:46; Mk 7:27).[14] Further, at least according to the first gospel, the restriction positively fulfills the promises made to the Jews (the temporal axis); it has no negative bearing on the gentiles at all.

The various arguments used to support the authenticity of Matt 10:5b-6 and 15:24 are all problematic. In no case is the restriction of the mission demonstrated to be antithetical to the gospel's universalism, and thus the first argument for assigning the problematic verses to a source fails. The historical arguments fail the *pro bono* test, and the theological arguments also do not support the claim to authenticity: both the early church and Matthew were theologically sophisticated, and both could have adopted either reading. And neither theological explanation ultimately holds for the gospel itself: representative universalism, if it is authentic, failed; and eschatological universalism is undermined by the Great Commission. Although the theological arguments provide some rationale for Jesus' mission to the Jews, they fail to explain why the mission to the gentiles was deliberately restricted. Since the arguments for authenticity are weak at best, and since none has offered a challenge to the claim that the exclusivity logia are at the most redactional or at the very least in harmony with the gospel's soteriological program, the quest for their origins moves to the next level.

Hooker, "Uncomfortable Words," p. 361: "The words offend our belief in the unlimited compassion of Jesus...."

[14]*Jesus' Promise*, pp. 71-73.

The Argument for a Jewish-Christian Origin

Like the criteria of authenticity, the tools used to reconstruct the *Sitz im Leben* or "setting-in-life" of a particular pericope have built-in difficulties. The difficulties of separating tradition from redaction reappear, and the problem of atomistic exegesis -- that is, of divorcing particular sayings from their narrative context -- runs rampant. Moreover, assigning a verse to a specific social and cultural setting requires substantial knowledge of the early church itself. But is the classification of the material to be based on *a priori* judgments about the early church (so Dibelius), or is the picture of the church to be reconstructed from interpretations of the pericopes (so Bultmann)? In either case a circular argument is unavoidable.[15] Thus any assignment of a logion to a source remains tentative at best, and the burden of proof consequently remains on those who would call such unique material as the exclusivity statements in the first gospel traditional.

Matthew 10:5b-6, often characterized as "Jewish-oriented [with] a certain narrow, parochial, even legalistic strain that runs quite counter to the broader, more prophetic, antilegalism that is the dominant motif" of the gospel,[16] is generally described as "the inheritance of the extreme

---

[15]M. Dibelius, *From Tradition to Gospel* (New York: Scribner's, 1935); R. Bultmann, *History of the Synoptic Tradition* (Oxford: Blackwell, 1963). For additional methodological shortcomings see Erhard T. Güttgemans, *Candid Questions Concerning Gospel Form Criticism: A Methodological Sketch of Fundamental Problematics of Form and Redaction Criticism*. 2d ed. (Allison Park, PA: Pickwick, 1979); J. A. Baird, *Audience Criticism and the Historical Jesus* (Philadelphia: Westminster, 1969), pp. 22-23.

[16]Baird, *Audience Criticism*, p. 116.

Judaizers."[17] Their traditions are represented by material from a hypothetical, pre-Matthean, Jewish-Christian, legalistic source usually designated "M" (referring to "special Matthew"). Descriptions of the community that produced M range from Hooker's benign Jewish-Christian group "opposed to evangelization of the Gentiles on the ground that there was enough to do within Judaism without going beyond its confines"[18] to Beare's "Jewish-Christian circles...which had little appreciation of the doctrine of freedom from law for which St. Paul contended so strongly."[19] This type of source

---

[17]Meier, *Antioch and Rome*, pp. 53-54; cf. Martin, "Recent Study," p. 134 (following F. Hahn, *Mission in the New Testament* [London: Allenson, 1965], pp. 54-55). See also S. F. G. Brandon, *Jesus and the Zealots* (Manchester, G.B.: Manchester University, 1967), p. 174, on anti-gentile prejudice; Gager, *Origins of Anti-Semitism*, pp. 26-27 ("non- or even anti-Gentiles").

[18]"Uncomfortable Words," pp. 363-64; Hooker herself, pp. 361-62, suggests the logion stems from a non-Marcan commission which "seems to lie behind Lk 9:2; 10:3-16" and which Luke omitted. See also T. W. Manson, *The Teaching of Jesus* (Cambridge: The University Press, 1945), p. 34; and *Sayings of Jesus*, p. 25; Meier, "Salvation-History," p. 204; *Law and History*, p. 27; *Vision of Matthew*, p. 31 and n. 34; and *Antioch and Rome*, pp. 16, 42, 53-54 (but see p. 53 n. 124 on Streeter's *Four Gospels*, p. 512); S. Brown, "Matthean Community," p. 221.

[19]Beare, "The Sayings of Jesus in the Gospel According to St. Matthew," in *Studia Evangelica* 4/*TU* 102, ed. F. L. Cross (Berlin: Akademie, 1968), p. 152; cf. his "Sayings of the Risen Jesus in the Gospel Tradition: An Inquiry into Their Origin and Significance," in *Christian History and Interpretation*, eds. W. F. Farmer et al. (Cambridge: The University Press, 1967), pp. 176-77; but see his revised opinion in "Mission of the Disciples," pp. 1-13; C. E. Carlston, "The Things That Defile (Mark vii.14) and the Law in Matthew and Mark," *NTS* 15 (1968): 90-91; and "Interpreting the Gospel of Matthew," *Int* 29 (1975):

criticism, not surprisingly, also works in reverse; just as the limitations are considered "Jewish," so the universalistic passages such as 28:16-20 are assigned to the "Hellenists," to Jewish Christians of "liberal persuasion," or, most often, to Christian gentiles.[20] Judaism is therefore viewed as narrow, and universalism must stem either from a watered-down "Hellenistic" Jewish-Christian group or, more likely, from gentile Christians.

Several problems immediately arise from such classifications. First is the tendency to equate ethnic identification with particular theological or soteriological beliefs: Jewish Christians are usually labeled "legalistic" (often used pejoratively to refer to communities who practiced ritual *Halachah*), yet gentiles may have been just as Law-obedient; gentile Christians are credited with developing and maintaining the universalistic impulses of the nascent community, yet Jewish Christians such as Paul had such universalistic goals as well. Nor need the retention of *Halachah* be judged contrary to a universalistic impulse: a Law-obedient church may well have sought converts from

---

8; Green, *The Gospel*, p. 31, cf. pp. 8, 108-9; E. P. Blair, *Jesus in the Gospel of Matthew* (New York and Nashville: Abingdon, 1960), pp. 33-34 (following Nepper-Christiansen); J. P. Brown, "The Form of 'Q' Known to Matthew," *NTS* 8 (1061/62): 32; Clark, "Gentile Bias," p. 165; J. A. Fitzmyer, "Anti-Semitism and the Cry of 'All the People' (Mt 27:25)," *TS* 26 (1965): 670; Dobschütz, "Matthäus als Rabbi," p. 344 (the logion expresses an opinion narrower than that held by Jesus).

[20]E.g., Meier, *Antioch and Rome*, p. 41: "The various universalistic traditions enshrined in Matthew probably found their impulse and their incubator among this Antiochene group of Gentile Christians"; cf. Rohde, *Rediscovering*, p. 54; Strecker, "Concept of History," p. 72; and *Der Weg*, pp. 34-35; W. Trilling, *Das Wahre Israel*, 3d ed. (Munich: Kösel, 1964), p. 192.

among the nations -- with the proviso that those converts enter fully into the practices as well as the beliefs of that community. The second, more heinous problem with such categorizations is the presence of value judgments often attached to the labels: Jewish Christianity is perceived either implicitly or explicitly to be narrow, primitive, prejudicial, or simply bad, while gentile Christianity becomes not only the historical winner but the moral winner as well. Retention of such titles as "*Jewish* Christianity" and "*Gentile* Christianity" thus also preserves the stereotypes of narrow, legalistic (Palestinian) Judaism and universalistic, liberal Hellenism and thus leads to classifications of monolithic "normative" groups rather than to an appreciation of the cross-ethnic diversity in the early religious communities. While certain Jewish-Christian groups may indeed have been anti-gentile, exclusivistic, and narrow, the historical evidence does not support the application of these characterizations to all or even the majority of such groups of the time. Until scholars agree upon exact definitions of the terms -- a consensus which does not appear to be forthcoming -- an alternative manner of classification is needed.

The observation by Raymond Brown that "'Jewish Christians' and 'Gentile Christians' are not helpful designations unless we know what type of Jewish/Gentile Christianity was involved"[21] offers one starting point. Brown proposes classifications of varying types of "Jewish-Gentile Christianity" based on observance of the Law. However, adherence to or dismissal of *Halachah* need not imply an ethnic

---

[21] *Antioch and Rome*, pp. 140-41, cf. his typologies on pp. 2-6, and R. Brown, "Not Jewish Christianity and Gentile Christianity but Types of Jewish Gentile Christianity," *CBQ* 45 (1983): 74-79. Also helpful is R. Murray, "Jews, Hebrews, and Christians: Some Needed Distinctions," *NovTest* 24 (1982): 196.

base, as the "Judaizing" (yet another loaded term which means, simply, obedience to the ritual Law and, usually, synagogue attendance) phenomenon among gentiles demonstrates. And while Meier's descriptions of the various groups that formed the early Antiochene church may be correct, his labels may ultimately be unusable: are his "ultraconservative Jewish Christians" to be distinguished from his "circumcision-insistent Jewish/Gentile Christians"?[22] Terms such as "liberal" and "conservative" are helpful when used, as Meier does, with respect to the Law (although they can lead to such oxymora as his description of Matthew as a "true liberal conservative" [p. 59]), but the application of ethnic signifiers to these terms is generally unhelpful. For example, some gentile Judaizers are more "conservative" than Jews such as Paul. Nor does the addition of qualifying terms clarify the situation. For example, Martin identifies Matthew as a "Christian church leader of the Jewish-Hellenistic wing of the church."[23] How is "Hellenistic" to be understood: neither Galilean nor Palestinian geographically and/or culturally? Does it indicate one who writes in Greek, one who has a Greek philosophical orientation, one from a Pauline school? And where should the emphasis be placed: on Matthew's Judaism, or Hellenism, or Christianity?

When these various difficulties are then reapplied to the problem of Matt 10:5b-6 and 15:24, the situation becomes even more entangled. Because the exclusivity pronouncements are judged to be part of the M source, and because this source is

---

[22]*Antioch and Rome*, pp. 126, 186. Both labels are assigned to "Group I." Blair, *Jesus in the Gospel of Matthew*, p. 29, describes the evangelist and the community as "liberalized Jewish Christians" who had "come to believe in the Church universal."

[23]"Recent Study," p. 136.

perceived to be "legalistic" and "anti-gentile," the first step in analyzing the logia would be to see if they are in fact involved either with Jewish Law or ethnic prejudice; the second is an analysis of those passages upon which the description of M is based. Both steps yield results confirming the temporal axis, and neither supports the argument that the restricted mission is the work of a source with which the evangelist was not in agreement.

The restriction of the mission as expressed in 10:5b-6 and reiterated in 15:24 does not concern obedience to any *Halachah* datable to the Herodian period, and its connection to such passages as 5:17-18 and 23:2-3, also usually assigned to M, is therefore tenuous at best. Further, Matthew usually states when a particular comment is in fulfillment of either biblical or traditional Law, so that even if the restriction were "legalistically" motivated, the evangelist does not appear to be aware of this factor. Matthew 10:5b-6 alone also fails to indicate a "movement [that] was presumably open to Gentiles, but only if they were prepared to accept the full responsibility of the Mosaic covenant."[24] While this theory may indicate the position of Matthew's source and church, the logion itself makes no provision for gentile converts to Judaism; it concentrates on the privileges of the Jews *as an ethnic group*. Fourth, Matt 10:5b-6 demonstrates no animosity toward gentiles, which is a common description of M in general and of the restriction of the mission in particular. The directive is pro-Israel, but this is not identical with being anti-gentile.

Although the verse itself has no explicit anti-gentile or anti-Samaritan connotations, it may yet be consistent with the hypothesis of an anti-gentile tendency in the gospel, and thus it may be part of a "narrow, Jewish-Christian, legalistic"

---

[24]Gager, *Origins of Anti-Semitism*, p. 130, seeing 10:5b-6 in contradiction to Matthean universalism.

source. But of the seven verses usually cited as direct evidence for anti-gentilism within the gospel -- 5:47; 6:7-8; 6:32; 18:17; 20:19; 20:25; and 24:9 -- only the first four are anti-gentile *qua* gentile, and even these are not direct evidence of ethnic bigotry. Matthew 20:19 and 24:9 illustrate the gospel's cross-ethnic division based on faith manifest in action. Matthew 20:25 is a foil for comparison: the members of the Christian community symbolized by the Jewish disciples are exhorted not to establish any system of government according to the Roman model of domination and exploitation. Thus this verse is comparable to the woes against the scribes and Pharisees in chapter 23. Indeed, while "rulers of the gentiles" (ἄρχοντες τῶν ἐθνῶν) is the subject of 20:25a, 20:25b keeps the emphasis on the rulers and the system of patriarchy they preserve rather than on the people being exploited. Not only do the rulers "lord it over" (κατακυριεύουσιν) their charges, their "great ones exercise authority" (οἱ μεγάλοι κατεξουσιάζουσιν) in a manner inconsistent with the *Basileia*. And, because the gospel continues to depict the shortcomings of the Jewish political system through the characterizations of the two Herods as well as of the priests, it would not be inappropriate to take the wider meaning of ἔθνη into account and translate 20:25a with reference to the "rulers of the *nations*."

Of the remaining four verses, Matt 6:32 is remarkably neutral in its attitude toward gentiles. Responding to the hypothetical questions of "What shall we eat, drink, and wear?" Jesus states simply that "the ἔθνη seek all these things, and your heavenly father knows that you need them all." Since these supplicants are not seeking personal benefits designed to distinguish themselves from their neighbors but necessities for human existence, their activities are not condemned. Rather, Matthew's Jesus emphasizes the universalism of the deity: heaven "knows" that food, drink, and clothing are needed and grants them to all. Moreover, because the verse concerns the universal care of the deity and the cross-cultural needs of humanity, the ἔθνη in question may refer to "nations" and not just to "gentiles."

Hare and Harrington and Meier, whose translations and interpretations of the expression πάντα τὰ ἔθνη in Matt 28:19 are pivotal for an understanding of the gospel's universalism, all translate the term ἔθνη in 6:32 as "gentiles," but the arguments are not conclusive.[25] First, Meier acknowledges that this translation is "not quite so clear, if taken by itself." Next, he argues that the context -- the address to a Jewish crowd -- increases the likelihood that ἔθνη is being used to refer pejoratively to gentiles. Yet the evangelist neither hesitates to condemn the general crowds and the Jewish leaders (cf. 6:5) nor refrains from specifying a gentile reference when the occasion warrants (5:46-47; 6:7; 18:17). Nor is the comment that the gentiles engage in practices which the Jews do as well a slight against the gentiles. If any insult lies behind the verse, then it is addressed equally to Jews and gentiles since both engage in the same type of behavior. Third, Meier appeals to the negative comment in 5:47, but the argument of "guilt by association" is weak: along with the "gentiles" "hypocrites" and "tax collectors" are condemned in the first discourse. Thus even if the term in 6:32 is translated "gentiles," it need not be viewed as an ethnic slur. In this case, the translation indicates that any distinction between the crowd at the Mount and the ἔθνη in 6:32 falls along the temporal axis: in the narrative present, Jesus simply exhorts his potential followers first to seek God. The gentiles, who now seek food and drink and

---

[25]J. P. Meier, "Nations or Gentiles in Matthew 28:19?," *CBQ* 39 (1977): 95; cf. D. R. A. Hare and D. J. Harrington, "'Make Disciples of All the Gentiles' (Mt 28:19)," *CBQ* 37 (1975): 362. For an analysis of their positions, see below, chapters 6-8.

clothing from sources other than the deity, will eventually hear the good news and reformulate their priorities.

Unlike 6:32, Matt 6:7-8 explicitly compares the gentiles with hypocrites (6:5-6), and both 5:47-48 and 18:17 equate the gentiles in negative terms with tax collectors. This shift from the more universal comment concerning life's necessities is accompanied by a change in terminology. Matthew 5:47-48; 6:7; and 18:17, the only three passages which condemn the gentiles *qua* gentiles, are also the only three statements in the gospel in which the term ἐθνικοί -- as opposed to ἔθνη -- appears. K. Tagawa's conclusion, that "Such expressions cannot be understood otherwise than as uttered in the spirit of extremely strong Jewish prejudice,"[26] is illustrative of the majority of scholarly treatments of the three verses. In some analyses an apologetic rationale is added: these anti-gentile expressions must derive from a Jewish-Christian source because "the contemptuous tone...is uncharacteristic both of Jesus and of Matthew."[27] Such classifications overlook the specific appearances of ἐθνικός in the first gospel, which is the only document in the Christian scriptures outside of III Jn 7 where the term appears. Matthew does not condemn gentiles as

---

[26]"People and Community in the Gospel of Matthew," *NTS* 16 (1970):153; C. H. Dodd, "Matthew and Paul," *ET* 58 (1946/47): 295; Manson, *Sayings of Jesus*, p. 210; Argyle, *The Gospel*, p. 141; Hill, *The Gospel*, p. 276; W. D. Davies, *Setting*, p. 233; and others.

[27]Green, *The Gospel*, p. 87; cf. Meier, *Vision of Matthew*, p. 132 n. 141: "Jesus openly associated with tax collectors and even performed miracles for Gentiles. The phrasing may come from the early, stringently Jewish stage of Matthew's church"; and Beare, "Sayings of Jesus," p. 150: "No doubt [18:17] felt itself to be directed by the spirit of Jesus, though we may ask ourselves whether Jesus would ever have used 'Gentile' and 'taxman' as terms of derogation."

a corporate group, nor are all tax collectors viewed as pariahs (cf. 9:9-13). According to the gospel, the "pagans" and "tax collectors" are those who have either rejected Jesus or who have not yet heard the message. In the context of the Matthean church, the individuals who fall under these designations have refused to heed the message of the gospel and, consequently, have deliberately absented themselves from the community of the *Basileia*.

These conclusions are reinforced by the temporal axis of Matthean salvation history. For 5:47-48 and 6:7-8, the narrative present of Jesus' restricted mission requires the less pejorative evaluation of gentiles and tax collectors. However, since 18:17 explicitly concerns post-resurrectional ecclesiastical structures, the negative connotations are appropriate. Therefore, the three passages do not indicate that the evangelist is anti-gentile any more than other sections of the gospel (e.g., chap. 23) are anti-Jews *qua* Jews. Just as "the Jews" (οἱ Ἰουδαίοι, 28:15) remains an operative category for Matthew's own community and refers to individuals of Jewish background who have not joined the church, so "the gentiles" or, better, "the pagans" (ἐθνικοί) are those non-Jews who have refused the Christian message.[28] There is, consequently, no manifest reason to assign these three references to a source. They do not demonstrate a contradiction of the gospel's universalism, nor do they indicate a negatively prejudicial attitude toward ethnic gentiles; they are instead consistent

---

[28]See the discussions in Meier, *Antioch and Rome*, p. 69 n. 157; Kilpatrick, *Origins of the Gospel*, pp. 117-18; Thompson, *Matthew's Advice*, p. 186 n. 41 (who suggests Kilpatrick has "exaggerated the derogatory tone in these passages"); E. Schweizer, *The Good News According to Matthew* (Atlanta: John Knox, 1975), p. 359; Hare and Harrington, "Make Disciples," p. 361.

with the program of salvation history articulated throughout the gospel text.[29]

Since those passages making specific reference to "gentiles" or "pagans" do not display ethnic prejudice, their support for the argument that 10:5b-6 and 15:24 derive from a narrow, Jewish, exclusivistic source is undercut. Matthew may have had access to several oral and written traditions which displayed ethnic bigotry, but this theory cannot be demonstrated on the basis of 5:47-48; 6:7-8; and 18:17. The argument from source criticism can also be redirected to claims for either the authenticity of the verses in question or for their redactional origin, and thus the reconstruction of M can be doubly challenged. For example, Jesus too might have expressed anti-pagan and anti-tax collector attitudes; while the tradition strongly suggests that he did heal gentiles,· it is not clear that he did so willingly. On the other hand, few would claim that he embarked on a universal program of evangelization. And while he did associate with tax collectors, he does not commend the profession. Nor would Matthew be exempt from possible anti-gentile or anti-tax collector feelings. If the redactor were indeed a tax collector by trade (9:9), then a negative depiction of those who did not "rise and follow" Jesus would not be surprising. But the gospel is not anti-gentile. Only the "pagans" (ἐθνικοί) are condemned and then only in conformity to the demands of the temporal axis. Thus

---

[29]Kilpatrick, *Origins of the Gospel*, p. 20, suggests 5:43-48 is Q material (cf. Lk 6:27-36); J. P. Brown, "Form of 'Q'," pp. 30-31 n. 4, suggests the reference is editorial. And while Kilpatrick, p. 29, cf. pp. 21, 28, also argues for an M or Q tradition behind 6:7 and 18:17, he adds that at least 18:16-17 "seem to refer to the conditions of a later period." See also Hill, *The Gospel*, p. 134; and esp. Tagawa, "People and Community," p. 154, on the possible redactional insertions (including the reference to ἐθνικοί) in 6:7 and 18:17.

the exclusivity statements need not be assigned to a source on the basis of a hypothetical connection with "other anti-gentile" passages, and indeed, the whole rationale for the M source deserves reevaluation.

In part, the source-critical arguments are based on the theory that the redactor is inconsistent. If it can be demonstrated that "the evangelist Matthew is a writer who blithely makes...contradictory utterances,"[30] then the case for locating the origins of the exclusivity statements in pre-Matthean tradition gains some strength. In addition to the common hypotheses that 10:5b-6 is in contradiction to 28:16-20, and that the "anti-gentile prejudice" of several gospel verses runs counter to the overall universalistic thrust of the text, the following passages have also been viewed as irreconcilable: 23:2f. with 15:3; 5:17f. with 5:21ff; 12:1-14 with 5:19; 23:13-16 with 23:3; and 5:22 with 23:17. Others, in turn, argue that although 10:5b-6 and 15:24 are inconsistent with Matthean universalism, the evangelist is competent. The clever redactor has simply accommodated special-interest groups within the church, and so, for example, inserted 10:5b-6 for the satisfaction of the "Judaizers" and 28:19 to address the concerns of the "Hellenists."[31] While a contradiction or two may slip past the watchful eyes of the most competent of

---

[30]Tagawa, "People and Community," p. 151; cf. pp. 150-53; Cope, *Matthew, A Scribe*, p. 11; Hare, *Jewish Persecution*, p. 82. See also Hill, *The Gospel*, p. 185; Manson, *Sayings of Jesus*, p. 180; Beare, "Sayings of Jesus," p. 176; Carlston, "Things That Defile," pp. 90-91 and nn. 1, 2; Gager, *Origins of Anti-Semitism*, pp. 129-30, 141; Baird, *Audience Criticism*, p. 117; J. P. Brown, "The Form of Q," p. 32; E. L. Abel, "Who Wrote Matthew?" *NTS* 17 (1971):142 (arguing for two redactors), 148; S. Brown, "Matthean Community," p. 193.

[31]See J. Kennard, "The Reconciliation Tendenz in Matthew," *ATR* 28 (1946): 163; Baird, *Audience Criticism*, p. 117.

authors, the passages cited as contradictions, upon close scrutiny, appear not to be so. And while writers may adapt their message to the needs of their audiences, an appeal to special-interest groups in order to explain the relationship between the limited mission charge and the gospel's universalism is unnecessary.

For example, Matt 23:2 and 15:3 convey different messages: the former concerns biblical interpretation; the latter, the Oral Law (the "tradition of the elders"). Similarly, while 23:3 refers to Pharisaic homiletics, 23:13-16 concerns Pharisaic behavior. Nor does 5:21 contradict 5:17f.; it extends and toughens it. Even the minor potential discrepancy between 12:1-14 and 5:19 on obedience to the Sabbath *Halachah* is transcended by the theme of Jesus' authority: both passages concern the "correct" interpretation of the Law, that offered by Jesus; he does not abrogate the Law in chapter 12. Finally, there is a difference between necessitated warning (23:17) given in the context of a polemic and unmotivated insult (5:22) given as part of instruction, as the early interpolation of the expression "without cause" (εἰκῇ) in 5:22 indicates. The argument of appeasement of special-interest groups is weakened not only by the difficulties inherent in the categorization of the two groups, it is also logically flawed: surely the members of the two hypothetical parties in the community would realize the discrepancy. It is doubtful these implied readers would have been satisfied with such obvious panderings.

The Capable Author

The discussion to this point has defined the talents of the evangelist in a negative manner: Matthew is neither inconsistent nor schizophrenic. On the positive side, the evangelist may be described as a careful artist who has deliberately constructed the mission discourse to highlight both the temporal and the social axes. Within the purview of this latter description, the case can be made for, at the very least, Matthew's agreement with the exclusivity logia of 10:5b-6 and 15:24 and, possibly, for their redactional origin. Adopting this perspective necessarily implies a reformulation of the traditional approach to the problematic verses. Rather than view them as peripheral to the gospel's soteriological program, the following analysis locates the restriction of the mission at its center.

That the limitation of the mission is not only consistent with the concerns of the redactor but central to them is immediately indicated by the placement of the exclusivity logion at the opening of chapter 10, the second discourse; following the list of the twelve, the restriction is the first command Jesus gives.[32] Its importance is further emphasized not only by its reiteration in 15:24 where the restriction is made specifically relevant to Jesus' own mission but also by its anticipation through the evocative imagery of the introduction to the discourse. According to the redactional summary in 9:35-38, Jesus has compassion for the crowd "because they were harassed and helpless, like sheep without a shepherd" (ὡσεὶ πρόβατα μὴ ἔχοντα ποιμένα, 9:36). The simile provides insight for understanding Matt 10:5b-6 in at least two ways. First, it indicates that the restriction does not establish the guilt of the corporate community: the leaders are implicitly condemned; the people are pitied; and the mission is motivated by Jesus' compassion. Moreover, although the

---

32 Hooker, "Uncomfortable Words," p. 361, suggests a possible connection to Mk 6:8, which opens the account of the mission with a reference to εἰς ὁδόν ("for the journey").

harvest motif which follows in 9:37-38 is a common metaphor for eschatological judgment (e.g., Isa 17:11; 24:13; Joel 3:13; Matt 13:30, 39), the "emphasis is on the richness of the opportunity, not on the menace of disaster."[33] Thus, the gospel appears quite sanguine regarding the ultimate salvation of the lost sheep. Second, the references to sheep in 9:36 and 10:6 reinforce the connection between the time of Jesus and the scriptural promises made to the Jews (e.g., Num 27:17; I Kgs 22:17; Zech 10:2-3; Jer 23:1-4; 50:6); the metaphors eliminate possible references to a gentile mission.

Matthew 9:35-38 also foreshadows the specific connections the second discourse draws between the activities of Jesus and those of the twelve. The mention of "all the cities and villages" (τὰς πόλεις πάσας καὶ τὰς κώμας) in verse 35 is a direct thematic foil to the restriction in 10:5b; it also anticipates the course of the mission described in 10:11, 14, 15, 23; and 11:1 (cf. 4:23). Further, the rehearsal of Jesus' miracles and preaching activity in 9:35 recalls 4:23, where the mission to Galilee is summarized, as well as emphasizes that the power of the disciples "is clearly an extension of Jesus' own power."[34] Giblin suggests that the connection between 4:23 and 9:35 indicates "*a wider perspective...precisely in terms of what seems at first to be a narrower perspective*": that is, the mission cannot be limited to the Jews.[35] However, 4:23-25 does not explicitly mention gentiles, and Jesus does not evangelize in gentile territories. Finally, the participation

---

[33]Beare, "Mission of the Disciples," p. 7; and against Hill, *The Gospel*, p. 182.

[34]Thompson, "Historical Perspective," p. 252 n. 23; cf. E. Schweizer, "Observance of the Law and Charismatic Activity in Matthew," *NTS* 16 (1970): 220; Hooker, "Uncomfortable Words," p. 362.

[35]"Theological Perspective," p. 655.

of the disciples in the restricted mission conforms to the Talmudic principle that a messenger's (שליח) authority cannot surpass that of the one who engaged the commission.[36]

Because the evangelist does not always specify how many comprise this group of messengers or "disciples," the presence of numerical markers in 10:1 is notable. The connection between the mention of the "twelve disciples" at the outset of the first commission and the notation that only "eleven disciples" appeared at the Great Commission (28:16) is yet more evidence of the gospel's structural unity and of the parallelism between the two scenes. Within the immediate context of the second discourse, the number twelve emphasizes the restriction of the mission: as in 19:28, the reference recalls the twelve tribes of Israel; in the context of the harvest imagery in 9:37 it may even suggest the gathering of all the tribes of Israel at the eschaton.[37] Not only does 10:1 thus confirm the gospel's interest in restoring the Jewish community, it is also indicative of the fulfillment of the Jews' soteriological prerogatives.

Like the introduction to the second discourse, the concluding comment in 11:1 reinforces the restriction of the mission. Here however the theme is implicit rather than explicit. Unlike the accounts of Mark (6:7, 12-13, 30) and Luke (9:6; cf. 10:1), the first gospel does not describe the mission of the twelve; Matthew simply notes that when Jesus had finished his instructions, "*he* went on" (μετέβη) to teach and

---

[36]H. Vogelstein, "The Development of the Apostolate in Judaism and Its Transformation in Christianity," *HUCA* 2 (1925): 114-15, citing e.g., *T.B. Ket.* 99b.

[37]Hooker, "Uncomfortable Words," p. 362. See also Thompson, *Matthew's Advice*, pp. 71-72; D. P. Senior, *Invitation to Matthew* (Garden City, NY: Doubleday/Image Books, 1977), p. 103.

preach in the cities. Argyle suggests the mission did not occur until after the resurrection; S. Brown proposes that anything which could not be applied to Matthew's own community was deliberately omitted; according to Hare "Matthew is interested solely in the instructions," not in their implementation; and Beare suggests that not only had Matthew no interest in this aspect of the Galilean ministry, but that, given the lack of information about the activities of the disciples, arguing for or against the historicity of the mission is time ill spent.[38]

Although the issue of a separate mission of the disciples has substantial historical implications, they are not necessarily relevant to the reconstruction of Matthew's agenda. The purposes of this study require only that the absence of the mission be studied in the context of the gospel. In Matthew's narrative, the omission of the journey of the twelve neither merely emphasizes the central role of Jesus during the era of Israel nor indicates the applicability of the second discourse only to the era of the church. The missionary injunctions in chapter 10 have two related foci. First, within the narrative world constructed by the evangelist, the words of Jesus are given to the twelve at a specific place and time. Therefore they serve as guides to the disciples' activities during the remainder of Jesus' mission to Israel (cf. 15:23). They cannot, however, be transferred directly to the age of the church. Only after the resurrection, when Jesus receives "all authority" (28:18), can he transfer his full power to his followers. And only after witnessing Jesus' suffering and death will the disciples be prepared to carry out an independent mission. Second, because the first mission is

---

[38]Argyle, *The Gospel*, p. 84; S. Brown, "Mission to Israel in Matthew's Central Section (MT 9:35-11:1)," *ZNW* 69 (1978): 75; Hare, *Jewish Persecution*, p. 97, cf. Hare and Harrington, "Make Disciples," pp. 366-67; Beare, "Mission of the Disciples," p. 3.

never brought to a close -- its focus is simply extended by the Great Commission -- the original directives remain valid for the era of the church. Thus the original charge to evangelize among the "lost sheep of the house of Israel" remains in force.

Attention to the present and future aims of the second discourse returns the discussion to the exclusivity logion's role in Matthean salvation history. Because allusions to the era of the church frequently have been viewed as corrections to or even antitheses of Matt 10:5b-6, the scholarly literature often suggests that the evangelist has thereby mitigated the force of the restriction. Some critics claim the exclusivity injunction is neutralized by its juxtaposition to 10:17-18; others interpret Matt 10:23b as an unfulfilled prophecy about the parousia and consequently claim that the gospel's program of salvation history is inconsistent. Both theories are based on a confusion caused by the dual temporal aims of the chapter, and both begin with the presupposition that the evangelist has retained traditional material no longer relevant for the church.

While Matt 10:5-15 is clearly relevant to the era of Israel and so applicable to the activities of the disciples during Jesus' earthly ministry, 10:16-23 presents a different emphasis and, according to some critical commentaries, requires a different audience. The first part of the discourse restricts the mission to the "towns and villages" (10:11) of Israel and comments on the actions the twelve are to take; the second part addresses what will happen to these disciples. In other words, 10:5-15 primarily concerns action (but cf. 10:14), and 10:16-23 concentrates on appropriate reaction. If this distinction is pressed, contradictions in the text begin to appear. For example, Kingsbury suggests that Matthew provides the mission with a "universal" dimension in 10:18 and so literally has the disciples go beyond the restrictions made in 10:5b. Argyle concludes that 10:1-16 is addressed to the twelve, and 10:17-33 is "addressed to the Christian Church rather than to the missionaries whom Jesus sent out." Hare in turn suggests that 10:17 has a past focus: "When Christians, ostracized from the synagogue, withdrew into the Gentile community for both fellowship and missionary activity, they were no longer liable to the disciplinary actions of the synagogue, nor could any legal charge be raised against them except before the civil courts"[39] -- therefore, Matt 10:17 cannot refer to the contemporary experience of Matthew's church. Finally, S. Brown observes that "*If* the gentile mission was taken for granted within the Matthean community, how is it that there is no direct reference to it in the Central Section?... In Mt 9.35-11.1 the evangelist has Jesus address his community in the person of the twelve disciples, and in the point-by-point assimilation of their missionary functions with those of Jesus, who sends them out, the Matthean community must be able to see the delineation of its own missionary task." Thus, for Brown, Matthew 10 does not depict "successive phases of missionary activity."[40] The first two positions misinterpret the future tenses employed in 10:17-18; the latter two underestimate them; and all four perceive a tension or contradiction within either the discourse or the gospel.

Once Matt 10:1-33 is read as a literary unity rather than as a collection of contradictory statements, such debates can be settled. The evangelist does not indicate that 10:5-15 is applicable only to the first era, 10:16-23 only to the time of the church. The carefully constructed parallels between the

---

[39] J. D. Kingsbury, "The Structure of Matthew's Gospel and His Concept of Salvation History," CBQ 35 (1973): 474; cf. Wilson, *Gentiles*, p. 15; Argyle, *The Gospel*, p. 81; Hare, *Jewish Persecution*, p. 105, cf. p. 113. See also Thompson, "Historical Perspective," p. 254; Gaston, "Messiah of Israel," p. 28.

[40] "Mission to Israel," pp. 79-80.

mission discourse and the Great Commission and the carefully developed association between Jesus and the disciples signal the continuing validity of the initial predictions and commands. Unless specifically abrogated or extended by the resurrected cosmocrator, therefore, all statements issued during the era of Israel are retained during the era of the church.

Appropriately, the second discourse emphasizes Jewish rather than gentile persecution: the disciples have been and will be persecuted by the Jews whom they encounter. Emphasis on such gentile rejection is reserved for the fifth discourse, which particularly addresses the era of the church (cf. 24:9-14). But while Matt 10:17-18 suggests that members of the church are dissociated from the Jewish religious establishment, contacts with and even sporadic persecutions by Jews have not necessarily ceased: the separation of Matthew's community from the synagogue does not eliminate the possibility that Christian missionaries either spoke to assemblies of Jews or were persecuted by them (cf. II Cor 11:24-25; Acts 14:19). The future tenses in 10:17-18 do not imply a temporal limitation, and the apocalyptic tone of such verses as 10:21-22 suggests that Jewish persecution will continue in the new era. The Jews of Matthew's own time might not be physically attacking Christians, but at the very least hostilitity between the two groups remains (cf. 28:15).

Conversely, the few references to gentiles in the second discourse do not compromise the temporal axis. Thus, for example, 10:18 should be associated with Jesus' activities in both 20:18-19 and 27:11; just as Jesus is dragged before gentiles, so the disciples must be prepared to suffer the same fate. Matthew has also added a mention of "the gentiles" (καὶ τοῖς ἔθνεσιν, 10:18; cf. Mk 13:9-10) to the group before whom the missionaries are to testify. This notice does not indicate that the gentiles in 10:18 receive Jesus' message indirectly through the suffering of the disciples.[41] The editorial insertion both creates a parallel to Jesus' own experiences and suggests that precisely this distinction between Jews and gentiles will be eliminated. During the era of the church, the message of the disciples will reach both Jews and gentiles; in turn some Jews and gentiles will persecute the church and some will join it. The future tense of Matt 10:18 maintains the temporal axis, and the specific mention of "governors and kings" (ἐπὶ ἡγεμόνας δε καὶ βασιλεῖς) as a separate group distinct from "the gentiles" is in accord with the social emphasis of Matthean salvation history. The ultimate division anticipated by the second discourse is not between Jews and gentiles but between those who rule and those who are ruled.

But because the emphasis throughout chapter 10 remains on the relationship between the disciples and the Jewish community, Matthew implies that the mission to the Jews is of continuing relevance for the church. The future tenses in 10:16ff. do not create an either/or, but a both/and impression. The second discourse is crafted to indicate that during Jesus' ministry the mission of both master and disciples was restricted to Israel; references to gentiles are cast in the future tense and are subordinated to the emphasis on the Jews. Too, the omission of the disciples' mission avoids a possible contradiction to the temporal axis: it eliminates the need to describe or even imply the contact between the disciples and the gentiles. And because the disciples' mandate to evangelize the Jews is neither described nor revoked, the Great Commission -- in which the outreach to gentiles is also not

---

[41]S. Brown, "Mission to Israel," p. 88, but see Hare, *Jewish Persecution*, p. 107; Thompson, "Historical Perspective," pp. 253-54, and his comments on Walker (*Die Heilsgeschichte*, p. 77) in n. 26.

described -- may be read as a continuation and expansion of the original mandate rather than as its abrogation or restriction.

The Matthean temporal axis is complemented in the second discourse by echoes of its social counterpart. While the cross-ethnic separation of elite from marginal, faithful from faithless, appears throughout chapter 10, the problematic, future-oriented verses 10:17-18 play upon them directly. Beare suggests that within the second discourse two "violent" transitions appear: the lost sheep of 9:36 and 10:6 become the wolves of 10:16-18, and the harvesters of 9:37-38 assume the role of sheep.[42] Thus the evangelist has at best created a mixed metaphor and at worst distinction and separation rather than continuity in the chapter. However, the gospel's metaphors do not require this tight one-to-one correspondence. Because of the future thrust of 10:17ff., the persecuted sheep correspond not only to the twelve harvesters but also to the members of Matthew's church, among whom are some of the "lost sheep of the house of Israel"; the repetition of the term "sheep" in 9:36; 10:6; and 10:16 indicates Jewish ethnic continuity among the crowds, the twelve, and the future members of the church. Nor are the wolves to be equated with all Jews. References to the extensive harvest (9:37), to those who receive the missionaries (10:11-13), and to family divisions (10:21-22, 34-46) all indicate that the Jewish community will be split, some following Jesus and others persecuting his representatives. These wolves are better equated with the false shepherds implied in 9:36 -- they are the rulers who, like wolves, have failed to sustain the sheep.

The particular descriptions of those involved in the persecution of Jesus' followers identify the lines of the split.

---

[42]See his "Mission of the Disciples," p. 7.

Those who will reject the disciples are synagogue members, members of the the Jewish "councils" (συνέδρια), governors, and kings. Again, the elite are negatively depicted, and the marginal position of the disciples is emphasized in turn by their limited holdings (cf. 10:9-10), perpetual mobility, and metaphoric association with sheep. To reinforce these social categories, the evangelist concludes the initial discussion about persecution with a warning to the disciples about the dangers of hierarchical relationships and the suitability of egalitarian structures within the church (10:24-25).

Immediately preceding Jesus' comment on the relationship between servants and masters, teachers and disciples is perhaps the most problematic verse in the second discourse. But although Matt 10:23 has been labeled "an insolvable problem,"[43] scholars have rarely hesitated to offer opinions on such issues as its origin, its possible functions in the nascent church, its redactional indicators, and the relationship between its parts. Among these various studies, the divergent claims that 10:23 provides "at least a hint that the mission to Jews may be broken off if it meets with rejection"[44] and that the verse is "an argument of conservative Jewish Christianity against any mission to non-Jews on the grounds of the imminence of the *parousia*"[45] have

---

[43]Franzmann, *Discipleship*, p. 93; cf. Beare, "Mission of the Disciples," p. 4.

[44]Green, *The Gospel*, p. 110; cf. Hooker, "Uncomfortable Words," p. 363. H. Frankemölle, *Jahewbund und Kirche Jesu. Studien zur Form- und Traditionsgeschichte des Evangeliums nach Matthäus* (Münster: Aschendorff, 1974), p. 132, connects 10:23 with the theme of judgment introduced in 10:14-15.

[45]Green, *The Gospel*, p. 111; cf. G. E. P. Cox, *The Gospel According to Matthew: A Commentary* (London: SCM, 1952), p. 76 ("...a refreshing Christian realism as to the limits of their resources, unless the restriction is due to Matthew's Judaizing

direct implications for a study of the exclusivity logia. Jesus' comment that the disciples "will not have gone through all the towns of Israel before the Son of Man comes" concerns the limitation of Jesus' mission to the Jews, but it is neither a warning to the Jews nor, within its Matthean context, a reference to the parousia. Rather, the verse indicates that the Jewish mission will continue at least until the turn of the soteriological era, and it carries the implications that during the time of the church both the mission to Israel will continue and the restriction against gentiles will be lifted.

The recognition that Matt 10:5b-6 is an affirmation of the promises made to the Jews rather than a warning to them undercuts the claim that 10:23 has negative implications. Further, the continuity between the beginning of the second discourse and the Great Commission, the incompletion of the first mandate signaled by the omission of the mission itself, the cross-ethnic factors pertinent to the eschatological judgment, and the various other component parts of the temporal axis[46] counter the argument that 10:23 portends the cessation of the mission to Israel. The argument that the verse is a remnant of the proverbial narrow Jewish-Christian source antithetic to the gentile mission is similarly countered. Moreover, there is no firm indication outside of 10:23 that "Jewish Christianity" limited the scope of its mission because of the nearness of the parousia; to adduce the verse in support of this hypothesis creates a circular argument, and the

---

source"); Manson, *Sayings of Jesus*, p. 180.

[46]See *Jesus' Promise*, p. 20; G. Barth, "Matthew's Understanding of the Law," in *Tradition and Interpretation in Matthew*, eds. G. Bornkamm et al. (Philadelphia: Westminster, 1963), p. 111; S. Brown, "Mission to Israel," pp. 81-82, 85; Franzmann, *Discipleship*, p. 83; Hare, *Jewish Persecution*, p. 111 (on 10:23a); Schweizer, *Good News*, p. 244.

concerns of the (gentile) Christians in Thessalonica combined with Paul's early opinions on the imminence of the eschaton offer conflicting rather than corroborating data.[47]

Analysis of the terms employed in 10:23 further attenuates possible connections to the parousia. The RSV translation of 10:23b as "You will not have gone through all the towns of Israel" and the NEB reading "Before you have gone..." lose the force of the verb τελέω (μὴ τελέσητε). The more literal "You will not finish" makes clear that the first mission will not have been completed at the time of the Son of Man's coming.[48] This translation in turn provides a basis upon which to interpret the reference to "Israel". Some consider it an allusion to Diaspora communities or to those "far-flung villages of the world to which the risen Lord has sent" the disciples,[49] others opt for a geographical interpretation with historical implications indicating that the original disciples concentrated their activities in Palestine,[50] and still others

---

[47]Cf. W. D. Davies's review of P. Nepper-Christiansen's *Das Matthäusevangelium. Ein judenchristliches Evangelium*, in *JBL* 79 (1960): 90. Against interpreting 10:5b-6, 23; 15:24 as "expressions of undiluted nationalism" see Wilson, *Gentiles*, p. 16.

[48]See esp. Giblin, "Theological Perspective," pp. 637, 646-48; Kümmel, *Promise and Fulfillment*, pp. 61-62. Plummer, *Exegetical Commentary*, p. 153, suggests incorrectly that "gone through" may mean "completely converted."

[49]Senior, *Invitation to Matthew*, p. 107; cf. Munck, *Paul and the Salvation of Mankind*, p. 256 n. 1; Kilpatrick, *Origins of the Gospel*, p. 119; Strecker, *Der Weg*, p. 41; Jeremias, *Jesus' Promise*, p. 20; Wilson, *Gentiles*, pp. 16-17; and see S. Brown, "Mission to Israel," p. 87 n. 52.

[50]E.g., Brandon, *Jesus and the Zealots*, p. 173; cf. Hare, *Jewish Persecution*, pp. 110-11 ("in its earliest form" the expression "referred exclusively to Palestinian cities").

take a more theological approach that emphasizes personal rather than geographic or ethnic connotations: Israel "stands for those to whom Jesus himself had come in fulfillment of God's word, and who are representative of the Church's universal mission."[51] But if the verse is read within the context of the second discourse and particularly in light of the geographical implications of 10:5b-6 and the force of τελέσητε, then "Israel" appears to be a geographical reference indicating that the disciples will remain on Jewish soil and preach to Jewish people until the "coming of the Son of Man."

This conclusion leads to the final interpretive crux, since "coming" could conceivably refer to the parousia and/or the eschaton, to the disasters of 70 C.E., or to the resurrected Christ who inaugurates the gentile mission in 28:16-20. Analysis of the verse's contextual placement yields the most helpful result. The instructions given by Jesus in the second discourse are framed by two statements referring to Israel, 10:6 and 10:23. The first indicates that the mission of the disciples is restricted to Israel; the second implies that at the coming of the Son of Man the disciples' mission will not have been expanded to include the gentiles. Because the gospel therefore has not yet achieved its universal application (28:19), the "coming" -- in its Matthean context although perhaps it is not in its original setting -- cannot refer to the eschaton. Nor is a connection with the Jewish War in 70 suggested by the context: the discourse primarily concerns persecution on the religious and familial levels, not on battles with the empire. Consequently, Matt 10:23 most likely refers to the appearance of the risen Jesus, the "son" in whose name the disciples are to baptize (28:19), at the Great Commission.[52] The Son of Man will remain with the disciples

---

[51]Giblin, "Theological Perspective," p. 658, cf. p. 641.

[52]See Meier, *Vision of Matthew*, p. 74 n. 48; Wilson, *Gentiles*,

until they have "completed" (τελέω) their journeys, "until the completion" (ἕως τῆν συντελείας) of the age (28:20).

The Translation of 10:5b-6

The actual location of these journeys is initially described in the exclusivity pronouncements. Because the first phrase in 10:5b, Εἰς ὁδὸν ἐθνῶν μὴ ἀπέλθητε, can be interpreted metaphorically rather than literally, this "road of the gentiles" has been mapped in some colorful ways. Together with the notice to avoid Samaritan towns, the order to eschew the "road" or even the "way" of the gentiles is interpreted by Hippolytus, Clement of Alexandria, Origen, Cyprian, and the author of the Didascalia as a warning against heresy, false doctrine, and pagan behavior. However, in the context of such geographical notices as the frequent references to cities and towns (9:35; 10:11-15; 10:23), a more literal rather than metaphorical reading of 10:5b is warranted. The disciples are exhorted not to extend their preaching tour literally to non-Jewish areas (e.g., the Decapolis, Rome)[53] and, both more generally and more accurately, to non-Jewish people (cf. 15:21-28). The extension of the reference to gentile individuals is demanded by the structure of Matt 10:5b-6; the "road of the gentiles" is the antithetic parallel of the "lost sheep of the house of Israel."

These same observations are also applicable to the "town of the Samaritans" (εἰς πόλιν Σαμαριτῶν).[54] Albright and Mann

---

pp. 24-25.

[53]The anarthrous construction implies a "generic character." See Giblin, "Theological Perspective," p. 656; cf. Manson, *Sayings of Jesus*, p. 179.

[54]Jeremias, *Jesus' Promise*, pp. 19-20 and n. 5; Hill, *The*

propose emending πόλιν to πάλιν, and read "do not enter a Samaritan (town -- implied from the first part of the sentence) again."[55] While this suggestion prevents a contradiction with Jn 4:1-42, the received version is consistent with Jesus' activities in the first gospel. Moreover, the geographical limitations specified in 10:5b and perhaps recapitulated by the mention of Galilee in the Great Commission suggest that Matthew not only wanted to distance the mission from gentiles and Samaritans, but also wanted to focus on the Galilee as opposed to Jerusalem. The directives given in the injunctions limit the disciples to the Galilee, which is bordered on the south by Samaria and on the other three sides by gentile territory.[56] The concern for gentile areas conforms to the dictates of the temporal axis, and the order to avoid the capital would not be unexpected given the gospel's association of Jerusalem with elitism and abuse of power.

Several explanations for the inclusion of Samaritans in the restriction appear in the scholarly literature: Giblin, for example, concentrates on their connection with the gentiles and concludes that the gentiles are rendered inappropriate targets of the missionary enterprise by "their conjunction with a group traditionally representative of anti-Israel." Similarly, Albright and Mann conclude that Jesus restricted the mission because "the disciples, having a Jewish ethnic and religious background, might antagonize the Samaritans

---

Gospel, pp. 184-85; and Hooker, "Uncomfortable Words," p. 362, retranslate the "town" (πόλιν) of the Samaritans to the Aramaic מדינה, or "province" although all three note that 'city' is also a possible reading.

[55]*Matthew*, p. 116; cf. pp. clxi, 119.

[56]See Jeremias, *Jesus' Promise*, p. 20; Hooker, "Uncomfortable Words," p. 362.

unwittingly." And Kilpatrick takes this argument one step farther in his claim that the verse "shows the point of view of Rabbinic Judaism";[57] in this last case the Christian text is exempted from any hint of direct ethnic bigotry and the perceived unpleasant comment in the gospel is assigned to a Jewish source. But because Matt 10:5b is the only reference to the Samaritans in the gospel, there is no indication that the text manifests anti-Samaritan ethnic prejudice. While there was substantial animosity between Jews and Samaritans in the first century, this attitude was not present among all members of each group, and it certainly need not have been present among the ethnic Jews in Matthew's congregation. Nor does the claim that the reference to Samaritans must have negative implications because it is associated with a mention of gentiles (ἔθνη) hold. Neither the second discourse nor the rest of the gospel is anti-gentile.

The association of the Samaritans with the gentiles in the exclusivity logion does not signal racial or religious hatred, and the restriction of the mission should not be viewed as a negative valuation of either non-Jewish group. Matthew 10:5b-6 -- like the rest of the gospel -- indicates that the mission of the first era is restricted to the Jews. Samaritans are not to be evangelized by the twelve because they are not "Jews." Albright and Mann are incorrect in their claim that the residents of Samaria would be considered among the "lost sheep of the house of Israel."[58] Arguing against them are not only Acts 8:1-25, the self-definition of the Samaritan woman of Jn 4:22, both biblical and rabbinic distinctions between those who worship in Jerusalem and those whose temple is on

---

[57]Giblin, "Theological Perspective," p. 656; Albright and Mann, *Matthew*, p. 119; Kilpatrick, *Origins of the Gospel*, p. 121.

[58]*Matthew*, p. 119.

Mt. Gerizim, and even Josephus, who generally classifies the Samaritans with gentiles and who in *Ant.* 12.5.5 calls them "Sidonians."[59]

Because of its parallelism with 10:6 as well as its role in the construction of the temporal axis, the reference to the gentile roads and Samaritan cities is appropriately expanded to include the native inhabitants of these areas. Consequently, the first part of the exclusivity logion, Matt 10:5b, negatively defines the parameters of the mission: the disciples are not to evangelize among the non-Jews (gentiles and Samaritans). The second part of the logion, Matt 10:6 (cf. 15:24), makes explicit the disciples' focus: they are to direct (lit., to "go" [πορεύεσθε]) their activites to the "lost sheep of the house of Israel" (τά πρόβατα τά ἀπολωλότα οἴκου Ἰσραήλ). While the translation is clear,[60] the function of the genitive and so the correct interpretation of the verse remain debated. Either the "lost sheep" refers to specific individuals within Israel who are lost "because those responsible for guiding them have failed (9:36; 13:10-15; 16:3)," in which case the term is a partitive genitive; or it refers to all of Israel which is in a lost state, and as such is an epexegetical or explanatory genitive.[61]

---

[59]Although *Ant.* 11.8.6 refers to the "apostates of the Jewish nation" (ἀποστάτων τοῦ Ἰουδαίων ἔθνων) who lived in Shechem; see G. Alon, *Jews, Judaism*, pp. 358-60 and n. 21; Brandon, *Jesus and the Zealots*, pp. 134-35;

[60]Jeremias, *Jesus' Promise*, p. 20 n. 2, again appealing to an underlying Aramaic construct state, proposes that οικος, meaning "tribe", "lineage", or "community" is a Semitism. However, the interpretation "extended family" is also appropriate, and this is a commonplace in classical Greek. Gager's rendition, *Origins of Anti-Semitism*, p. 130, of "last sheep" is likely the result of editors with wool over their eyes.

[61]See the discussions in D. E. Garland, *The Intention of Matthew 23* (Leiden: Brill, 1979), p. 128; Hill, *The Gospel*, p.

Both interpretations are grammatically correct. The immediate context of the verse also fails to offer a definitive response. While the association of the lost sheep with the gentiles and Samaritans -- who are not divided into good and bad, elite and marginals -- commends the explanatory function, the introduction to the discourse in which the crowds are described as "sheep without a shepherd" favors the partitive reading. Indeed, both readings are appropriate. The explanatory genitive (cf. 15:24) combined with the injunction against evangelizing among the gentiles in 10:5b reinforces the prerogatives of the Jews. However, the identification of the crowds as "sheep without a shepherd" in 9:36 combined with the discourse's necessary interest in mobility, in testimony before elites (10:17-18), and in ministry to the marginal (10:8) commends the partitive. The logion thus indicates that only some members of the community -- the marginal "sheep" as opposed to the elite "shepherds" -- will heed the preaching of the disciples and join the new community.

The exclusivity statement is, consequently, the point at which the temporal and social axes conjoin. The mission of the disciples is restricted to the Jews in order to fulfill the promises made to them. But even in his conforming to the demands of Jewish tradition, the Matthean Jesus indicates to the disciples and so to the readers of the gospel that the ultimate distinction is not between Jew and gentile but between the disenfranchised, the powerless, and the marginal who are the "lost sheep," and the elite, immobile rulers who, although now maintaining patriarchal structures, will eventually be cast into the outer darkness. This social interest

---

254; Meier, "Nations or Gentiles," p. 95; Hooker, "Uncomfortable Words," p. 362; Jeremias, *Jesus' Promise*, p. 26 n. 3.

is, indeed, a dominant theme of the gospel, as the following chapters on the genealogy, the infancy narrative, the gentile centurion and the Canaanite woman, and the erroneous claim that according to the first gospel the Jews have lost their opportunity for salvation demonstrate.

II

The Genealogy

The genealogy of Jesus recorded in the first chapter of Matthew has given birth to a series of exegetical offspring. That the five women listed in Jesus' ancestry have an import determined by a common factor other than simply their sex is not debated. Nor is it questioned that they are more than ancestral markers: unlike those rare women present in earlier biblical genealogies (e.g., Gen 22:20-24; 25:1-6; 35:22b-26; I Chron 2:3-4, 18-20, 46-47), the five do more than distinguish between clans or tribes, or between the children of concubines and those of wives. However, the connection between the genealogy and the rest of the gospel and the symbolic role of the women both remain topics for discussion. The two questions are interrelated, and literary criticism provides some guidelines for the resolution of each.

Since the evangelist has placed the genealogy at the beginning of the gospel it is not inappropriate to view this material as having some thematic consistency with, or indeed as programmatic for, the rest of the text. Further, while the genealogy may derive from a source, the evangelist has integrated it into and made it integral for interpreting the remainder of the gospel by retaining or including vocabulary and phrasing similar to that employed in the other twenty-seven chapters. Such contrived elements as the three divisions of fourteen generations, the omission of such well-known members of the Davidic line as Joash, Amaziah, Azariah, and Jehoiakim, and the inclusion of such seemingly superfluous elements as the mention of "and his brothers" (καὶ τοὺς ἀδελφοὺς αὐτοῦ) in 1:2, 11 portend underlying themes relevant for the remainder of the text. Finally, there is no convincing reason for the evangelist to have preserved this material were it incompatible with the remainder of the gospel. For example, the *Anchor Bible Commentary*'s assertion that the presence of gentile women indicates traditional rather than redactional composition -- "a Jewish-Christian would only have used [this motif] because tradition compelled him to do so" -- lacks appreciation for the author's narrative art, for the symbolic role of gentiles in the first gospel, and for the diverse views on gentiles expressed by both Jews and Jewish-Christians in the first century.[1]

While vocabulary and syntax shared by the genealogy and the account of Jesus' ministry can point to redactional and even thematic connections, the interpretation of these connections remains problematic. Shared vocabulary is hard data; analysis of the various motifs depicted in the genealogy in part relies on artistic judgment. The critic continually faces the dangers of a circular argument: is the presence of the women in the genealogy to be explained in terms of the depiction of gentiles in the rest of the gospel, or are these gentile characters and the comments about the ἐθνικός throughout the gospel to be interpreted in relation to the genealogy? The critic's first step is to look at the genealogy

[1]W. F. Albright and C. S. Mann, *Matthew* (New York: Doubleday, 1971), p. 5. On the connection between the genealogy and the rest of the gospel see K. Stendahl, "Quis et Unde? An Analysis of Mt 1-2," in Stanton, p. 57; and on redactional elements, M. D. Johnson, *The Purpose of the Biblical Genealogies with Special Reference to the Setting of the Genealogies of Jesus* (Cambridge: University Press, 1969), pp. 210-28; W. B. Tatum, "The Origin of Jesus Messiah (Matt 1:1, 18a): Matthew's Use of the Infancy Traditions," *JBL* 96 (1977): 524; R. Brown, *The Birth of the Messiah* (New York: Doubleday, 1979), esp. p. 48 and n. 13.

on its own terms, and then to see whether the conclusions reached are supported by the remainder of the gospel. If they are, then the exegesis of Matthew 1 has been successful; if they are not, then three options remain open: either the exegesis in question is incorrect; or, the analysis of the remainder of the gospel needs correction; or, the evangelist is an inept author who has not harmonized the introductory chapter with the remainder of the narrative. The third option can be bracketed by the literary critic interested in the wholeness of the text; the reader demands closure and will create it even when it is not immediately present. With the first gospel, however, such extreme machinations are unnecessary: a literary-critical reading of the genealogy -- one that departs from the traditional interpretations in favor of a deconstructionist-feminist reading -- points to a plausible interpretation both of the five women in Jesus' ancestry and of the connection between the first chapter and the remainder of the gospel.

In the search for the common factor by which the presence of the women in the Matthean genealogy can best be understood, Krister Stendahl has expressed most clearly the theory that the women "represent an 'irregularity' in the Davidic line" indicated by their somewhat unorthodox and certainly unexpected sexual activities.[2] The competing theory, which establishes the genealogy as a pivotal chapter for Matthean universalism, claims that four women are united by their gentile backgrounds. Any conclusion based on these theories must, in turn, address two issues. First, because of the five women only Mary is mentioned in the gospel outside of the genealogy, the connection among the first four must be

---

[2]"Quis," p. 60, cf. p. 65 n. 31; cf. R. Bloch, "Juda engendra Phares et Zara de Thamar, Matt 1,3," in *Mélanges Bibliques* (Paris: Bloud and Gay, 1957), pp. 381-89.

established on the basis of evidence external to Matthew's work: biblical, pseudepigraphical, rabbinic, patristic. Second, the interpretation of the factor must be shown to be consistent with themes developed in the remainder of the gospel. While the common denominator of the first theory, the unorthodox manner of perpetuating the line, is easily demonstrated on the basis of the outside sources, both its interpretation and its connection with the remainder of the gospel remain elusive. The converse of this situation characterizes the second theory. Based on the other twenty-seven chapters of Matthew, several plausible interpretations of the presence of gentiles in Jesus' genealogy can be formulated. But proving from external sources that for the evangelist all five, or even four, of the women are non-Jews is impossible. Thus the presence of the five women must anticipate something more than the inclusion of gentiles in either the messianic line or the Matthean church.

That these two interpretations have stood for so long reveals both a lack of consensus among biblical scholars and the incompleteness of each explanation. After examining the weaknesses of these two theories this chapter offers a third alternative incorporating the helpful elements of both: the women represent people oppressed by dominant political, religious, and social systems. While the genealogy does foreshadow the inclusion of gentiles in the Christian community, it does more than address ethnic concerns. Jesus' lineage symbolizes the welcome of his church to the marginal and the excluded, to all denied status or privilege by members of elite groups, to all whose higher righteousness is undervalued by structures of patriarchy. In turn, the genealogy encourages the powerless to act. Achieving righteousness is not a passive process, and no one -- including if not only women -- should therefore capitulate to an unjust social structure.

Irregularities in the Davidic Line

The theory that the common factor uniting the first four women in the genealogy is their somewhat unusual sexual activities is substantially supported by biblical descriptions: Tamar posed as a prostitute and seduced her father-in-law; Rahab was a prostitute; Ruth enticed the drunken Boaz on the threshing floor; and Bathsheba committed adultery with David. This theory has the added merit of beginning with the internal content of the genealogy rather than with a presupposed interpretation of the gospel as a whole. Complications arise, however, over the best *interpretation* of the data. Not even those hypothetical antinominians, against whom Matthew may have included material on the retention of the Torah, would argue that the gospel commends seduction as a form of higher righteousness. Yet the traditional interpretations of the four women are not without problems. When the extended descriptions of the women in the Hebrew scriptures as well as in rabbinic and pseudepigraphic commentaries, the association of the four with Mary, and the likely reconstruction of the Matthean church engaged in debate with the local Jewish community are taken into account, the three principal explanations of these "irregularities" -- the women are sinners in need of [Christian] redemption, they respond to controversies over the messiah's lineage, and they are evidence of the entry of God into history -- are all found to be inadequate.

The first interpretation, offered by church fathers such as Origen and Jerome, proposes that the women represent all sinners redeemed by Jesus. This fine example of patristic patriarchal attitude finds expression even in the modern era. As Franzmann succinctly observes, the women "are anything but paragons of virtue."[3] Yet the explanation has problems both historical-critically and ideologically. While dominant members of the apostolic church may have perceived Matthew's women, or all women, to be trapped in as well as agents of sin, the Jewish sources are much less explicit in equating these particular women with improper action. Tamar's favorable mention in Ruth 4:12 is adopted by Philo, who views her as a model of virtue and chastity,[4] and rabbinic discussions of Bathsheba usually place responsibility on David.[5] Jubilees 41

---

[3]*Discipleship*, p. 11. On the patristic commentaries (e.g., Origen *Homily on Luke* no. 28; Jerome *In Matt.* 9), see A. D. Heffern, "The Four Women in St. Matthew's Genealogy of Christ," *JBL* 31 (1912): 70; Brown, *Birth*, p. 71. J. C. Anderson, "Matthew: Gender and Reading," in M. A. Tolbert (ed.), *The Bible and Feminist Hermeneutics* (= *Semeia* 28 [1983]), p. 9, addresses the "Eve/Mary polarity" in which "women, sexuality, and sin are linked."

[4]*Quod Deus* 136 (on Gen 38); *On the Virtues* 220-22. See also, e.g., *Gen Rabbah* 85 and *T. B. Hor.* 10b (R. Ulla, ca. 260): "Tamar committed adultery and Zimri also committed adultery. Tamar committed adultery and kings and prophets descended from her; Zimri committed adultery and through him many tens of thousands in Israel fell." *T. B. Sotah* 10a and *T. P. Sotah* 5a, 16d are rare vindications of Judah accomplished by attributing sinful activity to Tamar.

[5]See *Mid. Sam* 25:2; *T. B. Kidd.* 43a (a baraita of Shammai presented apparently as an alternative to the prevailing view); and *T. P. Taan.* 2:10. In *Mid. Ps* 3:3 (cf. 4:2) David prays: "Master of the Universe! It is revealed and known to thee that Bathsheba was held ready for me from the six days of creation, yet she was given to me for sorrow." Here blame is placed on the deity rather than on the woman. Johnson, *Genealogies,* pp. 159-75 extensively discusses these and other primary sources relevant to the four women in Matt 1:3-6.

and the Testament of Judah 10:6, while admitting that Tamar's activities were less than kosher, ascribe blame neither to her nor to Judah but to Judah's Canaanite wife, who refused to allow Shelah to fulfill his Levirate duties. And *CD* 7:7 claims David's actions were not punished "save only the blood of Uriah," Bathsheba is not mentioned. Even the association of Rahab with what was considered a socially improper form of sexual activity is modified in the later sources. Josephus, for example, calls her an innkeeper (which may be a euphemism), and the rabbinic materials emphasize her sinful past only to provide a contrast to her repentance and conversion.[6] Thus the first association many Jews would make with Rahab would be "ideal convert" rather than prostitute or sinner. Finally, Ruth is not accused of sin in either the biblical or the rabbinic traditions. Her actions on the threshing floor, undertaken on the advice of her mother-in-law no less, may have been seductive and wily, but they were neither illegal nor, at least according to the various accounts of the event, immoral. While her Moabite ancestry -- which recalls the incestuous relationship between Lot and his daughters -- was construed as tainted, discussion of her ancestry properly belongs to the second general theory: that the women are united by their

---

[6]*Ant* 5.1.1; cf. *Targ. Josh* 2:1. In Heb 11:31, "Rahab the prostitute" (Ῥαὰβ ἡ πόρνη) is an example of proper faith and is placed in the company of Abraham and Moses; cf. I Clem 12; and the discussion in B. Bamberger, *Proselytism in the Talmudic Period,* rev. ed. (New York: KTAV, 1968), p. 194. Johnson, *Genealogies,* p. 162, suggests Rahab is more extensively exonerated in the rabbinic tradition because she has no explicit association with the house of David. For a helpful study of the Rahab tradition in the rabbinic documents, see esp. J. R. Baskin, *Pharoah's Counsellors: Job, Jethro, and Balaam in Rabbinic and Patristic Tradition* (Chico, CA: Scholars, 1983), pp. 45-54, 74.

gentile backgrounds. Ultimately, the emphasis on "sin" in the patristic commentaries reveals more about the patriarchal interpretations of the critics than about the agenda of Matthew's genealogy. What the church fathers perceived to be sin was neither necessarily considered sinful by the women themselves nor by the several Jewish writers -- men not usually reknowned for their positive assessment of women's activities -- who either exonerated them or used them as moral exemplars, nor by the first gospel. If Matthew did view the four as particularly in need of redemption, then the lack of explicit connection between women (as opposed to men) and sin in the rest of the gospel is surprising. Finally, as Heffern concludes, the evangelist had no "need to seek in them the types of sin, since a selection from the genealogical line of the men would equally or better serve such a purpose."[7]

These observations are confirmed when Tamar, Rahab, Ruth, and Bathsheba are compared to the fifth woman in the genealogy, Mary. While the accusation of sin might have been made against her -- "Before they came together she was found to be pregnant" (πρὶν ἤ συνελθεῖν αὐτοὺς εὑρέθη ἐν γαστρὶ ἔχουσα) -- she is guiltless; in 1:18 the agent of her pregnancy is clearly noted: "the Holy Spirit" (ἐκ πνεύματος ἁγίου). The association of the four women with Mary does not, however, rule out the theory that the common denominator uniting them is their sexual activity. Rather, it leads to a second interpretation of this shared factor.

As early as 1751, Wettstein suggested that the five women are intended to refute Jewish charges that Jesus was

---

[7]"Four Women," p. 72; cf. Johnson, *Genealogies,* p. 156; R. E. Brown et al., *Mary in the New Testament* (Philadelphia: Fortress; New York: Paulist, 1978), p. 81; and even F. Spitta, "Die Frauen in der Genealogie des Matthäus," *ZWT* 54 (1912): 1-8.

illegitimate.[8] The genealogy would then be analogous to Matt 28:11-15, in which the evangelist counters the Jews' claim that the disciples had stolen Jesus' body. But the analogy is weak support for the theory of Jewish calumny, and four other factors render the conclusion improbable. First, it cannot be determined when Jewish accusations of an illegitimate birth began; the infancy narratives of Matthew and Luke may well be the source of and not the answer to the charge.[9] Second, the argument that Mary conceived by the Holy Spirit seems unlikely to convince doubters that she did not commit adultery. Indeed, the inclusion of Bathsheba in the genealogy would suggest that Mary did engage in some sort of moral impropriety. The better argument would have been either not to mention the circumstances of Jesus' birth or to make explicit Joseph's paternity. Matthew would have known of the former option from Mark, and might have settled for the latter given the gospel's familiarity with the tradition of Joseph's paternity (e.g., 13:55). Similarly, the evangelist could have responded directly, on the model of 28:11ff., to this hypothetical Jewish charge. Thus, third, the argument based on consistency of style is attenuated by both structural and grammatical observations. While the claim that the disciples stole the body is explicit -- "Tell people, 'His disciples came

---

[8]Followed by Zahn, Allen, Klostermann, and J. Weiss. See the summaries in Heffern, "Four Women," p. 75; A. H. McNeile, *The Gospel According to St. Matthew* (London: Macmillan, 1915), p. 5; R. Leany, "The Birth Narratives in St. Luke and St. Matthew," *NTS* 8 (1961/62): 165; and Johnson, *Genealogies,* p. 158.

[9]The charge first appears in Christian sources: the Acts of Pilate 2:3 (second century); cf. Origen *Contra Celsum* 1.29, 32, 69. On Jn 8:41, see Brown et al., *Mary,* p. 205. On the Ben Stada and Ben Panthera traditions, see M. Goldstein, *Jesus in the Jewish Tradition* (New York: Macmillan, 1950); and Johnson, *Genealogies,* pp. 147-48.

by night and stole him away while we were asleep'...and this story has been spread among the Jews to this day" (28:13, 15; cf. the other direct accusations in 9:11, 14; 12:2) -- the charge of illegitimacy is not. Matthew does not hesitate to condemn the Jews for such explicit claims as the assertion that Jesus is in league with the Devil and the proclamation that he is mad; the absence of the charge of illegitimacy is therefore striking. Finally, W. D. Davies observes that "polemic seldom creates poetry, and we can be sure that the motive of combating Jewish slanders against Mary's chastity is inadequate to account for the richness of the infancy narrative."[10] Ultimately, even if the first gospel is responding to charges of Jesus' illegitimacy, this conclusion insufficiently explains the presence of the four women.

Also arguing from the perspective of the controversies surrounding both Jesus' ancestry and his messianic qualifications, Johnson suggests that the unexpected activities of the women in the royal line were criticized by those who favored a Levitical or Aaronic heavenly representative (the Sadducean position?) rather than a Davidic messiah.[11] According to this interpretation, by specifically mentioning Tamar, Rahab, Ruth, and Uriah's wife, Matthew lends support to the Pharisaic expectations. This explanation is weakened by the lateness of the sources that document the controversy (e.g., *Midrash Rabbah* 8:1 on Ruth 4:18-21) as well as by the lack of external evidence connecting Rahab with the Davidic line.[12] Further, the remainder of the gospel suggests

---

[10] *Setting*, p. 66; cf. Hill, *The Gospel*, p. 77; Johnson, *Genealogies,* pp. 158-59; and esp. Senior, *Invitation to Matthew*, p. 27.

[11] *Genealogies*, pp. 176-77, cf. pp. 205, 209.

[12] On the former point, see Brown et al., *Mary,* p. 80; on the latter see R. H. Gundry, *Matthew: A Commentary on His Literary and Theological Art* (Grand Rapids: Eerdmans, 1982), p. 164.

that the debate with the Sadducees is a thing of the past (cf. the identification of their theological beliefs in 22:23).

The third interpretation proposes that these women represent the mysterious workings of the deity in salvation history. In other words, "their presence may be intended to suggest the lack of convention in the process of divine providence."[13] Not only does this conclusion fail to address what is specifically unconventional -- their sexual activity -- it is also too general. The same conclusion can be drawn from the theory that the women are united by gentile descent or association. Indeed, given the rarity of women's appearance in genealogies, their very mention can be invoked to support this theory. Moreover, one may well ask whether the presence of several of the men named in the genealogy -- Solomon, who is condemned for his consorting with foreign wives, Manasseh the archetypal sinner, etc. -- provides a better example of the deity's surprising program for redemption. While these particular women may draw readers to the text, the contrived nature of the genealogy as a whole suggests the evangelist had more in mind than enticing an audience.

A related interpretation, which focuses on the entry of the Holy Spirit at specific times in Israel's history, also incompletely explains heaven's lack of convention. According to this view, the Spirit appears at key moments in Jesus' life (3:16; 4:1; 28:19) just as the women appear at significant stages in Israel's history: Tamar in the patriarchal period, Rahab at the entry into Palestine, Ruth in the time of the judges, and Bathsheba during the monarchy.[14] While not inaccurate, this interpretation receives little support from the gospel itself. The genealogy makes specific reference to only

---

[13]Hill, *Gospel*, p. 74; cf. Franzmann, *Discipleship*, p. 11.

[14]Franzmann, *Discipleship*, p. 11; cf. Brown, *Birth*, p. 73; Bloch, "Juda engendra," pp. 386-87.

one of the four stages, and this indirectly ("David the King" in 1:6). The other key period mentioned in the first chapter, the exile to Babylon (1:11), is not associated even indirectly with a woman. Nor is the Holy Spirit a major motif in either the biblical or the extracanonical characterizations of the first four women. For Matthew, the Spirit provides a partial link between the genealogy and Mary, but it does not explain the presence of the first four women.

The five women in the genealogy clearly share one common factor: their activities all involve a form of unconventional sexual activity. Yet the major interpretations of this shared factor are neither comprehensive nor adequate. Rabbinic exonerations of Tamar, the tendency to shift the blame to David for the affair with Bathsheba, the rehabilitation of Rahab, the generally positive assessments of Ruth, and Mary's innocence argue against the patristic view of the women as sinners redeemed by Jesus. Even though Matthew's gospel is, like all the New Testament documents, an androcentric text produced by a patriarchal culture, this observation does not give the critic leave to assert an overriding negative association between women and sin. Not only are the men in the genealogy better examples of sinners who require redemption, throughout the gospel it is primarily men rather than women who require the instruction of and mercy of Jesus. The arguments based on Jewish slanders or on the debate between Pharisaic/Davidic and Sadducaic/Aaronic parties are also flawed: the infancy narratives may have provoked the Jewish charges; the sources employed to support the interpretations are late; the tone of the infancy accounts suggests more than merely apologetic interests; the remainder of the gospel indicates that Sadducaic concerns are a thing of the past; and, in any case, the women themselves fail to provide an adequate rebuttal to either Jewish calumnists or

Sadducaic supporters. Finally, the explanation based on "lack of convention" is too general: it simply reiterates the common factor rather than deals with the genealogy's focus on sexual activity.

These various interpretations also fail to address the *distinction* the evangelist makes between the first four women and Mary. The references to the first four are all preceded by the formula "X the father of Y by (ἐκ τῆς) Z" (1:3a, 5a, 5b, 6b); Mary's name stands as a possessive genitive: "Joseph, the husband of Mary, of whom Jesus was born" (τὸν Ἰωσὴφ τὸν ἄνδρα Μαρίας, ἐξ ἧν ἐγεννήθη Ἰησοῦς, 1:16).[15] And Mary was a virgin not only preceding but also following her conception of her son; this claim cannot be made for the other four. Finally, the genealogy is that of Joseph, not Mary, and thus she is clearly distinguished from the first four women: Tamar, Rahab, Ruth, and Bathsheba are all related by blood to Joseph; Mary has merely an unconsummated marriage. Any interpretation of the Matthean genealogy consequently must address both the connections among the five and the differences between the first four and Mary.

Gentile Descent

According to one critic, "It is highly probable that at the time of the composition of Matthew, each of the four, in Jewish tradition, was considered to be of Gentile stock."[16]

---

[15]H. C. Waetjen, "The Genealogy as the Key to the Gospel According to Matthew," *JBL* 95 (1976): 216.

[16]Johnson, *Genealogies,* p. 153; cf. H. Stegemann, "'Die des Uria': Zur Bedeutung der Frauennamen in der Genealogie von Matthäus 1,11-17," in G. Jeremias et al. (eds.), *Tradition und Glaube* (Göttingen: Vandenhoeck and Ruprecht, 1972), pp. 246-76; Schweizer, *Good News*, p. 25; H. Milton, "The Structure of

Given the concentration placed by certain Jews of the Second Commonwealth on genealogical purity[17] the Matthean depiction of Jesus' ancestry would then be doubly anomalous; not only are women included but also these women are gentiles. This observation leads to two related interpretations which are both consistent with themes established elsewhere in the first gospel: the women foreshadow Jesus' concern for gentiles,[18] and they reveal the power of the deity to accomplish the unfolding of salvation history through the actions of people outside the covenant community. Matthew's later explicit interest in opening the church to the gentiles thus plays the major role for this theory in determining the connection among the first four women. The conclusion that their gentile ancestry is the common denominator can also be related to the frequently proposed reconstruction of the Matthean *Sitz im Leben*. This predominantly Jewish church has begun a gentile mission, and ethnic non-Jews are entering the new community. The Jewish congregants need to be reminded that the gentiles have a legitimate place within salvation history, and the gentiles need the support for their new status that their compatriots in the genealogy as well as in the remainder of the gospel provide. Thus the four women justify

---

the Prologue to St. Matthew's Gospel," *JBL* 81 (1962): 176-77; Franzmann, *Discipleship*, pp. 10-11; Gundry, *Matthew*, pp. 14-15; and others.

[17]Johnson, *Genealogies,* pp. 85-89 (*Mid. Ps* 87:6; *Num Rabbah* 8:8; *T. B. Kidd.* 72a; *T. B. Pes.* 62b; I Chron 1:1-9:44); H. B. Green, *The Gospel According to Matthew* (London: Oxford, 1975), p. 53.

[18]Johnson, *Genealogies,* pp. 154-55, citing Origen, Chrysostom, Jerome, Ambrose, Luther, and a host of modern scholars. Heffern, "Four Women," p. 80, adds that the universalism of Rom 9-11 also begins with a genealogical reference. See also Stegemann, "Die des Uria," pp. 246-76; Brown, *Birth*, p. 72; J. Daniélou, *The Infancy Narratives* (New York: Herder and Herder, 1968), p. 17.

the entry of the gentiles into the church.

While Matthew's gospel evinces substantial interest in non-Jews (e.g., 8:5-13; 15:21-28; 28:19), the theme of universalism is anticipated less by the women than by the Magi in the second chapter.[19] Further, the difficulties of ascribing a gentile background to Mary, Tamar, and Bathsheba as well as the evidence that Ruth and Rahab were regarded by first-century Jews not as gentiles per se but as proselytes substantially weaken the second theory.

The assertion of Mary's gentile ancestry is, while an excellent example of anti-Jewish propaganda,[20] impossible to support on the basis of the New Testament materials. Matthew portrays her as a well-known member of the Galilean Jewish community; Luke corroborates her fidelity to Jewish

---

[19]Connecting the genealogy's universalism with the mention of Abraham are Meier, *Vision*, p. 53 n. 14; Milton, "Structure," p. 176; Kingsbury, *Matthew*, p. 37; Brown, *Birth*, p. 67 (calling the theme "subtle"); Johnson, *Genealogies*, p. 169 (citing *T. B. Yeb.* 63a); Hill, *Gospel*, p. 93. On the reference to Abraham in 3:9, cf. Hare, *Jewish Persecution*, p. 157, who notes that "this motif is not developed in relationship to Gentile believers." Abraham is the hope of Jews (3:9) and of all marginal peoples (8:11; cf. 22:29-33), but he is not the explicit hope of the gentiles. Moreover, the tradition of messianic descent from Abraham (TLevi 8:15) could account for the patriarch's prominent position in Matthew 1. Finally, Abraham's Matthean prominence relies on his association with other figures in biblical history and not on his connection with the promise in Gen 12:3.

[20]E.g., R. Seeberg, "Die Herkunft der Mutter Jesu," *Theologische Festschrift für G. N. Bonwetch* (Leipzig: Deichert, 1918), pp. 13-24, cited by Brown, *Birth*, p. 73 n. 29; and both F. Delitzch, *The Great Delusion*; and E. Jung, *Die Herkunft Jesu* (which claims Mary was a Samaritan raped by the Roman Panthera), cited by J. S. Bloch, *Israel and the Nations* (Berlin/Vienna: Benjamin Harz, 1927), p. 415.

traditions; and Rom 9:5; 15:8 leave no room for debate. Nor can Lohmeyer's related theory that, on the basis of Matt 2:19-22, Mary's Galilean background makes her analogous to the gentile women in the genealogy be accepted.[21] Although more plausible than the arguments for Mary's gentile ancestry, this suggestion is attenuated by the gospel's initial portrayal of Mary not as a native of Galilee but of Bethlehem. Further, the Pharisaic presence in Galilee throughout the gospel combined with the explicit mention of Galilean synagogues undercuts the gentile connection. According to the first gospel, Galilee is no more and no less "Jewish" than Jerusalem. The distinction between the two locations is one of social divisions and power structures, not one of ethnic or religious orientation. If it could be determined that of the five women mentioned in Matthew 1 only Mary is Jewish, the hypothesis that gentile descent unites the women of Joseph's ancestry would remain viable. The distinction between the four and Jesus' mother might be employed to explain the syntactical shift present in the introduction of Mary. However, this approach has two substantial drawbacks: first, it obviates the concern for an element common to the five; and second, the evidence that the other four are gentiles is not at all clear-cut.

While Mary's background is not in doubt, the ancient sources present no consensus on Tamar's ancestry. Because the

---

[21]E. Lohmeyer (and W. Schmauch), *Das Evangelium des Matthäus* (Göttingen: Vandehoeck and Ruprecht, 1958), p. 5 (cited by Johnson, *Genealogies*, p. 155): "Alle vier Frauen treten als Fremd, sei es nach Blut und Glauben oder nach ihrem Leben und Schicksale, indie Verheissung des Messias-Geschlechtes ein; wenn Mt vorausgesetzt hat, dass Maria aus dem fernen und verfemten Galiläa stammte (s.zu 2:19-22), so ware damit eine gewisse Analogie gegeben." This connection by *either* blood and belief *or* life and fate is also strained: "foreignness" need not be so broadly defined.

biblical text does not mention her background, Jewish writers sought to fill in the gap. According to Philo (*De Virtutibus* 220-22; *De Nobilitate* 6), Pseudo-Jonathan (on Gen 38:3), and *T. B. Sotah* 10, she is a gentile convert to Judaism.[22] In Jubilees 41:1 and TJud 10:1; 12:2 she is called a "daughter of Aram"; the designation relates her to the Jewish community while preserving the original ambiguity in the Hebrew account (cf. the targumim to Num 23:9; Dt 33:15, and *Sifre Dt* 33:15). Occasionally, she is identified as a daughter of Shem, who is himself considered to be a Hebrew priest.[23] In light of these various identifications, it cannot be determined if either the author or the earliest readers of the first gospel would have considered Tamar a gentile.

Her presence in the genealogy is further complicated by the accompanying mention of her son Zerah, who is not part of the messianic line. This apparently superfluous reference

---

[22]*De Virtutibus* identifies Tamar as "a woman from Syria-Palestine who had been brought up in her own native city, which was devoted to the worship of many gods." *Sotah* recreates the following dialogue: R. Samuel b. Nachmani (ca. 260 C. E.) said, "When [Judah] solicited her, he asked her, 'Are you perhaps a Gentile?' She replied, 'I am a proselyte.' 'Are you perhaps a married woman?' She replied, 'I am unmarried'....'Perhaps you are unclean?' She replied, 'I am clean.'" See Johnson, *Genealogies*, pp. 159-60, 271-72; J. A. Raisin, *Gentile Reactions to Jewish Ideals with Special Reference to Proselytes* (New York: Philosophical Library, 1953), p. 112; Bloch, "Juda engendra," pp. 381-89; Bamberger, *Proselytism*, pp. 180, 210; Brown, *Birth*, p. 72.

[23]*Genesis Rabbah* 85:11 (on Gen 10:22): "Ephraim Mikshaah, a disciple of R. Meir, said in the latter's name, 'Tamar was the daughter of Shem, for it is written: And the daughter of any priest, if she profane herself by playing the harlot...she shall burn with fire (Lev 21:9); consequently, Judah said: "Bring her forth and let her be burned"' (Gen 38:24)" (cited by Johnson, *Genealogies*, pp. 270-71, cf. p. 133 on *Ruth Rabbah* 8:1).

suggests that more than either sexual irregularities or gentile descent is to be associated with Tamar. Johnson proposes that the extraneous element may be dependent on I Chron 2:3-4 and "intended merely to distinguish Judah's sons with Tamar from his sons with Bath-Shua the Canaanitess."[24] But not only is the necessity of this distinction questionable, the appeal to the Chronicler fails to explain either Matthew's willingness to omit others mentioned by that earlier writer or the absence of Bath-Shua from the gospel account. Nor would Matthew's audience have required this explicit distinction. Finally, since Bath-Shua was a Canaanite (Gen 38:2), had the first gospel a dominant interest in connecting gentiles to the messianic line, the reference to Bath-Shua rather than to Zerah would have been more appropriate. Gundry, on the other hand, suggests that such additional references as "and his brothers" and "Zerah" are prefigurations of "the brotherhood of the church."[25] While not implausible, the explanation fails to indicate why other brothers (e.g., the other children of Jesse, David, and Solomon) are also not mentioned. Rather, the mention of the brothers in Matt 1:2, 11 seems to indicate the extent of the community's exiles: according to the genealogy, the entire people participated in the move first to Egypt (a theme further developed in chap. 2) and later to Babylon. The evangelist thus places the entire Davidic line in the context of weakness and disenfranchisement. Further, Gundry's explanation is attenuated by the functions of the brothers of both Perez and Jechoniah: these individuals are clearly not part of the messianic line, and so they appear as branches grafted onto the family. Perhaps Matthew is here indicating that a divine plan is being followed not only by Jesus in his ministry, but also by the deity in establishing the messiah's ancestry. Just as the

---

[24] *Genealogies*, p. 152.
[25] *Matthew*, pp. 14-19.

mission of Jesus can only go to the Jews, so Jesus' own lineage can only go through one male ancestor at a time. The gentiles, like the men from whom Jesus does not descend, have a place in the ministry of the church, but not an equal one during the era of Israel. Finally, given that Zerah's line produced the unrighteous Achan, the reference to this twin suggests that membership in the ethnic community to which the promises were given and from which the messiah was to descend is no guarantee of salvation. In light of these various observations, both the issue of Tamar's ancestry and the appearance of Zerah in the genealogy place stumbling blocks in the way of theories emphasizing her gentile associations.

Bathsheba is identified in Matthew's genealogy as "she of Uriah" (τῆς τοῦ Οὐρίου); hence she obtains her association with gentiles through her husband. In some rabbinic sources her marriage alone casts doubt on Bathsheba's Jewish origins.[26] However, the same notation that associates her with Uriah undercuts her connection with Matthew's interest in gentiles in two ways. First, Uriah is not explicitly identified as a Hittite in the genealogy; second, he is identified as a husband. Thus Bathsheba's conjugal activity rather than her gentile association is emphasized.

Unlike Tamar, Bathsheba, and Mary, the gentile backgrounds of Rahab and Ruth are unquestioned. Nevertheless, because both these women were regarded as ideal proselytes, the claim that they should be equated thematically with Matthew's interest in non-Jews is weakened. And because the first gospel manifests no explicit concern for conversion to Judaism (e.g., the Great Commission issues a command to baptize, not to circumcize or give a donation to the Temple),

---

[26]Raisin, *Gentile Reactions,* p. 71, claims Bathsheba was regarded as a Hittite whose name is a Semitic slurring of Kuti-Kheba. See also Johnson, *Genealogies,* pp. 152-53, 173.

the two women are also unlikely representative models for the church's missionary endeavors. Matthew likely expected gentile members of the new community to conform to Jewish *Halakhah*, and therefore the women may in part function as models for the gentile Christians. However, this symbolic role concerns behavior within the church rather than the mission to the gentiles itself; the ethnic interest is subordinated to the concern for Jewish orthopraxis. The association of Ruth and Rahab with Tamar, Bath-Sheba, and Mary as well as the descriptions given in the Hebrew Bible of their alliances with Israel argue too against any programmatic emphasis on gentile origins.

Rahab's gentile background is the necessary precondition for the accounts of her conversion, but it receives scant attention in the early sources.[27] Indeed, these documents are more likely to comment on her daily profession of prostitution than on her gentile profession of faith. Concerning the other exemplary woman proselyte, Ruth, Jewish legend even suggests that her conversion was foretold: to Abraham (*T. B. Yeb.* 63a), Lot (*Gen Rabbah* 41:4; 50:10), and Moses (*T. B. Bikk.* 38a, b).[28] Unlike Rahab, however, Ruth's dissociation from her gentile background rather than her sexual activity receives the bulk of the later commentary. Also unlike Rahab, Ruth is explicitly named as an ancestor of David by the Hebrew scriptures. Yet her participation in this messianic line is

---

[27]Bamberger, *Proselytism*, pp. 190 (citing e.g., *Cant Rabbah* 1:15), 193-94; Brown, *Birth*, p. 72 (citing Heb 11:31; and I Clem 12:1); Johnson, *Genealogies*, pp. 163 n. 1 (citing *Cant Rabbah* as well as *Num Rabbah* 3:2; *Eccl Rabbah* 5:11; *Pesikta Rabbati* 9; *M. Ber.* 2:8), 164; and Baskin, *Pharoah's Counsellors*, p. 73 (citing Aphraates).

[28]Bamberger, *Proselytism*, pp. 195-99; I. Abrahams, *Studies in Pharisaism and the Gospels*, vol. 1 (New York: KTAV, 1967), p. 36.

almost invariably accompanied in the rabbinic literature by extended discussion. The *Halachic* problem revolves less around her non-Jewish background per se than around the specific group of gentiles from which she is descended. According to Dt 23:3, "No Ammonite or Moabite shall enter the assembly of the Lord, even to the tenth generation." Ruth's presence is ultimately justified by a fine example of rabbinic exegesis. The rabbis note her gender and proclaim "not a Moabite [may enter], but certainly a Moabitess."[29] Had the evangelist wished to emphasize Ruth's Moabite origins, then it is strange that the mother of Rehoboam, the Ammonite Naamah (I Kgs 14:31; II Chron 12:13) goes unmentioned in Matthew 1. The frequent pairings of Ruth and Naamah in rabbinic commentary as well as the particular opportunity the genealogy offers to include her provide the argument from silence with a relatively strong voice.[30]

---

[29] *T. B. Yeb.* 76b-77a; cf. *M. Yeb.* 8:3: "An Ammonite or a Moabite is forbidden for all time, but their women are permitted forthwith"; and *Ruth Rabbah* 4:1. Josephus *Ant.* 5.9.4 expresses some concern over Ruth's Moabite origins but concludes that she demonstrates heaven's ability to elevate the poor and despised. See the sources cited in Johnson, *Genealogies*, pp. 167-70; W. G. Braude, *Jewish Proselytizing in the First Five Centuries of the Common Era* (Providence, RI: Brown Univ., 1940), pp. 49-52.

[30] *T. B. Yeb.* 77a: "Rabba (d. 352) made the following exposition [of the saying, 'An Ammonite but not an Ammonitess; a Moabite but not a Moabitess'] -- What is meant by 'Thou hast loosed my bonds' (Ps 116:16)? David said to the Holy One, blessed be He, 'O Master of the World! Two bonds were fastened on me and you loosed them: Ruth the Moabitess and Naamah the Ammonitess.'" A similar connection is made by R. Eleazar (3d cent.) in *T. B. Yeb.* 63a (cf. Johnson, *Genealogies*, p. 159). Biblical information on the other women in the messianic line is incomplete. The majority appear to be ethnically Hebrew. The mothers of Joram, Shealtiel, and Zerubbabel are not mentioned, nor is the

For the first theory the common denominator of unexpected sexual behavior can be determined, but its interpretation remains uncertain. The second theory offers an interpretation consistent with interests manifested throughout Matthew's gospel, the eventual entry of gentiles into the church, yet the common factor itself -- the gentile origins of the women -- cannot be established as the principal explanation for the women's presence. Thus a search for a third theory which incorporates both the 'irregularities' of the first and the interest in gentiles of the second is warranted.

Overcoming Exclusion

This third theory incorporates the central points of the two major arguments: sexual irregularities and an interest in Jesus' gentile background. Although the interpretation of the sexual activities of the five women remains elusive, the activities themselves must be considered in any new reading. To address this common factor, the alternative applies a focus generally associated with sociological and feminist criticism: the importance of social roles and relationships. And while

---

mother of Ahaz. In this last case, the omission may reflect a possible gentile background. Ahaz himself was known for idolatrous practices (II Kings 16:2b-4; II Chron 28:1b-4; Isa 2:8, 20). Abijam's mother Maacah, the daughter of Abishalom, "had an abominable image made for Asherah" (I Kings 15:13), which at least suggests gentile sympathies if not a gentile background. However, worship of the Goddess was not found only among non-Hebrews. The mother of Amos (Amon) is identified as Meshullemeth the daughter of Haruz of Jotbah (II Kings 21:19). While Jotbah is probably in the Galilee (Gr: Jotapata), there is nothing to indicate that Meshullemeth is a gentile.

Mary is not a gentile and the non-Jewish backgrounds of both Tamar and Bathsheba can be questioned, certainly the genealogy includes gentiles in the messianic line. In addition to its consideration of Matthean universalism, the new reading simultaneously reveals the gospel's cross-ethnic emphasis on categories of elite and oppressed. Finally, this new reading emphasizes the integrity of the text: a theme expressed in the genealogy should find some connection with motifs developed elsewhere in the gospel. Indeed the genealogy can be seen not only as consistent with but actually as central to the remainder of the text. Combining both sexual and ethnic categories, this multidisciplinary approach indicates that what unites the women is their manifestation of a faith which outstrips that of their partners.

The grammatical pattern noted in connection with the first theory offers a helpful starting point: each of the four women is introduced by the specific formula ἐκ τῆς plus the name. However, because of the unexpected appearance of these women, because of their even more unexpected association with sexual irregularities, and because of the critical need both to associate and to distinguish the first four women from Mary, an important implication of the prepositional phrase is overlooked. The women are not active in the genealogy; their partners are. The men -- Judah, Salmon, Boaz, and David -- are the subjects; the women are the objects of their actions as well as of the preposition. Yet the biblical records of the four women indicate that they were the ones who made history happen: they acted in order to secure their fate. Conversely, in 1:18-2:23, Joseph is consistently active: all decisions are his; all omens are addressed to him; even the genealogy is his. His role demands that the actions of the men explicitly connected to women in the genealogy proper should be examined. And it is Joseph's internal debate over the ritually and socially proper manner by which to resolve his unexpectedly complicated relationship with Mary that leads to the recovery of the third common factor -- faith manifested in action -- and the alternative interpretation. In other words, the focus on the anomalous presence of the women should not blind the interpreter to the presence of their partners.

The four women in the genealogy become part of the messianic line by fulfilling their true destinies -- or the intent of Providence -- and all, in so doing, overcome obstacles created by men in authority who were unwilling to fulfill their own responsibilities in salvation history. The women are socioeconomically and cultically powerless, yet they exhibit the faith by which the divine program is accomplished. Like the Pharisees and Herod, like the disciples of Jesus and of John the Baptist, the men associated with these women are negatively contrasted by the evangelist with the underprivileged, the oppressed, the cultically impure, and the outcast.

Tamar was forced to pose as a prostitute because Judah refused to accept his responsibility for her. Only when he concludes that she has disgraced him does he acknowledge any accountability; he states "Bring her out and let her be burned" (Gen 38:24b). And only when he is confronted with the evidence of his own participation in Tamar's actions does he realize the obvious: "She is more righteous than I, inasmuch as I did not give her to my son Shelah" (Gen 38:26a). Judah's lack of cultic as well as familial responsibility is highlighted by the unorthodox behavior of his daughter-in-law, and she ironically is most righteous while posing as a prostitute.

The placement of the only acknowledged professional prostitute among the four women, Rahab, in Matthew's genealogy is substantially more problematic. The Hebrew Bible does not place her in the Davidic line, and while the rabbis hail her as the ancestor of such worthies as Jeremiah and Hilkiah, she is not directly associated with the lineage of the messiah or the royal house. Moreover, Rahab lived at the time of the entry of the tribes into Palestine and, at least according to rabbinic legend, married Joshua.[31] Compounding these difficulties is Salmon's undeveloped character in both biblical and noncanonical literature. He is mentioned in Ruth 4:20-21, where he is in fact called the grandfather of Boaz; he is also implicitly associated with Tamar by the mention of Perez in Ruth 4:18. Because of the lack of evidence for a relationship between Rahab and Salmon, therefore, Salmon may be viewed as a cypher for others with whom Rahab is paired or contrasted. Given the anomalous association of Rahab with this shadowy husband, the text seems to urge the reader to focus on Rahab herself.

Such a search is not disappointing. Because the prostitute from Jericho demonstrates faith in Yahweh (Josh 2:9-11), she offers a strong contrast to the King of Jericho (2:3) who, familiar with the same evidence that convinced Rahab, orders the spies to be handed over. This same pattern is repeated in Matthew 2 with the Magi in Rahab's role and Herod the substitute for the king of Jericho. Second and more significant, the gentile prostitute is ironically contrasted with unfaithful Israelites. Joshua issued two commands regarding the destruction of Jericho: that Rahab be spared and allowed to leave the city and that the goods reserved "for the treasury of the Lord" be set aside for later destruction (6:17-19, 23-25). This pairing of Rahab and the treasure, repeated twice, prepares the reader for the third notice of Rahab and the *Herem* in 7:1. Yet in this last reiteration not only the pattern is interrupted: "But the people of Israel broke faith in

---

[31] Johnson, *Genealogies*, pp. 152, 164-65 (citing *Ruth Rabbah* 2:1 and *Sifre Num* 78).

regard to the devoted things: for Achan the son of Carmi, the son of Zabdi, son of Zerah, of the tribe of Judah, took some of the devoted things; and the anger of the Lord burned against the people of Israel." Rahab, the faithful gentile on the periphery of her city's social structure, is thus contrasted with both the unbelieving king of Jericho and the faithless Israelite Achan. And the inclusion of an individual named Zerah in Achan's own genealogy offers a subtle reinforcement to the explanation of the otherwise unexpected presence of Tamar's other son in Jesus' lineage. Merely being part of the messianic line or, more broadly, of the ethnic group upon which the covenant community is based, is neither an indication of righteousness nor a guarantee of salvation. Thus Rahab's significance for the first evangelist lies not simply in her origins or her profession but in the contrast she provides with two men in more powerful positions, two men who demonstrated an ultimately damaging lack of faith.

Ruth is, like Rahab, frequently considered the epitome of faith because of her statement to Naomi: "Your people shall be my people, and your God my God" (Ruth 1:16). But her assertion is more indicative of her loyalty to her mother-in-law than of her faith in God. Ruth actually manifests her faith less by such verbal profession than by action (e.g., 2:7b); it is she who convinces Boaz to fulfill his responsibilities to a close relation (3:9). Only through the perception of Naomi and the persistence of Ruth -- the resolve of two poor widows -- does Boaz come to state: "Also Ruth, the Moabitess, the widow of Mahlon, I have bought to be my wife, to perpetuate the name of the dead in his inheritance" (Ruth 4:10). The underlying theme of this episode, substantiated by Boaz's discourse, is clearly economics. Boaz must first secure Ruth's release from a relative with a better claim, and this cousin in turn forgoes his Levirate responsiblity because he is concerned about his own children's inheritance rights. The episode consequently heightens the distinction between the rich and the powerful (Boaz and the selfish relative) and the poor and disenfranchised (Ruth and Naomi). The narrative's concern for "restoring the name of the dead" (4:5) combined with its explicit mention of Tamar in 4:12 confirms this social connection between Ruth and Judah's daughter-in-law. They are related neither through gentile descent nor, primarily, through using seduction for achieving their goals but through their fidelity to the tradition of Levirate marriage: each perpetuates the name of her husband in the face of opposing circumstances. Judah and Boaz must be tricked into performing their duties; the widows are the ones with the motivating and, in contrast, overriding faith.

Matthew identifies the fourth woman in the genealogy, Bathsheba, not by name but as "the wife of [lit.: she of] Uriah." The two explanations for this divergence from the pattern of explicitly naming the woman that have been offered -- that τῆς τοῦ Οὐρίου emphasizes Bathsheba's adulterous relations with David and that she gains a symbolic connection to gentiles through her association with Uriah, a Hittite -- should be expanded in a pair of ways. On the one hand, the mention of Uriah reinforces David's guilt: he was the one who summoned Bathsheba, and he was the one who ordered the death of her husband. On the other hand, the divergence in the syntactical pattern makes Uriah and not Bathsheba the individual paired with David. Here again the person in control, the individual whose royal title is explicitly and otherwise unnecessarily mentioned in 1:6, breaks the law while the soldier (cf. Matt 8:5-13) -- both a subordinate and a gentile -- manifests faith: "The ark and Israel and Judah dwell in booths, and my lord Joab and the servants of my lord are camping in the open field; shall I then go to my house, to eat and to drink, and to lie with my wife?" (II Sam 11:11a). Uriah argues for egalitarianism. David, already in an elite position, abuses his authority and arranges the soldier's death.

Thus, the first four figures in the genealogy identified by the phrase ἐκ τῆς share a common factor other than their sex, their participation in somewhat unusual sexual activities, and their alleged gentile origins: they all demonstrated faith when the men with whom they are associated in the Hebrew narratives did not. This motif is in turn reiterated throughout the remainder of the gospel: the privileged, the leaders, the elite (Pilate, disciples, Pharisees) are unfavorably contrasted with the excluded, the despised, the cultically disenfranchised, and the poor (the centurion in 8:5-13, tax collectors, prostitutes, and sinners). The proper way for members of the church to behave is suggested by the presence of the women in the genealogy, but it is made explicit by the actions of the fifth pair: Mary and Joseph.

Like Judah, Achan, Boaz, and David, Joseph must address a question of moral propriety. Yet unlike these others, and so accounting for the syntactical shift in Matt 1:16, Joseph immediately demonstrates proper righteousness (1:19). The first men actively deny their responsibilities; Joseph goes to extremes to manifest his. This observation leads directly to the oppositional pairs set up in the second chapter of the gospel: Joseph and the Magi take extraordinary measures to manifest their faith; Herod, the chief priests, and the scribes refuse to accept the responsibilities of proper leadership and obedience to God.

The third theory answers the questions raised by the first two positions. It recognizes the importance of the sexual "irregularities" and of the gentile origins of at least two of the women. It also offers a plausible rationale for the shift in the identification of Mary which preserves her connection with the first four women as well as indicates the unique position she and Joseph hold. At the opening of the gospel, then, Matthew indicates two major themes of the text: ethnic divisions are subsumed under social categories of elites and marginals, and in the final analysis the separation of individuals is based on faith manifested in action.

The feminist implications of this interpretation are bittersweet. The first gospel presents women as exemplars of active faith, suggests that categories of sex as well as of race are made irrelevant by the Christ event, and even can be read as celebrating a woman's prerogative to make a sexual advance. However, the domestication of these women's sexuality through its incorporation within a structure that subordinates their individual needs to the fulfillment of divine purpose reveals the narrative's androcentric perspective. Further, that the four women were forced to use sex as a tool either for economic existence (Rahab; Ruth), for political safety (Bathsheba), or for a reason to exist (Tamar) undercuts rather than underscores notions of egalitarianism. In all five cases, too, the women's unconventional activities receive an initially negative assessment: even Joseph is scandalized by Mary. These activities are not fully reassessed as positive; rather in each case the end is seen as justifying the means. Finally, they are certainly not examples that should or can be repeated. Ultimately, these women were forced to use their bodies in order to write themselves into history. They are to be lauded for surviving, but they cannot be viewed as having achieved a break in patriarchal attitudes. Indeed, because the history into which they have written themselves is one of patriarchy, they have perpetuated rather than undermined structures of social inequity. Such feminist-hermeneutical observations are not inconsistent with Matthew's transcending of gender roles as well as ethnic distinctions by the more general thematic concern for socioeconomic, religious, and political egalitarianism. The gospel does offer hints of an egalitarianism coupled with the abolition of patriarchy, but the ideal world of the *Basileia* of Heaven is, for the first gospel, still culturally determined. While egalitarian impulses appear throughout, the focus of the gospel remains centered on men: the Son of God, the disciples entrusted with both missions, and the Father in Heaven.

III

The Infancy

Since Augustine identified the Magi as "the first fruits of the nations to recognize Christ" and proclaimed their adoration of Jesus as "that humility which was more in those who were from the nations than in the Jews,"[1] Matthew's second chapter has been viewed as a foreshadowing of the passion narrative in which evil Jews persecute Jesus while good gentiles worship him. Nor have theological interpretations of this ethnic division escaped critical studies. For example, J. C. Fenton writes:[2]

> In this chapter Matthew introduces the major theme of his Gospel: the Jews have rejected the offer of salvation, but the gentiles will accept it. Herod, his son Archelaus, and the people of Jerusalem are the representatives of the Jews; and the wise men (Magi) from the East are the representatives of the Gentiles. The Gentiles will be brought into the place which the Jews had forfeited by their unbelief....

Both church father and modern scholar base their interpretation on two premises: that the Magi are in fact gentiles; and that the gospel's principal distinction between those to be saved and those to be damned is drawn along ethnic (often synonymous

---

[1]Sermo CC, *Epiphania Domini.*

[2]*Saint Matthew* (Philadelphia: Westminster, 1963), p. 44. On Matthew 2 as a "proleptic passion narrative" see Meier, *Vision of Matthew*, pp. 32, 52; Senior, *Invitation to Matthew*, p. 34 and his *Passion Narrative According to Matthew: A Redactional Study* (Louvain: Leuven University, 1975), pp. 2, 226; Tilborg, *Jewish Leaders*, pp. 154-55 and references cited there.

with confessional) lines. The following pages address both these positions, but support only the first.

Although never explicitly identified as such, for the first gospel the Magi are best viewed as gentiles. The term "magoi" (μάγοι) originally indicated members of the Persian priestly caste (so Herodotus *Hist* 1.101, 132), and by the turn of the era the Magi were associated with sorcery and perhaps charlatanism (Acts 8:9); in neither case however were they usually associated with Jews (but cf. 13:6-8). The first gospel provides additional clues to their non-Jewish background. The reference to their gift of "gold and frankincense" (2:11) is reminiscent of the prediction in Isa 60:3-6 that "all the nations shall come to your light... they shall bring gold and frankincense";[3] their probable home in the East (ἀπο ἀνατολῶν, 2:1) distinguishes them from the population within Jewish border; and their reference to the "king of the Jews" (βασιλεὺς τῶν Ἰουδαίων, 2:2) confirm their non-Jewish origin. This phrase is used consistently in the first gospel by gentiles, most notably in the passion narrative (27:11, 29, 37). Matthew's Jewish characters usually refer either to "the Christ" (2:4) or to "the king of Israel" (27:42). Exegetical problems arise, however, when the meaning of the visit of the Magi is sought. Like the prevailing approach to the genealogy, interpretations of Matthew 2 tend to focus on ethnic distinctions and so miss the cross-ethnic implications of the gospel's program of salvation history.

---

[3]For gentiles bringing gifts to Israel cf. also Ps 72:10; I En 53:1; and PsSol 17:32-33. Brown, *Birth*, p. 36, notes the connection between the Magi and Balaam, "a type of Magus from the East who saw the star rising out of Jacob," cf. pp. 117 and n. 46, 168, 196. J. E. Bruns, "The Magi Episode in Matthew 2," *CBQ* 23 (1961): 53, cites parallels between the Magi and the Queen of Sheba (I Kgs 10:1-13; cf. Matt 12:42).

Patristic sources explain the visit of the Magi as indicating the overthrow of pagan magic by the messiah, and C. S. Mann even suggests that the wise men are Babylonian Jews who give up their occult practices to worship Jesus.[4] Yet at this stage of the gospel, the conflict between the power of magic and the might of the deity is not apparent, and the Magi's lack of familiarity with Jewish lore coupled with their other gentile associations indicates the several weaknesses of Mann's position. The most that can be retained of this theory is that magic is a less profitable activity than proper study of the Torah: the Magi can use the tools of their trade to follow a heavenly portent, but to determine where the sign specifically leads they are dependent on Jewish learning. While their ultimate manner of proceeding, their "other way" (δι' ἄλλης ὁδοῦ, 2:12), is determined not by astrological observation but by a heaven-sent dream, even here the change in route is less a subtle reference to a shift in their religious perspective than it is a connecting link between the activities of the gentile wise men and the Jewish Holy Family: Joseph too is warned by a dream not to return from Egypt to Judea; he travels another route to the Galilee. Finally, there is no notice in the text that these wise men have abandoned their profession: they rather return "to their own region" (εἰς τὴν χώραν αὐτῶν).

W. D. Davies also interprets the Magi as representative of pagan culture, but he offers the more plausible suggestion that they represent the "submission of the Gentile world to Christ."[5] This theory would be better expressed in terms of potential: the Magi indicate the appeal Jesus will have for

---

[4]Ignatius *Ephesians* 19:3; Justin *Dial. Trypho* 78:9; Origen *Con. Celsum* 1.60; Tertullian *De Idol.* 9; etc.; and C. S. Mann, "Epiphany -- Wise Men or Charlatans?" *Theology* 61 (1958): 495-500.

[5]*Setting*, p. 327, cf. p. 66.

some gentiles and their resulting entry into the church. They are not, however, typical of all gentiles portrayed either in the remaining chapters of the first gospel or by church history in general. Just as Matthew does not depict a "typical Jew" so there is no "typical gentile." The gospel emphasizes that quite a number of gentiles -- Pilate, his soldiers in 27:27-31, the residents of Decapolis in 8:34, and the ἐθνικοί of 6:7 and 18:17 -- do not respond favorably to Jesus' message. Moreover, the journey of the Magi does not serve as a catalyst for other gentiles to approach Jesus or even for the mission to be extended beyond Israel's borders. While this chapter may foreshadow the positive role some non-Jews will play in salvation history, their actual enrollment in the church must wait until the Great Commission. The presence of gentiles in Matthew 2 thus should not be confused with the church's universal mission. Gentile wise men do worship the child, but at this time they do not become his disciples.[6] The evangelist simply states that they returned to their "own country" (2:12), and so they depart from the text.

The Magi are consequently best compared to the two other non-Jews in the gospel who approach Jesus: the centurion in 8:5-13 and the Canaanite woman in 15:21-28. In none of the three cases does Jesus extend the offer of discipleship to the gentiles; in the first pericope he does nothing, and in the latter two he discourages the gentiles from seeking his help. In all three, moreover, the gentiles approach Jesus because of some external indicator which he does not control: a star or his reputation rather than his preaching.

---

[6]Contrast J. D. M. Derrett's claim, "Further Light on the Narratives of the Nativity," *NovTest* 17 (1975): 105, that "in return for their sumptuous gifts they must have obtained supersubstantial benefits...this summarises the mission to the gentiles, who should give what is appropriate for worship."

Although the infancy narrative is frequently identified as programmatic for the reception of the gentiles and the rejection of the Jews, Matthew 2 actually serves to establish the temporal priority of the Jewish people. A comparison between the two groups classified as faithful -- the Holy Family and the Magi -- indicates that preceding the resurrection the Jews retain their privileged position in salvation history, and a comparison of the gentile wise men and the Jewish Joseph with "Herod and all Jerusalem" produces a cross-ethnic social separation between the faithless, here characterized by authority and stasis, and the faithful, characterized by subordination and movement.

A principal reason why earlier studies of the Magi remain committed to an ethnic emphasis is the exegetical tendency to concentrate on individuals rather than to analyze the relationships among various groups. Compounding the problem is the tendency to view all the Jewish characters who support Jesus as "proto-Christian" and therefore no longer as members of the Jewish community. But just as the import of the genealogy takes on a sharper focus when the women are associated with their partners, so too the parallels between the gentile astrologers and the two Jewish contingents mentioned in the account, the Holy Family and the inhabitants of Jerusalem, indicate that all three groups are mutually informing. The Magi provide a contrast to "Herod and all Jerusalem" and so highlight the faithlessness of the Jewish leadership; and they parallel Joseph's actions and so underscore his higher righteousness as well as the privileged position of the Jew in this era of salvation history. And because the chapter aligns the gentile Magi and the Jewish Joseph against the Jewish king and his Jerusalem cohorts, it eliminates any emphasis on ethnic lines.

Ethnicity is, to be sure, a factor in the contrast between

Herod and the Magi, but it is not the major one. Through the use of several narrative ploys Matthew moves the reader away from the issues of nation and cult and toward a political and social agenda. The political aspect of the chapter is signaled by the repetition of a governing office three times within the opening verses. The wise men's request to find the "*king* of the Jews" (ὁ ... Βασιλεύς, 2:2) is framed by two references to Herod which stress his royal title: "in the days of Herod the *king*" (ἐν ἡμέραις Ἡρῴδου τοῦ Βασιλέως, 2:1); and "the *king* Herod" (ὁ Βασιλεὺς Ἡρῴδης, 2:3; cf. 2:7, 12, 13, 16, 19, in which the title is absent). Herod's desire to retain political power becomes thematically as well as aesthetically the glue which holds the plot together. This political interest is recapitulated and extended in the passion narrative, where the gentile Pilate replaces the Jewish Herod. Pilate too is concerned about Jesus' royal status (27:11), and the sign above the cross reveals Jesus' legitimate appropriation of Herod's title: king of the Jews (27:37).

A second ploy indicating Matthew's subordination of ethnic to political interests is the gospel's paucity of specific detail concerning the background of the wise men. The evangelist does not explicitly identify the Magi as gentiles, nor is Herod directly identified as a Jew. Additionally, both the wise men and the king are odd exemplars of their ethnic groups. The gentile astrologers worship the Jewish messiah while the Jewish king, who should manifest some familiarity with the traditions of his people, is forced to rely on his advisors (2:4) to ascertain the location of the child. Herod's ignorance of the Hebrew scriptures may indicate not only his theological distance from Judaism, but also his Idumaean ancestry. Just as the real "king of the Jews" has gentile women in his family tree, so the false, earthly king has gentile ancestors. Through its omission of specific ethnic identifications for both Herod and the Magi therefore, the chapter may also be interpreted as undercutting rigid ethnic distinctions. Further, Herod can be easily associated with the half-gentile Laban who, according to the Passover midrash, attempted like Pharoah to kill all the Hebrew children. This secondary association is supported not merely by the absence of explicit ethnic categorizations within the chapter but also by the several allusions to the Passover tradition in the infancy account.

The actual relationship between the Magi and Herod indicates the third technique whereby emphasis shifts from religious and ethnic divisions to political categories. The king summons the wise men to obtain information and then sends them as his agents to Bethlehem. By commanding them to go and search diligently for the child (2:8), he coopts their plan into the fulfillment of his wishes; the Magi are ordered to do exactly what they originally planned to do at the outset of the story. Herod's policies even indirectly determine their route home. While the earthly king remains in Jerusalem, the wise men are warned by a dream to take a different road home.

Herod's connection to Jerusalem is in striking opposition to the Magi, whose major activity in the narrative is traveling. This contrast plays upon a major thematic device the gospel employs to distinguish the faithful from the faithless. In the infancy account and again in the passion narrative, people in elite positions -- Herod, Caiaphas (26:57), Pilate (27:2), the Roman soldiers (27:27) -- are all associated with particular locations, and all have Jesus brought to them. Yet the Magi who journey from the East to Judea and back, Joseph, who is forced to flee to Egypt (2:13) and then commanded to return, and especially Jesus himself are characterized by movement rather than stasis.[7] Being well-positioned, geographically as

[7]On "wandering" as a characteristic of discipleship see Gerd

well as politically, is a characteristic of those removed from the *Basileia* of Heaven.

The category of movement offers a helpful departure point for comparing as well as contrasting the gentile Magi with the Jewish Holy Family. On the one hand, both groups are fully mobile and both are faithful; thus they reveal the presence of the social axis: ethnic divisions are ultimately superseded by social categories. On the other hand, the contrast between the two groups retains Matthew's temporal axis: Joseph and Mary, the Jews, remain with Jesus; the gentiles are advised to part from him. Jesus' movements may be similarly contrasted with those of the Magi. Even though Jesus recreates the travels of the Magi in reverse -- they travel to and from Jewish lands; he is brought temporarily to Egypt -- he does not come into contact with the Egyptians. Further, while the Magi actively seek the sign of the star and protect the child from Herod's plans, the infant remains entirely passive: he is born (2:1-2); seen (2:11); worshiped (2:11); offered gifts (2:11); taken to Egypt (2:14); and returned to Israel (2:21). Matthew is thereby able to depict Jesus as mobile without having him inaugurate the gentile mission. The chapter's silence concerning Egyptian people and Egyptian towns reinforces this distancing of the Jewish messiah from the gentiles. Compared to the number of people referred to in Palestine -- Herod, the chief priests, the scribes, the personified Jerusalem, all the male children, Jesus, Mary, Joseph, Herod Archelaus, etc. -- the absence of any Egyptian individuals cannot be ignored. And while the first evangelist records a checklist of both major and minor Palestinian regions -- Bethlehem, Jerusalem, Ramah, Nazareth, Judea, and the Galilee -- Egypt is depicted as a single unit. Thus the focus

---

Theissen, *Sociology of Early Palestinian Christianity* (Philadelphia: Fortress, 1977).

of the narrative and consequently of the early years of the messiah remains on Jewish people and in Jewish territory. The reference to Egypt provides the occasion for the fulfillment quotation in 2:15, establishes parallels between Jesus and both Moses and Israel, and foreshadows the peripatetic nature of discipleship. It does not reveal an interest in the gentile mission.

Similar observations about stasis and mobility, past allusions and the narrative present's focus on the Jewish people can be applied to the genealogy, although in that case the patterns are more subtle. While both Judah and Tamar journey to the crossroads, Tamar's movements are emphasized in that they contradict the commands issued to her by her father-in-law. Judah had sent Tamar back to her father's house (Gen 38:11), and ordered her to "remain a widow there." Thus her first act of higher righteousness was to disobey Judah's order: she refused to sit still. Conversely, he disobeys the moral command of abiding by the contract of Levirate marriage precisely by sitting still. Judah is further characterized by lack of action following his encounter with the unknown prostitute. Rather than travel to the supposed prostitute to pay his debt and reclaim his pledge, he sends his friend Hirah the Adullamite. An analogy can even be drawn here to the Jewish Herod's sending the gentile Magi, bearing gifts, to a woman and child. Nor does Judah claim the suspected adulteress from her father's house; he rather commands that she be brought out (Gen 38:24). Here again a connection to Herod may be drawn: just as the king ordered the destruction of the children, so Judah ordered the burning of his daughter-in-law; in each case the command was thwarted.

The second and third women in the genealogy, Rahab and Ruth, are clearly mobile: both leave their native lands in order to live among the Israelites. In turn, Achan and Boaz are not associated with movement. The former is actually imprisoned with "a great heap of stones that remains to this day" (Josh 7:26) above his head, and Boaz "went to lie down at the end of the heap of grain" on the threshing floor (Ruth 3:7). Both Bathsheba and Uriah also travel: she is summoned to the king's house, and he shuttles back and forth to the front while David sits in his palace. Finally, because Joseph is commanded to flee to Egypt, Mary too enters the ranks of world travelers.

Such geographical notices as the distinction between Herod's Jerusalem and the Egypt of the Holy Family have of course provided data for those who see the primary division in the infancy accounts as well as throughout the gospel to be between wicked Jews and faithful gentiles. Two phrases in the opening verses of Matthew 2 also hold a prominent position in the arsenal of this critical camp. First, not only Herod but "all Jerusalem" (πᾶσα Ἱεροσόλυμα, 2:3) is described as troubled by the words of the wise men. From this statement Daniélou, for example, draws the conclusion that "Israel's rejection [is] manifest even during Christ's infancy."[8] Second, Herod obtains his information about the location of the child not simply from any religious experts, but from the "chief priests and scribes *of the people*" (πάντας τοὺς ἀρχιερεῖς καὶ γραμματεῖς τοῦ λαοῦ, 2:4). The phrase has been interpreted as "another way of broadening the responsibility" of the Jewish community and has been associated with the condemnation of Jesus by "all the people" in Matt 27:25.[9]

---

[8] *Infancy Narratives*, pp. 91-92, concluding also from the personification of Jerusalem that the break between church and synagogue was complete. Conversely, Hill, *The Gospel*, p. 83, states the personification indicates simply that the entire population was disturbed, and notes this particular Matthean motif in 3:5; 8:34; 21:10b.

[9] Brown, *Birth*, p. 175, also citing Matt 26:59 (cf. Mk 15:1). Gundry, *Matthew*, p. 28, makes the helpful observation that πᾶς

The separation between the Jewish leadership and Jesus can by no means be ignored: the theme is established in the infancy account and is continued throughout the gospel. However, to claim that the entire Jewish world has aligned itself against Jesus and his church is incorrect. The Jewish leaders are most accurately to be compared not with coreligionists such as the sinners, prostitutes, and lepers lacking full or equal participation in the cultus but with members of other elite, exploitative groups: the Roman rulers, those who attempt to control the church through domination rather than those who guide through service, even the disciples of Jesus and of John who on occasion perceive themselves to be better than those more distanced from the prophetic figures. Similarly, distinctions in Matthew 2 are not drawn strictly according to religious and ethnic lines: the gentile Magi and the Jewish Joseph are both contrasted to Herod. And it is this contrast based on categories of authority and control, rather than the alignment of the entire Jewish community against Jesus, which is indicated by the various phrases invoked by the those who advocate a reading emphasizing divisions between Jew and gentile: the personification of Jerusalem, the various fulfillment quotations and specific geographical references, the mention of the "chief priests and scribes *of all the people*," and the reference to the members of the Jewish establishment who "gather together" (συνάγω).

The personification of Jerusalem in Matt 2:3 does not symbolize Judaism as a whole. Rather, Matthew places emphasis on the city's central role in Jewish tradition and polity as well as in the story of Jesus: this is the city where Herod and the Sanhedrin sit, where the Temple is located,

---

and πάντας modify the capital city and the chief priests, not the people.

where history is made (cf. 21:10). Jerusalem is the center of the world, and every center has a periphery. According to the ruling elite -- to those who control the people's mythology -- all other locations are therefore peripheral and consequently insignificant, evil, or to use Eliade's term, profane.[10] But Matthew rejects both centrality per se, because it maintains as if divinely ordained the social distinctions between elite and despised, and Jerusalem, because it personifies and epitomizes this distinction. Jerusalem cannot therefore be replaced by an alternative physical center since this would merely create a new periphery. Consequently, the evangelist first indicates the rejection of Jerusalem's claim to centrality by comparing the city unfavorably with locations despised because of their distance from the center, their heterogeneous ethnic composition, and their historical associations. Second, the gospel makes it clear that these locations are not established as new centers: the true locus of the church is revealed in 28:20 to be the abiding presence of Jesus within the community. Sacred space is anywhere disciples gather.

Bethlehem is directly addressed and so personified also in the chapter's first fulfillment quotation. This text from Micah 5:1 (MT), independent of any Marcan trigger, addresses not the division between Jewish and gentile territory but the distinction between apparently powerful and ostensibly weak areas. A comparison between Matthew's Greek and the Hebrew version highlights the evangelist's agenda. The first evangelist changes "Ephrathah" to "land of Judah"; adds "by no means"; and

---

[10]See *The Sacred and the Profane* (New York: Harcourt, Brace and World, 1959), pp. 42-47, using Jerusalem as the example; Jonathan Z. Smith, "Earth and Gods," chap. 5 of *Map Is Not Territory* (Leiden: Brill, 1978), pp. 104-28; and, from the perspective of biblical criticism, J. Munck, *Paul and the Salvation of Mankind*, p. 258.

changes (revocalizes?) the reference to "clans of Judah" (אלפי יהודה) to read "rulers of Judah." Thus Micah's "But you, O Bethlehem Ephrathah, who are little to be among the clans of Judah, from you shall come forth for me one who is to be ruler in Israel" is changed to read: "And you, O Bethlehem, in the land of Judah, *are by no means least among the rulers of Judah* (οὐδαμῶς ἐλαχίστη εἶ ἐν τοῖς ἡγεμόσιν Ἰούδα), for from you shall come a ruler who will govern my people Israel." By changing Ephrathah to "land of Judah" (cf. 2:1, 5), Matthew highlights the comparison to Jerusalem. "By no means" shifts the connotation of the Hebrew version: Bethlehem's minor status is transformed into an affirmation of its ultimate importance. Finally, by changing "clans" to read "rulers," the evangelist reinforces the political focus of the chapter.[11] The other locales mentioned -- Egypt, the gentile land which ironically provides a haven for a Jewish male infant; Ramah, the Jewish city located to the north of Jerusalem and which is with Bethlehem tainted by death and in mourning for the Jewish children; Nazareth, the new refuge for Joseph and his family -- are comparably despised and cultically unclean areas which attain glory through their sympathy with and sheltering of the child. By contrast, the final mention of Judea is again associated with political authorities: "Archelaus reigned (βασιλεύει) over Judea in place of his father Herod" (2:22); the evangelist thereby recapitulates the theme of danger associated with that region.

These observations run counter to the conventional wisdom on fulfillment quotations and geographical references. For example, Green suggests that Jeremiah is deliberately mentioned in 2:17 to recall the destruction of the first Temple

---

[11]Stendahl, *School of Saint Matthew*, p. 200; Gundry, *Matthew*, pp. 29-30; and his *Use of the Old Testament in St. Matthew's Gospel* (Leiden: Brill, 1967), pp. 91-93.

and thus foreshadow the destruction of the second; both, he adds, were destroyed because of "Jewish obduracy."[12] Yet this line of argument imposes lapses in narrative continuity upon the text. First, the children slaughtered by Herod's soldiers had no part in the rejection of Jesus; to condemn both these children and their parents, all of whom are Jews, for the rejection of Jesus is simply to blame the victims of governmental persecution for their own deaths. It is not impossible that the evangelist would use this line of argument, but it is inconsistent with Matthew's concern for those victimized by society (cf. 25:31-46) and with the gospel's overriding distinction not between Jews and gentiles but between elites and marginals, faithless and faithful. Second, the "Slaughter of the Innocents" is perfectly consistent with the "new Moses" and "new Israel" motifs well-known to any reader of the first gospel. Because of these analogies as well as the evocation of the Exodus tradition, the reference to Jeremiah brings Jesus closer to the Jewish community rather than distances him from it.

The fulfillment quotation in 2:23b is also problematic. While the comment that "he shall be called a Nazarene" (Ναζωραῖος) is unique to Matthew, at the very least it indicates the evangelist's interest in associating Jesus with the Galilee. Because the Galilee was pejoratively viewed by the residents of Jerusalem and Judea, the quotation moreover may reinforce

---

[12] *The Gospel*, p. 60. See also Senior, *Passion Narrative*, p. 226; A. Vögtle, "Die Matthäische Kindheitsgeschichte," in M. Didier (ed.), *L'Evangile selon Matthieu: Rédaction et théologie* (Gembloux: Duculot, 1972), esp. pp. 172-73. Conversely, Brown, *Birth*, p. 217, suggests that Bethlehem, Egypt, and Ramah offer "a theological history of Israel in geographical miniature. Just as Jesus sums up the history of the people named in his genealogy, so his early career sums up the history of these prophetically significant places."

the division between elite and marginal members of Jewish society. Jesus is not to be remembered for his birth in "Bethlehem of Judea" but for his residence in "Nazareth of the Galilee": he is "Jesus *of Nazareth*." Since the town itself appears neither in the rabbinic literature nor the works of Josephus, the silence of the sources indicates its insignificance. Even Jesus leaves this village for the larger city of Capernaum (Matt 4:13). If John 1:45-46 ("Can anything good come out of Nazareth?") can be taken as historically accurate, then the town was marginal in another sense: it had a negative reputation. The association of Jesus with Nazareth indicates therefore that even the most marginal, the seemingly most insignificant of both people and places are perhaps the most worthy of recognition. In turn, it is to these people and places that Jesus is sent.

Yet another phrase usually seen as indicating ethnic divisions, the inclusion of "all the people" to modify "chief priests and scribes," is also best explained in terms of authority and lack of power. The emphasis of the complete phrase, πάντας τοὺς ἀρχιερεῖς καὶ γραμματεῖς τοῦ λαοῦ, falls not on the people but on the officials. Rather than indicate union between the sheep and shepherds, the expression may be read as a partitive genitive and so seen as reinforcing the separation between ruled and ruling. The verse thus provides an "implicit contrast between the religious authorities 'of the people' and Jesus, 'a ruler who will shepherd my people Israel' (2:6)."[13] The mention of the religious authorities in turn reinforces the elite nature of the Jerusalem contingent: the priests and scribes, members of the ruling classes, are aligned with the king, and the people, implicitly, are connected with the families whose sons were killed in Bethlehem. The

---

[13]Brown, *Birth*, p. 175.

ultimate separation is thus between the Jewish establishment and Jesus, and the people remain the lost sheep caught in the power struggle. This same conclusion is applicable to a third phrase in the opening paragraph of the chapter. It is the elite members of the Jewish establishment who "gather together" (συνάγω), not the people as a whole. The verb "alludes to the unbelieving synagogue, dominated by the chief priests and scribes."[14]

The powerless position of the faithful, both Jewish and gentile, is clearly indicated in the infancy account. But because of the wealth of allusions presented in the second chapter (Herod and Pharoah/Laban, Jesus and Moses/Israel, the Magi and the various gentile visitors to Israel, etc.), and the contrast between the surprisingly receptive gentiles and the surprisingly malevolent king, the connections between the Magi and Joseph are frequently overlooked or undercut in favor of ethnic categories. For example, John Meier comments on the dream of Pilate's wife (27:19), "as in the case of the Magi, God's message comes to the Gentiles, while the Jews remain obtuse."[15] Yet in addition to his travels and his concern for the child, the Jew Joseph shares with the Magi the gift of prophetic dreams. Indeed, this righteous Jew bases all of his recorded activity upon such revelations: through a dream he agrees to marry Mary (1:20), to take his family to Egypt (2:13), and to return (2:19). He thus shares more than his name with the other well-known Joseph -- a figure also for whom ethnic categories are superseded by concerns for the correct use of power, and for whom both geographical and social mobility are

---

[14]Gundry, *Matthew*, p. 28; cf. Brown, *Birth*, pp. 174-75. The same verb is used in the passion narrative for gatherings of the religious authorities (26:3, 57; 27:27, 62; etc.).

[15]*Vision of Matthew*, p. 198.

dominant tropes. While the Magi and Joseph are both beneficiaries of signs, this form of heavenly communication also indicates a distinction between them. The wise men are directed to Palestine by a natural sign visible in the East to all who cared to look rather than by direct supernatural communication. In addition, the portent they observe requires interpretation available only from the Jews. Reminiscent of Paul's natural theology in Romans 1-2, the Matthean account indicates that the gentiles do not have the same types of divine contact in terms of either quantity or quality that the Jews possess.

A qualitative difference also distinguishes the travels of the various characters. While the Holy Family and the Magi are, in contradistinction to and because of Herod, associated with movement, Joseph's journeys are undertaken because of divine commands, and the reasons for the trips are more substantial than those of the Magi. The Magi seek to worship Jesus; Joseph is concerned with preserving the child's life. Moreover, by recapitulating part of Jewish history, the sojourn in Egypt indicates the comparably greater richness of Joseph's movements. The connection to the Exodus also serves to emphasize social rather than ethnic divisions: Herod and the Pharoah are clearly parallel, but what they share in common is not their religious or ethnic background. Each is, instead, concerned with preserving his leadership position.

Finally, a temporal difference, necessitated by the events themselves but nevertheless significant for the Matthean presentation of salvation history, is depicted between the wise men and the Holy Family. The first acts of righteousness related to the child are performed by Joseph (1:18-23); the gentiles come to worship the child, but his mother is already there (2:11); the gentiles depart for their home without any notice that they will recount to their compatriots the wonder they encountered in Bethlehem, but Joseph and Mary remain linked to the child; the wise men return to gentile terrority after a brief stop in Judea, but Joseph and Mary can be located in both Judea and the Galilee and so travel with the child to all the future sites of his mission. Thus, while the first gospel aligns the Jewish family and the gentile wise men against the Jerusalem establishment, it preserves a consistent distinction between the faithful Jews and the faithful non-Jews.

These comparisons between the Holy Family and the Magi express two themes developed throughout the gospel: both gentiles and Jews are to be numbered among the faithful; and, during Jesus' tenure on earth, the Jews retain their privileged position in salvation history. Like the genealogy, the infancy narrative conforms to a temporal axis revealing that the mission is to the Jew first, and also to the Greek; and to a social axis stating that in the post-resurrection church there will be neither Jew nor Greek, center nor periphery, elite nor marginal.

IV

The Centurion and the Sons of the Basileia

Characters in the Gospel of Matthew are clearly divided into three oppositional pairs. First, the Jewish religious and political elite are negatively contrasted with individuals on the periphery of either the socioeconomic or the cultic system: lepers, women, tax collectors, and sinners. Next, differences between Jews and gentiles are highlighted in narrative (2:1-10; 15:21-28), instructional (6:7; 10:5b), and prophetic material (24:14). And the ultimate distinction is that between those who are received into the *Basileia* of Heaven (ἡ βασιλεία τῶν οὐρανῶν) and those who are cast into the outer darkness (8:11-12; 25:31-46). Because these divisions appear throughout the text, because they are familiar to readers of other documents in the Christian scriptures, and because, admittedly, academics like to compartmentalize, readers frequently privilege one element within each pair and then combine the valued and devalued terms into separate groups. On the one hand are the oppressed -- usually identified either implicitly or explicitly with the creedal signifier "church members" rather than with the ethnic designation "Jews" -- and the gentiles; these are considered the future residents of Heaven. On the other hand fall the elite and the Jews (groups often viewed as synonymous); they will not be so fortunate.

Analysis of the contexts in which these characters are placed does not, however, support such categorizations. Those Jews who are not members of the elite groups do not somehow lose their ethnic identity. They remain Jews, and the reservations at the heavenly banquet of those who do the will of the host must be honored; otherwise, commentators will have paid the cover charge of reductionism. The assignment of gentiles to the category of the redeemed also overlooks the social distinctions drawn throughout the text among the non-Jewish characters. The gentile community consists of Romans who rule and Canaanites who serve, officers who command and soldiers who follow orders, guards who mock and guards who believe, those who will become disciples (28:19) and those who will not (18:17). Matthew's soteriological perspective does not divide individuals along ethnic lines; the text establishes a cross-ethnic pattern of salvation with the powerless who manifest faith accorded seats at the heavenly table and with the elite who rely on their own rather than on Jesus' authority denied entry to the feast.

The healing of the centurion's son[1] offers an excellent occasion to examine these general observations. The context of the pericope, the roles and role-reversals of the participants in the dialogue, and the eschatological logion appended to the healing narrative all depict ironic exchanges of power and eschatological position. The point of the pericope is not that the Jews, who fail to acknowledge Jesus, lose their benefits and are consequently replaced by gentiles. According to the first gospel faith in Jesus separates members of both ethnic groups into those who will attain salvation and those whom

---

[1]While Παῖς is usually here and elsewhere in the New Testament and LXX translated "servant" [עבד] (*BAG*, p. 609), Hill, *The Gospel*, p. 158, opts here for "son" [בן] (citing Jn 4:46-54, where ὁ υἱος appears). The Lucan parallel in 7:1-10 reads δοῦλος, "servant". "Son" provides a better contrast to the servant (τῷ δούλῳ μου) of 8:9 and a greater parallel to the daughters of both the Canaanite woman (15:21-28) and the synagogue ruler (9:18-26). I have been unable to obtain a copy of U. Wegner's *Der Hauptmann von Kafarnaum* (Tübingen: Mohr, 1985 [WUNT 2/14]), in which, I suspect, this question as well as others addressed in this chapter are treated at some length.

Jesus ultimately will deny.

Matthew 8:5-13 is part of a narrative unit comprised of ten miracle stories and several controversy accounts. Framed by the Sermon on the Mount (chapters 5-7) and the Second Discourse (chapter 10), the various pericopes in this self-contained section depict Jesus' first substantial contact with individuals who might become his disciples. The message of the inbreaking *Basileia* has been given, and the disciples now require edification in dealing with the crowds who have heard the good news. Only by marking the lessons these encounters provide will Jesus' followers be prepared for the harsh demands made in chapter 10. Thus the section's ecclesiastical and theological thrust actualizes the message of the Sermon on the Mount and prepares the way for the missionary instructions.

The evangelist's social and political concerns are also revealed in chapters 8-9. No longer talking primarily to an amorphous crowd (ὄχλος, 5:1), Jesus now encounters individual Jews and gentiles, rulers and pariahs, men and women, all with distinct needs and distinct responses to his message. By focusing particularly on the interaction between Jesus and those who are outcasts of or marginal participants in the Jewish cultic establishment[2] -- lepers (8:1-4), women (8:14-

---

[2]Thompson's conclusion in *Matthew's Advice*, p. 87, that "by choosing these people the evangelist taught the Christian community to embrace the sick and needy excluded from Judaism" is too harsh. "Excluded" implies that these people had no role in the cult rather than that they lacked power or status within it. See, for example, Thompson's comment on the same page that "a woman's rights and privileges within the community were restricted." On the marginal status of the various groups suggested by the supplicants see, e.g., H. J. Held, "Matthew as Interpreter of the Miracle Stories," in Bornkamm et al., *Tradition and Interpretation*, pp. 291, 259 n. 2; and esp.

15), demoniacs (8:16, 28-34; 9:32), tax collectors (9:9-13), sinners (9:11-13), the cultically impure (9:20-22), and the very marginal and impure, the dead (9:23-26) -- the section exposes an interest in social rather than ethnic divisions. The centurion's gentile background and thereby his peripheral relation to the various forms of institutionalized Judaism is continuous with rather than antithetical to the majority of the Jews whom Jesus encounters.

To aid the reader in reaching this conclusion, and so avoiding any overemphasis on Jewish-gentile polarities, Matthew both sets up specific parallels among pericopes within these two chapters and separates the narrative section into distinct blocks. The reader is consequently encouraged to analyze each account in terms of its internal development and characterization, its more immediate context of contiguous accounts, and its relation to the general context of chapters 8 and 9.

The Characters

Distinctions between those who claim authority (ἐξουσία) and those kept on the periphery of power find their strongest expression in Matt 8:5-13. In this pericope, three conventional structures are reversed: the political division between the conquering Romans and the oppressed Jews; the military division between the centurion's role as commander and his new position as Jesus' subordinate and supplicant; and the final distinction made by Jesus between those who expect salvation (both the Jewish religious establishment and the members of the church) and those who, although condemned by

---

E. P. Sanders, *Jesus and Judaism* (Philadelphia: Fortress, 1985), pp. 174-218.

the controlling factions of the religious organizations, nevertheless manifest faith. Throughout the narrative, only one expected division remains constant: Jesus remains faithful to the soteriological promises granted the Jews by the Hebrew Bible and reinforced by the exclusivity logia in 10:5b-6 and 15:14. Yet the abolition of this privilege and so the full equality between Jews and gentiles in the era of the church is also anticipated in 8:11-12.

The centurion's willingness to subordinate his own authority to that of Jesus is indicated twice in Matt 8:5-6. The soldier is described as "beseeching" (παρακαλῶν), an unexpected stance for a member of the occupying forces to adopt when conversing with one of those under occupation. And by addressing Jesus as "Lord" (Κύριε) the centurion confirms the role-reversal. His earthly and transient power must yield to Jesus' heavenly and eternal authority. Even his request reverses expected positions of authority. He approaches Jesus on behalf of the παῖς, one who, whether child or servant, would normally carry out orders on behalf of the master (Matt 8:9).

Like the soldier, Jesus too has a commission which involves leaders and followers. His, however, is the only position of authority which is neither based on nor contaminated by a desire for power or status (cf. 20:25-28). But because of his own restraints -- a mission only to the lost sheep of the house of Israel -- and not because of any prejudice against the gentile, Jesus expresses reluctance to grant the centurion's request. Matthew 8:7, Ἐγὼ ἐλθὼν θεραπεύσω αὐτόν, should be translated as a question: "Shall I come and heal him?" and it anticipates a negative answer.[3] Recognizing

[3]W. C. Allen, *A Critical and Exegetical Commentary on the Gospel According to St. Matthew*, 3d ed. (Edinburgh: T. and T. Clark, 1912), p. 77; McNeile, *The Gospel*, p. 104; Held, "Matthew as Interpreter," pp. 194-95; Jeremias, *Jesus'*

Jesus' reluctance and implicitly acknowledging the privileged position of the Jews in Jesus' ministry, the centurion is motivated by faith to continue.

It is not the case, as the *Anchor Bible* asserts, that "whichever way the translation is made, the essential point is that Jesus is prepared to have dealings with a Gentile, and by implication to enter his house."[4] In neither of the two healings of gentiles (8:5-13; 15:21-28) does Jesus set foot in a non-Jewish home or even on non-Jewish soil. This observation is reinforced by the evangelist's omission of the gentile indicators from Mark's rendition of the Gadarene exorcism. While the herd of swine may indicate a gentile setting, the pigs are "at some distance" (μακράν) from the demoniacs. Matthew's demoniac does not use the term "son of the Most High God" (υἱὲ τοῦ θεοῦ τοῦ ὑψίστου, Mk 5:7; Lk 8:28), which is an expression commonly placed on the lips of gentiles in the Hebrew Bible, and Marcan references to "Legion" (a Latinism perhaps suggesting the Roman occupation) are absent. The first evangelist has so cleansed the pericope of gentile connotations that the focus of the story remains squarely on Jesus' battle with malevolent supernatural forces. Ethnic descent is no longer an issue. Indeed, lest some early readers were familiar with the gentile associations of this account, the evangelist ensures that Jesus has no undue dealings with non-Jews. For example, like the opening of 15:21ff., Matt 8:28 describes the

---

Promise, p. 30 (citing Jn 4:48); Wilson, *Gentiles*, p. 12; W. Trilling, *Das Wahre Israel*, p. 105; Hill, *The Gospel*, p. 158 (noting that the positive meaning is also appropriate); Green, *The Gospel*, p. 99 (citing Matt 15:21-28); and Thompson, *Matthew's Advice*, pp. 90-91 n. 18. Held, following Zahn and Lohmeyer, adds that the strongly emphasized "I" ('εγώ) gains significance only if the phrase is read "as the astonished or indignant" question of Jesus.

[4]Albright and Mann, *Matthew*, p. 93.

demoniacs as coming to meet Jesus; he does not "come out of the boat" (Mk 5:2) to meet them. Nor is the cured demoniac invited to follow Jesus; the final scene of this encounter depicts the herders begging Jesus to leave their neighborhood. Matthew has preserved the salient points of the Marcan account -- the demoniac, the exorcism, the pigs -- but has omitted overt gentile signifiers and downplayed any suggestion that Jesus had self-motivated dealings with non-Jews.

The centurion thus faces one stumbling block that the leper, Peter's mother-in-law, and even perhaps the demoniac, do not: as a gentile he is not entitled to participate in this phase of Jesus' ministry. But he persists. Like the Canaanite woman of chapter 15, he repeats the respectful title "Lord" (Κύριε). Next, he acknowledges the restricted mission by making Jesus' word ἐλθών ("I come," 8:7) the basis of his statement in 8:8 that he is not worthy for Jesus to come under his roof (οὐκ εἰμὶ ἱκανὸς ἵνα μου ὑπὸ τὴν στέγην εἰσέλθῃς, 8:8a).[5] The ethnic borders of this pericope receive additional reinforcement in the following account, which conversely begins, "And when Jesus entered Peter's house" (Καὶ ἐλθὼν ὁ Ἰησοῦς εἰς τὴν οἰκίαν Πέτρου, 8:14).

Finally, the centurion mounts an argument based on the question of authority, and here the ironic reversal of positions of authority finds its specific focus. Rather than emphasize the power associated with his position, the centurion stresses its limitations. He can give orders, but he himself is "under authority" (ὑπὸ ἐχουσίαν) and must comply with orders from above.[6] And whatever authority he holds is rendered impotent

---

[5]See Held, "Matthew as Interpreter," pp. 195, 237, cf. p. 171 on composition by catchword in 8:8.

[6]C. H. Dodd, "The Portrait of Jesus in John and in the Synoptics," in W. F. Farmer et al. (eds.), *Christian History and*

by powers which do not recognize such distinctions, such as disease. By acknowledging that his powers are both worthless when compared to Jesus' worthiness and meaningless when confronted with problems political or military position cannot control, the centurion reverses his religious and political alignments. His contextual relation with those Jews on the periphery of the official cultus is reinforced by his recognition of Jesus' power, and this recognition in turn separates him from not only the Jewish leaders (scribes, Pharisees, Sadducees) but also from the gentile political and military establishment (Pilate, his soldiers) with whom he is most naturally associated.

Although the centurion has made a confessional shift by expressing faith in Jesus, he remains a gentile. Jesus, consequently, can not answer him directly. To indicate that his response is not restricted to this particular gentile at this particular stage in the ministry, the evangelist explicitly states that both the assessment of the appeal (8:10) and the predictions that follow from it (8:11-12) are addressed to those who follow Jesus (καὶ εἶπεν τοῖς ἀκολουθοῦσιν...). The switch in audience from soldier to church also places the ensuing cure in its proper perspective: by turning to his followers and away from the centurion, Jesus symbolically notes that his mission is still to the Jews.[7] Moreover, since "those who were

---

Interpretation: Studies Presented to John Knox (Cambridge: University Press, 1967), p. 93, adds that "because he is himself loyal to his commanding officer, he can give orders to his men with all the authority of the Empire behind him. Therefore, he argues, Jesus can similarly exercise effective authority." On the problems of translating 8:9, see Hill, *The Gospel*, p. 158; and S. H. Hooke, "Jesus and the Centurion: Matthew viii.5-10," *ET* 69 (1957/58): 79.

[7]Hummel, *Auseinandersetzung*, p. 140; Jeremias, *Jesus' Promise*, p. 31; Blauw, *Missionary Nature*, p. 68; Manson, *Jesus*

following him" implies an audience already sympathetic to and allied with Jesus rather than a crowd either hostile to or unfamiliar with his message, the comments in 8:10-12 should be interpreted more as a warning to those, both Jews and gentiles, who believe their religious or ethnic affiliation guarantees them salvation than as a promise to those excluded from the religious establishment.

Jesus' comments do, however, indicate the means by which the marginal and the oppressed can obtain the privileges which the Jewish leadership considers officially theirs. By affirming that the centurion's faith (πίστις, 8:10; cf. 8:13) surpasses that of the Jews, since "with no one [or "not even"] in Israel have I found such faith" (παρ'οὐδενὶ τοσαύτην πίστιν ἐν τῷ Ἰσραὴλ εὗρον), Jesus reverses the expected soteriological conclusion. Here the Jews, or perhaps even more specifically, those living in Palestine -- the center of Judaism -- are the elite group, but they are negatively depicted. Conversely, the gentile who may not be native to Palestine and who is certainly outside the cult receives the positive evaluation. Matthew's definition of faith goes beyond the belief that Jesus can work miracles, and it implies more than group membership (7:21) and adherence to certain rituals. It is a trust which is manifest in action. This faith is the reason for Jesus' willingness to perform miracles on behalf of gentiles (cf. 15:21-28), and it is the means by which gentiles will gain access to the privileges now held only by the Jews.[8]

---

and the Non-Jews, p. 22.

[8]Held, "Matthew as Interpreter," pp. 196, 280-81; Hare, *Jewish Persecution*, p. 161; G. Barth, "Matthew's Understanding," p. 112; and C. H. Giblin, "Theological Perspective," p. 55 (who suggests that "Jesus' own mission to the lost sheep of Israel is not such as to exclude gentiles"). On the centurion's foreshadowing the extension of the mission see esp. Meier, "Salvation-History," p. 205; and his volume cowritten with

The General Context

While the centurion's position introduces the section's thematic interest in the proper valuation of authority, the gentile soldier is not the only character in a leadership position whom Jesus encounters. In Matthew 8-9, the cross-ethnic concern with power gained through group association is eloquently depicted in the portrayals of both scribes and disciples. The encounters Jesus has with members of these religious establishments reveal the incompatibility of stasis and discipleship, of complacency and faith. They also serve as warnings to anyone who believes that membership in a group, be it the synagogue, the church, or the state, conveys ultimate meaning or guarantees eschatological rewards.

The reference to "another disciple" in 8:21 (ἕτερος δὲ τῶν μαθητῶν) implies that the scribe (γραμματεύς) in 8:19 may have been among Jesus' followers. If this is the case, the forceful statement he makes in 8:19 ("Teacher, I will follow you wherever you go") can be read as the oath of a new enthusiast. Yet this member of the Jewish establishment remains apart from the church. His professional identification is highlighted by the narrative whose rhetoric implies his distance from the new community of equals. The scribe is directly rebuffed through Jesus' words, and the evangelist's stylistic juxtapositions confirm the character's connection with personal position rather than with the demands of true discipleship. Jesus' comment in 8:20 that the Son of Man lacks permanent comforts while foxes have holes and birds have nests not only emphasizes the peripatetic nature of

---

Raymond Brown, *Antioch and Rome*, p. 23; Hummel, *Auseinandersetzung*, p. 25; C. H. Lohr, "Oral Techniques in the Gospel of Matthew," *CBQ* 23 (1961): 413 (on "new sons of Abraham"); Stendahl, *School of Saint Matthew*, pp. xii-xiii; and the parallel pericope, Matt 15:21-28.

discipleship, it underscores the scribe's ultimate concern for stability and ease.[9] Matthew in turn has provided subtle clues to indicate that the scribe might not be fully motivated to follow Jesus. Pejorative connotations are implicit in his addressing Jesus with the redactionally inserted "teacher" (Διδάσκαλε, cf. 12:38), a term used sarcastically by the Pharisees in chapter 12, rather than with the more frequent and respectful Κύριε which even the centurion managed to employ. Since the abrupt end of the dialogue cuts off not only the conversation but also the scribe's chance of salvation, Jesus' own final statement may be indicative of this disciple's shortcomings. Too, the negative association this failed follower has with the other hostile scribes who appear in chapter 9 suggests that his final decision was to return home. In both appearances of scribes within this narrative section, their dominant concern has been with staying put: the potential

---

[9]Because "the birds of the heavens" (τὰ πετεινὰ τοῦ οὐρανοῦ) connotes gentiles in I En 90:33 as well as, perhaps, Matt 13:32, T. W. Manson, *Sayings of Jesus*, pp. 72-73, suggests the phrase here (cf. Lk 9:58) also refers to gentiles: the birds symbolize the Roman overlords and the foxes (cf. Lk 13:32) the "Edomite interlopers." Matthew 8:19-20 would thus indicate that everyone is at home in Israel except the true Israel. However, in the Lucan parallel no connotation of gentiles appears, and the same phrase is employed in Matt 6:26 where the equation with gentiles is impossible (cf. Lk 12:24). Christian apocryphal literature also argues against Manson's theory. In the Protevangelium of James 3:2, Anna states: "Woe to me, to what am I likened? I am not likened to the birds of heaven, for even the birds of heaven are fruitful before thee, O Lord"; in the Acts of Pilate, the Jews threaten Joseph of Arimathea: "Know that the hour forbids us to do anything against you, because the Sabbath dawns, but know also that you will not even be counted worthy of burial, but we shall give your flesh to the birds of heaven" (cf. Rev 19:17-21).

disciple is unable to leave his own bed, and his compatriots in 9:3 do not believe the paralytic can leave his.

The reluctant scribe is a negative foil to the supplicant who appears in the verses immediately following 8:19-20. This second petitioner is identified as a "disciple" (ἕτερος δὲ τῶν μαθητῶν [αὐτοῦ]) and so is connected to Jesus rather than to the Jewish system. Appropriately, he addresses Jesus with the confessional title "Lord." And while this disciple is also concerned with his home life -- "Let me first go and bury my father" -- he has already agreed to Jesus' mobile existence: the implication of "first" (πρῶτον) is that he will next follow Jesus. Thus the scribe who returns is numbered among the dead; his foil, whose choice to follow Jesus rather than expected social custom is suggested by the repetition of the technical term οἱ μαθηταὶ ("the disciples") in 8:23, takes the first step toward salvation.

While the disciple has passed the first test of faith, he has not yet obtained admission into the *Basileia*. Because the disciples, by virtue of their group membership and proximity to Jesus, have the potential to abuse their privileged position or to turn an egalitarian group into a hierarchically based institution, they too must receive lessons in service and humility. Only in light of such instruction can Jesus later provide lessons in ecclesiastical organization. Consequently, like the Jewish leaders, the disciples of both Jesus and John the Baptist are contrasted to, rather than compared with, individual Jewish and gentile faithful. The blind men whose eyes are opened and the woman who touched Jesus in the crowd are characterized by faith (Κατὰ τὴν πὶστιν, 9:29; ἡ πίστις σου σέσωκέν σε, 9:22), but Jesus' disciples are ὀλιγόπιστοι (8:26), those of little faith. The portrayal of John's followers is only slightly more positive. Following Jesus' declaration that he has come to call sinners and not those considered "righteous" by the religious authorities (οὐ γὰρ ἦλθον καλέσαι δικαίους ἀλλὰ ἁμαρτωλούς, 9:13), the representatives of the Baptist ironically inquire about the proper interpretation of the Law, about a practice they consider "righteous." Their subtle claim to an exclusive jurisdiction over Truth is further indicated by the content of the question in 9:14. The issue of fasting is the converse of the previous subject of eating and drinking, which was introduced by an apparently hostile Pharisee. The Pharisees and the disciples of both Jesus and John are thus depicted as mirror images of each other. Structurally, topically, and through their privileged position as members of select and consequently potentially elite groups, the disciples of John and of Jesus are related to the scribes and Pharisees, and they are distanced from the sinners and sufferers.

Matthew's particular concern for eliminating hierarchies and incorporating peripheries reappears in this section in the association of two healings not usually viewed as corresponding accounts. The strong parallels between the gentile centurion in 8:5-13 and the Canaanite woman in 15:21-28 have virtually occluded the striking connections between the centurion and the ruler of 9:18-26. Not only do these two accounts have strong structural similarities, but the evangelist's packaging of chapters 8-9 commends such an internal analysis. There are ten miracle stories within the narrative section, but these are the only two in which the supplication is done by a mediator: both men seek help for a beloved child. Further, both subordinate their positions of authority to Jesus' higher claim of power; neither is present when the healing is accomplished; and both healings occur only after an interruption. In 8:10-12, Jesus stops to turn the centurion's words into a lesson for the crowd; in 9:20-22, the woman with the hemorrhage stops Jesus. Most striking, however, are the main characters' lack of group identification.

The Jewish supplicant is not called -- contrary to the pattern of this narrative section as well as of the complete text -- a Pharisee or a scribe; he is simply identified as a "ruler" (ἄρχων) and not as, in Mk 5:22, a "ruler of the synagogue" (ἀρχισυνάγωγος). By omitting Mark's reference to the synagogue the first evangelist has done more than indicate the separation of the church from the synagogue system (cf. 10:17), the symbolic value of the father becomes generalized: he can be any ruler of any group or institution. The centurion -- again surprisingly -- is not identified as a gentile or as a member of some particular non-Jewish national group. That this latter omission may be a redactional modification is suggested by the parallels in Lk 7:1-10 and Jn 4:46-53 as well as by the explicit identification of the woman in chapter 15 as a "Canaanite" (γυνὴ Χαναναία, 15:22). Thus the gentile centurion and the Jewish ruler are stylistically comparable not only to each other but also to the unaffiliated paralytics, lepers, and sinners, and they are therefore contrasted with the disciples, the scribes, and the Pharisees whose group membership is emphasized. Although in positions of authority, the centurion and the ruler subordinate themselves to Jesus; although commissioned to serve, the disciples as well as the Pharisees seek to retain their potentially exploitative leadership roles.

The ethnic distinction between the two characters cannot, however, be overlooked. The centurion's gentile background is highlighted by the comparison between his account and that of the Canaanite woman, by Jesus' unwillingness to accede to his request, and by the more narrow context of his story. The evangelist has grouped three healing narratives into the beginning of chapter 8: the leper in 2-4; the centurion in 5-13, and Peter's mother-in-law in 14-15. The break at 7:29/8:1 is signaled by the shift from discourse to narrative and by the accompanying shift in Jesus' position: no longer upon the mountain, he is now physically and symbolically on the same level as the people (Καταβάντος δὲ αυτου ἀυτοῦ τοῦ ὄρους...). Thus the first practical lesson is presented: in his personal interactions Jesus does not exploit his superior background, status, or knowledge. The break at 8:17/18, which is less major because the narrative section continues until chapter 10, is indicated by the summary fulfillment quotation from Isa 53:4 and by Jesus' plan to relocate: "he gave orders to go over to the other side" (ἐκέλευσεν ἀπελθεῖν εἰς τὸ πέραν). Here two other Matthean motifs appear: Jesus' message remains in continuity with the pattern established in the Jewish scriptures and the messenger remains perpetually in motion.

The narrative frame provides a corrective to previous schema suggested for the symbolic value of the leper, the centurion, and Peter's in-law. For example, Allen proposes that chapter 8 highlights three typical diseases -- leprosy, paralysis, and fever -- to illustrate Jesus' power to heal.[10] Yet the accounts which follow the subsection depict equally typical ailments: blindness, the inability to hear and speak, even death. Further, the descriptions of the various illnesses are both lacking in detail (especially when compared to their Marcan parallels) and subordinated to the portrayals of the various characters.[11] The centurion is introduced before the

---

[10]*Critical and Exegetical Commentary*, p. 74. Held, "Matthew as Interpreter," p. 254, suggests that "Jesus appears thematically as the miracle-working Saviour" only in 8:2-17, the narratives in 8:18-9:17 are not accounts of healings, and 9:18-31 concerns faith." This focus on christology too de-emphasizes the events in the narratives. The pericopes in 9:18ff. are healing stories first, and lessons on faith second.

[11]Held, "Matthew as Interpreter," pp. 214-42, esp. on the approximation of the miracle stories' form to that of controversy and scholastic dialogues.

paralysis of his son is mentioned, his personality is described only through dialogue, and the announcement of the healing itself appears almost as an afterthought (8:13).

The evangelist's interest in characters and dialogue rather than in pathology or aretalogy is continuous with the narrative frame's emphasis on fidelity to Jewish tradition and on interpersonal relations. Looking first at the connection of the three characters in 8:2-15 to the cult, the reader finds a subtle interest in legal issues. Unlike many receiving Jesus' gifts of healing and safety in the later accounts of chapters 8-9, the leper, the gentile, and the woman would be physically capable of full participation in the cult only if certain legal restrictions were abolished. While those possessed by demons are unable to participate because they lack personal control and those who are blind or deaf cannot participate fully in worship because they cannot, respectively, see the scrolls or hear their exposition, the leper, the centurion, and the woman all have sanity, sight, and hearing. The leper -- read "disenfranchised" -- is introduced through a dialogue that stresses the cultic rather than the physical aspects of his illness and cure (8:4). The centurion -- read "gentile" -- is excluded from the cult by an accident of birth; his parents were not Jews. And Peter's mother-in-law -- read "woman" -- is only a marginal participant in the Temple cult. She has her own religious responsibilities and privileges, but she has little control over their form or extension (e.g., she cannot enter the inner court of the Temple). Thus the immediate context of the healing of the centurion's son emphasizes the cultic ramifications of social divisions.

This theme is reinforced in the progression from Jewish man to gentile man to Jewish woman. Leprosy might be cured, but regardless of his health the man was still a member of the Jewish community. Matthew underscores this ethnic identification through Jesus' order that the man show himself to a priest and "offer the gift that Moses commanded, for a proof to them" (8:4).[12] The gentile centurion could become a proselyte. It may be ironic that his story is juxtaposed to that of the leper: while the leper regains status in the Jewish cult by being provided with new skin, the centurion remains outside the fold because he is still in possession of his foreskin. In other words, the former was barred from full participation in the Jewish community because of his "mutilation of the flesh," while the latter could obtain membership only through it. But the woman could not become male.

Matthew does not, however, make any implicit case for the subordination of women. Mark 1:30b, which suggests that the woman's companions brought her case to Jesus, is omitted from the first gospel. The healing of Peter's mother-in-law consequently becomes the only healing narrative in the first gospel in which Jesus takes the initiative.[13] And, if her action of "serving him" (διηκόνει αὐτῷ, 8:15) has ecclesiastical connotations, then Matthew has depicted the first deacon in the church. Indeed, Peter's mother-in-law is the first character in the gospel aside from Jesus to manifest ecclesiastical authority properly: one demonstrates wholeness through service. The woman does not debase herself to perform her function; rather, she rises to do so (καὶ ἠγέρθη καὶ διηκόνει). Expectations are reversed: the sick are made well; the Roman soldier subordinates himself to a Jew from the Galilee; a

---

[12]Held, "Matthew as Interpreter," p. 229, observes that προσκυνέω (cf. 9:18; 15:25) suggests "genuine adoration" (contrast Mk 15:19). S. H. Hooke's claim, "Jesus and the Centurion," p. 80, that the leper had "a type of faith in Jesus' ability to heal him which does not seem to have met with Jesus' approval" is incorrect.

[13]See Held, "Matthew as Interpreter," p. 169.

woman serves Jesus; and the disciples all receive instruction in service and faith.

The Couplet

The meaning of these several reversals is summarized in the eschatological couplet which concludes the pericope. Matt 8:11-12 transcends the ethnic distinction made in 8:10 by means of its concentration on the cross-ethnic categories of elite and marginal.[14] Thus it both complements and reinforces the themes of the pericope as well as of the narrative section as a whole.

The logia do not explicitly identify either the many (πολλοὶ ἀπὸ ἀνατολῶν καὶ δυσμῶν) or the sons of the *Basileia* (οἱ ...υἱοί τῆς βασιλείας).[15] The majority of commentators, however,

---

[14]Like 8:19-22; 14:28-31; and 15:22-24, 8:11-12 is apparently a Matthean insertion and probably did not follow the healing narrative in the earliest traditions. See Held, "Matthew as Interpreter," pp. 168, 196; Tagawa, "People and Community," p. 154; and cf. Lk 13:28-29. Green, *The Gospel*, p. 100, suggests that Matt 8:12 is a redactional composition (cf. 13:42, 50; 22:13; 24:51; 25:30). Jeremias, *Jesus' Promise*, pp. 55-56 and n. 3; and Wilson, *The Gentiles*, p. 3, appeal to an Aramaic retranslation of 8:11-12 and to "Semitic elements" (e.g., antithetic parallelism, Jewish imagery) in claiming the couplet to be early and possibly authentic Jesus material.

[15]The expression is unknown in rabbinic usage. Hill, *The Gospel*, p. 159, offers the remote parallel to "the sons of the *Basileia*" in the expression "the sons of his covenant" found in IQM 17:3. The rabbis do speak of a "son of the world to come"; see Abrahams, *Studies in Pharisaism*, vol. 2, p. 187 (citing *T. B. Ber.* 4a; *T. B. Taan.* 22a; etc.; as well as Philo *De Execrationibus* 6); G. Dalman, *The Words of Jesus* (Edinburgh: T. & T. Clark, 1902), p. 115.

assert that the many are clearly gentiles, the expelled sons the Jews.[16] This conclusion is in part correct: the entry of gentiles into the church and the rejection of certain Jews is foreshadowed in the infancy narratives;[17] it is also consistent with the comparison made in 8:10. The claim that "in Israel" (ἐν τῷ Ἰσραήλ) in 8:10 has a geographic as well as an ethnic connotation does not mitigate this observation. The phrase may suggest that Diaspora Jews -- those unable to fulfill the *mitzvoth* related to the land and the Temple -- have more faith than Jews living in Palestine. Nor, too, is assigning ethnic labels to the various characters in this section improper: the exegetical richness of the centurion and the ruler becomes fully apparent only when the unidentified backgrounds of the characters are entered into the analysis. However, such ethnic distinctions should not be exaggerated. While the couplet has been read as an emphasis on the rejection of all Jews [i.e., ethnic Israel],[18] this conclusion can be demonstrated neither

---

[16]Among others, Tagawa, "People and Community," p. 153; Hill, *The Gospel*, p. 159; Hooker, "Uncomfortable Words," p. 363; Held, "Matthew as Interpreter," p. 196; Jeremias, *Jesus' Promise*, pp. 56 n. 3, 62ff.; cf. his *Rediscovering the Parables* (New York: Scribner's, 1966), p. 52; Argyle, *The Gospel*, p. 67; and Wilson, *Gentiles*, p. 3.

[17]See Brown, *Birth*, pp. 178-81, on the connections among the Magi, the centurion, and the soldiers at the cross.

[18]Cf. Rohde, *Rediscovering*, p. 84 and references there; Hare, *Jewish Persecution*, p. 161; D. Senior, "The Death of Jesus and the Resurrection of the Holy Ones (Mt 27:51-53)," *CBQ* 38 (1976): 325; G. Barth, "Matthew's Understanding," p. 112; Jeremias, *Jesus' Promise*, p. 51; Hummel, *Auseinandersetzung*, p. 153; and see the discussion of Gnilka's position in Rohde, *Rediscovering*, pp. 246-47. See also Garland, *Intention*, p. 212; and Trilling, *Das Wahre Israel*, pp. 68-70, who suggests that 8:11-12 not only condemns the Jews but also eliminates the possibility of their future conversion. Scholars are divided on

by the specific words of the couplet nor the gospel as a whole. Indeed, the conclusion that the many are only gentiles and the sons Jews is reductive as well as incomplete.

The relationship of the couplet to its various contexts (the block of the three healings, chapters 8-9, the entire gospel) provides the first clue that the distinction drawn in 8:11-12 follows socioeconomic rather than ethnic categories. Although the juxtaposition of the eschatological verses to 8:10 suggests the πολλοί are gentiles, the overall context indicates these otherwise unidentified individuals are both gentiles and Jews not immediately involved in the dominant religious system: Peter's mother-in-law, the leper, the paralytic, tax collectors, sinners, and if 8:10 is interpreted with reference to geographic considerations, Diaspora Jews.[19] Their social rather than ethnic status is also indicated by the direction in which they move: from the periphery to the center. Indeed, like the Magi, the Holy Family, the disciples from Galilee, and Jesus himself, these marginal members of official society are characterized by movement: the woman rises and serves Jesus, the leper approaches him, the paralytic takes up his pallet and walks. Their counterparts -- the sons of the realm as well as

---

whether the couplet reflects past history or prophetic threat. See G. Baum, *Is the New Testament Anti-Semitic?* rev. ed. (Glen Rock, NJ: Paulist, 1965), p. 98, for a succinct discussion.

[19]Jeremias, *Jesus' Promise*, p. 55 n. 2, states that πολλοί has an "inclusive meaning." W. L. Knox's claim that 8:11 means "the many would enter the Kingdom as proselytes" for "the Jewish law holds good for the new kingdom" (cited in Blair, *Jesus in the Gospel of Matthew*, p. 29 n. 39) overlooks the separation between Jews and gentiles depicted throughout the gospel as well as the distinction between the church and the Jews implied in 28:15, 19. While the many may keep Jewish law, they are not an ethnic part of the Jewish community or an extension of it; they comprise a new body, the church.

Pilate, Herod and Herod Antipas, the chief priests and scribes -- are characterized by stasis. The many actively "will come" (ἥξουσιν); the sons, passively, "will be thrown" (ἐκβληθήσονται). These many, in turn, move within a sphere encompassing ethnic Judaism: their dinner companions, the patriarchs of the Jewish community, signal a continuity with the Jewish people rather than an exclusion of them from the *Basileia*. At the eschaton, Jews and gentiles will be equals, having no legal barriers or soteriological privileges separating them.[20] The motif of the eschatological banquet itself has cross-ethnic implications: similar imagery in a context stressing social status rather than ethnic origin appears in Matt 22:1-14.

Grammatical considerations also lead to the conclusion that the eschatological logion has a social emphasis. Although 8:10 may imply that the Jews are the correct referent of the "sons," the first indication of the more precise reading is offered by the antithetic parallel of "many." If those coming from the East and West are both Jews and gentiles, then the "sons" should also have a cross-ethnic referent. Since the leper

---

[20]Jeremias, *Jesus' Promise*, p. 63; Abrahams, *Studies in Pharisaism*, vol. 1, p. 56. S. Brown, "Matthean Community," p. 196, follows Jeremias, *Jesus' Promise,* pp. 55-56 and *Rediscovering the Parables*, p. 52 (cf. Hill, *The Gospel*, p. 159) in suggesting that the logion combines two traditional images: the pilgrimage of the nations (Isa 2:2f.; Mic 4:1-7) and the eschatological banquet (Isa 25:6f.). Brown's further claim on p. 198 n. 25 that the association of the gentiles with "the resurrected patriarchs" represents a "significant shift from the Old Testament conception, according to which the gentiles come to join with Israel" is overstated: the patriarchs are difficult to separate from the community they founded. However, the shift may be a subtle indication that at the eschaton judgment has a cross-ethnic basis: individuals will be separated according to their works rather than according to their national origin or religious affiliation.

and Peter's mother-in-law are examples of faithful Jews, they must be included in the group coming in from the outside. Further, in 8:11, Jesus describes those who will sit at the heavenly banquet simply as "many" (πολλοί); the definite article is absent. Conversely, those to be expelled belong to a specific group: they are "*the* sons of the *Basileia*" (οἱ υἱοὶ τῆς βασιλείας), the elite. And, while "many" is almost completely obscure without a context or a subject, the "sons of the *Basileia*" has immediate connotations of status and privilege.

The general term "many" can easily change meaning depending upon its context;[21] the "sons of the *Basileia*" is a more descriptive and therefore more recognizable phrase. Consequently, its repetition in 13:38 has a direct bearing on its meaning for 8:12. This explanation of the Parable of the Weeds equates οἱ υἱοὶ τῆς βασιλείας with τὸ καλὸν σπέρμα ("the good seed"), with the members of the church.[22] Thus, while those condemned to the outer darkness include Jews, the phrase also serves as a warning to church members of both Jewish and gentile backgrounds.[23] The association of the "sons of the

[21]A similar difficulty occurs in exegetical studies of Mk 10:45. The πολλοί for whom Jesus gives his life have been identified as gentiles, as the poor, and as "the many of Israel, over against Jesus." See Hooker, "Uncomfortable Words," p. 364 n. 8; Wilson, *Gentiles*, pp. 7-9.

[22]Cope, *Matthew, A Scribe*, p. 51 n. 92, states "one would hardly expect the 'sons of the Kingdom' to mean just Israelites, as it must here [8:12], if the use of the same term in the parable interpretation of 13:37ff. is kept in mind"; cf. Tagawa, "People and Community," p. 160; and E. Schweizer, "Observance of the Law," p. 230 (opposing Tagawa). Cope's problem is solved when the inclusive connotation of the term is recognized.

[23]See the discussion in Thompson, *Matthew's Advice*, pp. 50-58, 65-68, 98. Bornkamm, "End-Expectation," p. 19; and Hummel, *Auseinandersetzung*, pp. 103-6, interpret the pericope

Basileia" in 8:12 and 13:38 with the members of the church receives subtle reinforcement from the discussion of the Temple tax in Matt 17:24-27. Here the "sons who are free" are church members -- Jews as well as gentiles who have affiliated with the Jewish community -- who, Matthew suggests, should continue to pay the *fiscus Iudaicus*.

The many Jews and gentiles will move from an ambiguous and general location of the "East and West" to the table, which is even more difficult to locate spatially. Similarly, the "sons of the *Basileia*" move from the center (implied by the authoritative connotations of the title) to the outer darkness, an area also apart from standard definitions of time or space.[24] Thus these potential synonyms for heaven and hell are made both ambiguous and complicated. At the eschaton, a noncentric emphasis prevails not only for those to be saved but also for those condemned. A reversal of the categories of obvious and obscure is in progress,[25] and the connection of centers with heirarchies is thereby undercut. Where new believer and ancient patriarch are united as equals is a goal and a reward, but it is not a place where earthly authority is exercised.

The context of the pericope, the centurion's comments on the limitations of authority, the ambiguous and obscure terminology of the eschatological logion, and the Matthean

---

as indicating the continuing attachment of Matthew's congregation with Judaism; Trilling, *Das Wahre Israel*, p. 79; and Strecker, *Der Weg*, pp. 34-35, deny this association. The compromise view that the Matthean community had split with the synagogue but still identified with the Jews (e.g., through preservation of *Halacha*) is the most helpful.

[24]Cf. Matt 22:13; 24:51; 25:30; as well as IV Ezra 7:93; I En 63:10; PsSol 14:9; 15:10; WisSol 17:21.

[25]Suggested by Wesley A. Kort.

technique of addressing the church through Jesus' words all indicate that the major theme of Matt 8:5-13 is *not* the rejection of the Jews and the eventual salvation of the gentiles. The division expressed by this pericope as well as throughout the gospel is between the complacent elite -- Jewish disciple, gentile procurator, church member, anyone in a position of authority -- who does not have faith and act upon it, and those excluded from or marginal to the ruling religious, social, or political system -- sinners, women, lepers, gentiles -- who manifest πίστις.

V

Gentile Puppies and Jewish Sheep
The Canaanite Woman in Context

During the early part of his ministry, as he teaches his disciples both the content of the good news and the means by which to convey it, Jesus consistently indicates that his mission and message are for the Jews. Not only does he hesitate to heal the centurion's son, he explicitly instructs his disciples "to go nowhere among the gentiles and enter no town of the Samaritans." Matthew 15:21-28, the healing of the Canaanite woman's daughter, recapitulates both Jesus' interaction with a gentile supplicant and the soteriological grounding behind it. Both centurion and Canaanite -- the only two gentiles depicted in healing narratives -- are positively portrayed, engage in dialogue with Jesus, and have their requests granted. Both healings are accomplished at a distance, in neither case does Jesus enter the gentile's home, and neither the woman nor the centurion becomes a disciple. Finally, both pericopes emphasize the faith of the gentile supplicant. But in the later account, Jesus explains to his supplicant the exact reasons for his hesitance to bestow the blessings of the *Basileia* upon her: "I was sent only to the lost sheep of the house of Israel" (15:24). Thus the second healing account reinforces as well as intensifies the message of the first.

Not surprisingly, the interpretations of the two pericopes have also been similar. For example, several scholars have proposed that the faith of the Canaanite woman presents a deliberate contrast with Jewish unbelief,[1] just as the comments about the "sons of the *Basileia*" in 8:12 are viewed as signaling the rejection of the Jewish people. Similarly, Jesus' invocation of an ethnic factor to explain his refusal to heal the gentile girl (15:24) is viewed as not only antithetical to Matthew's universalistic outlook but also as prejudicial and appalling. Jeremias states that "Matthew's only reason for preserving the logion in spite of its repellent implication was that it bore the stamp of the Lord's authority."[2] Yet a comparison between the Matthean and Marcan versions of the healing narrative as well as an analysis of the exclusivistic statement within both its immediate context of Matt 15:21-28 and its general setting of Matt 13:53-16:12 calls into question this negative evaluation. Rather than either repellent or inconsistent, the restriction of the mission in chapter 15 reveals Matthew's fidelity to the promises made to the Jews. Further, a contextual analysis of Matt 15:21-28, like that of 8:5-13, indicates both that the Jews retain their privileges during Jesus' earthly mission (the temporal axis) and that the cross-ethnic distinction manifested through the categories of center and periphery (the social axis) is a dominant theme in this section.

Matthean Elements in 15:21-28

Although both Mark and Matthew present the same story,

---

[1]Munck, *Paul and the Salvation of Mankind*, p. 262; Carlston, "Interpreting the Gospel," p. 12; Hahn, *Mission*, p. 32.

[2]*Jesus' Promise*, p. 27. Similarly, Schuyler Brown, "Matthean Community," p. 195, n. 7, "wonders whether the author may not, perhaps unconsciously, have been moved by a desire not to attribute to Jesus a statement which suggests that he was not exempt from the tribal prejudices of his nation and age."

the two versions convey substantially different impressions. Through changes in vocabulary and content, Matthew transforms the Marcan extension of Jesus' evangelism to the gentiles into a reaffirmation of the restricted mission.[3] The temporal priority of Israel is retained, and the entry of the gentiles into the church is, at the most, only foreshadowed.

Two subtle changes to Mk 7:24a -- "And from there he arose and went away (ἀπῆλθεν) to the region of Tyre" (εἰς τὰ ὅρια Τύρου)[4] -- prepare the reader for the major distinctions to come. First, Matthew adds to the opening line of the pericope the notice that Jesus not only "went away from there" but also "withdrew (ἀνεχώρησεν) to the district (εἰς τὰ μέρη) of Tyre and Sidon" (Matt 15:21). The favorite Matthean expression for avoiding danger, "he withdrew" (ἀναχώρησεν), is the first indication of the redactor at work. Of the six occurrences of the term, five and possibly all six can be associated with gentile environs: 2:14 depicts Joseph's departure to Egypt; 2:22 concerns the return to Galilee, classified as "of the gentiles" in 4:15; 4:12 is Jesus' withdrawal again into Galilee following the arrest of John; 12:15, the escape from the hostile Pharisees following a healing in their synagogue, is modified by a fulfillment quotation emphasizing the one who will "proclaim justice to the gentiles...and in his name will the gentiles hope" (12:18, 21); and 15:21 explicitly mentions Tyre and Sidon. In all six cases, however, the withdrawal is

---

3Even if Matthew is not dependent on Mark, the differences between the two accounts can serve to highlight particular Matthean motifs. These motifs can, in turn, be checked through analysis of the pericope within its own narrative context.

4The addition of καὶ Σιδῶνος ("and Sidon") in A, B, K, X, Pi f1, f12, etc. appears to be an assimilation to Matt 15:21. The inclusion in Mk 7:24 is redundant, since 7:31 suggests a progression from Tyre to Sidon.

occasioned by the actions of the Jewish religious and political establishment. The sixth appearance of the term, 14:13, concerns Jesus' flight from Herod Antipas following the execution of the Baptist. And because the previous connections drawn in 4:12 among Jesus, the Baptist, and withdrawing conclude with a reference to gentile territories, it would not be inappropriate to interpret the escape to a "lonely place" in 14:13 as indicating at the very least a removal to a place that might have gentile associations. Thus the technical expression "to withdraw" has both ethnic and political implications. Ethnically, the term foreshadows the mission to the gentiles, and it indicates to future missionaries that gentile territory can be a place of refuge. Politically Jesus' withdrawing implies a deliberate separation of his mission from the agendas of the Pharisees and the Herodians. There is even a veiled hint that, for the church to survive, future disciples must remove themselves from the influence of those whose positions are characterized by stasis: the members of the establishment remain in cities, palaces, and synagogues; Jesus and his followers withdraw. It is in the lonely places, that is, the places apart from the center, where refuge is found.

The second modification of Mk 7:24a both confirms Matthew's interest in stasis and mobility and leads to a cross-ethnic application of these categories. By conjoining Tyre and Sidon in 15:21, the first evangelist recalls three themes depicted in the narrative's earlier mention of the cities (11:21; cf. Lk 10:14). First, large urban areas (τὰς πόλεις; 11:20) are characterized by an unwillingness to repent and thus are implicitly contrasted with wilderness areas where the faithful crowds follow Jesus and John (cf. 11:7). This comparison is grounded in part in the categories of center/periphery: the accentuation of Capernaum's high self-opinion in 11:23 -- "and you, Capernaum, will you be exalted to heaven?" -- repeats the gospel's challenge to the authority of centers.[5] Next, although the gentile cities are positively portrayed in comparison to Chorazin and Bethsaida, they are nevertheless classified as evil and unrepentant. Matthew 11:22, "It shall be more tolerable on the day of judgment for Tyre and Sidon than for [Chorazin and Bethsaida]," is a lesson about the failings of the Jewish cities, not about the righteousness of the gentile ones. The parallel associations of Capernaum with Chorazin and Bethsaida on the one hand and Tyre and Sidon with Sodom on the other confirm the negative valuation of all the cities, both Jewish and gentile. Consequently, the evangelist undercuts the simplistic division between good gentiles and evil Jews.

The personification of the cities in chapter 11 evokes yet a third motif: it takes up the gospel's stance against the establishment's ethos. This literary technique creates a distinction between the cities per se and their few faithful inhabitants. While the cities are condemned, great faith had recently been demonstrated in Capernaum by the friends of the paralytic (9:2), the tax collector (9:9), the ruler and the woman with the hemorrhage (9:18-26), and others "in his own city" (τὴν ἰδίαν πόλιν, 9:1). Like the personification of Jerusalem in chapter 2, the condemnations in Matthew 11 ultimately focus on issues of center and periphery, stasis and mobility, rather than -- as those who focus on the references to Tyre, Sidon, and Sodom might suspect -- on ethnic origins. One gains a chance at salvation by dissociating from the cities. Mere residence within these locations is not, conversely, necessarily indicative of future damnation, since the gospel indicates that the faithful may be found anywhere.[6]

---

[5]See Theissen, *Sociology*, pp. 47-51, on the "tension between the cities and the country."

[6]J. A. Comber, "The Composition and Literary Characteristics

However, these various references to gentile cities like Tyre and Sidon do reveal the temporal aspect of salvation history. The evangelist not only implies that any reward to be accorded to the gentiles is reserved for the eschaton (11:22, τύρῳ καὶ Σιδῶνι ἀνεκτότερον ἔσται ἐν ἡμέρᾳ κρίσεως ἢ ὑμῖν; in light of the comparison with the unrepentant Jewish cities as well as the parallel to Sodom, this is not much of a reward) but, by stating that no miracles were performed in the gentile cities, recalls the restriction of Jesus' mission. Regardless of their actions, the Jews retain their privileged role during Jesus' lifetime.

To dissociate Jesus from inaugurating the gentile mission, Matthew combines Mark's separated references to Tyre and Sidon. By specifically locating Jesus first in Tyre and then in Sidon, as well as by including references to other gentile areas Mark 7:31 -- "Then he returned from the region of Tyre, and went through Sidon to the Sea of Galilee, through the region of the Decapolis" -- produces a missionary tour of the gentile cities. Matthew, conversely, conveys the impression that Jesus traveled only to the general region, and no hint of investment in gentile territories is produced.[7] This

---

of Matt 11:20-24," *CBQ* 39 (1977): 498, noting that each comparison of Jewish to gentile city concludes with the reference to the day of judgment, states "Jesus totally and unequivocally excludes the cities from eschatological salvation"; cf. Hare, *Jewish Persecution*, p. 14, who describes the passage as indicating the "rejection of the community-as-a-whole."

[7]Hooker, "Uncomfortable Words," pp. 362-63; S. Brown, "Matthean Community," p. 195. Kilpatrick's claim, *Origins of the Gospel*, pp. 130ff., that the setting is emphasized (cf. 11:21-22) because it is the location of Matthew's church is attenuated by the change of the Marcan "Syrophoenician" to "Canaanite" and by the association of Tyre and Sidon with areas such as Sodom (11:23). Hill, *The Gospel*, p. 203, helpfully

dissociation is reinforced by the changes apparent in the next verse. Mark 7:24b-26a reads: "And he entered a house (εἰσελθὼν εἰς οἰκίαν), and he would not have any one know it; yet he could not be hid. But immediately a woman...came and fell down at his feet. And the woman was a Greek, a Syrophoenician by birth" (ἡ δὲ γυνὴ ἦν Ἑλληνίς, Συροφοινίκισσα τῷ γένει). According to Matthew, Jesus does not enter a house: he only travels toward Tyre and Sidon, and he may not have crossed the border. Matthew 15:22a simply announces that "a Canaanite woman came out from that region" (γυνὴ Χαναναία ἀπὸ τῶν ὁρίων ἐκείνων ἐξελθοῦσα).

By omitting Mark's notice that Jesus entered the woman's house, Matthew remains consistent in separating Jesus from a gentile mission. The flight to Egypt removes the child from both the Jewish king and the Jewish land, but no contact with native Egyptians is mentioned, and no mission is inaugurated; the pericope of the Gadarene demoniacs (Matt 8:28-34; cf. Mk. 5:1-20) has been revised to undercut gentile connotations; and the healing of the centurion's son in 8:5-13 is depicted as an exception to Jesus' general practices. It is therefore unlikely that, according to the first gospel, Jesus entered the region of Tyre and Sidon.[8] Rather, the Canaanite woman comes out; by

---

observes that the juxtaposition of the two cities may derive from the traditional linking in condemnatory pronouncements by the prophets (e.g., Joel 3:4; Isa 23:1-12; and Zech 9:2). See also Gundry, *Matthew*, p. 310, who, however, claims that the references are combined "to make the story a dominical example of ministry to Gentiles."

[8]Against Hill, *The Gospel*, pp. 253-54; Albright and Mann, *Matthew*, p. 187. Conversely, Gundry, *Matthew*, p. 310, suggests that the Matthean reading of "districts" (εἰς τὰ μέρη, 15:21) instead of "boundaries" (εἰς τὰ ὅρια, Mk 7:24) is intended to "forestall an inference that Jesus went up to the borders of Gentile territory but did not enter."

meeting Jesus not only on his own terms but also on his own turf she acknowledges the temporal priority of the Jews. Matthew 15:22 is, moreover, exceptional among miracle stories in the first gospel because it does not employ any form of προσέρχομαι, "to approach" or "to associate with" (cf. Acts 10:28), in describing the supplicant's first encounter with Jesus.[9] In 8:5-13 the term is used because the centurion represented one among many individuals marginal to the ruling Jewish and gentile powers; his connections to others apart from their respective centers rather than his uniqueness as a gentile receive Matthew's attention. In chapter 15, however, the woman's Canaanite nationality is specifically emphasized, and therefore the division between her and the messiah to the Jews is reinforced.

Along with the women's actions, the narrator's rhetoric also expresses Israel's temporal priority. Matthew calls her not a Syrophoenician Greek but, in the only use of the term in the New Testament, a Canaanite (Χαναναία). Even if this were a first-century Semitic idiom for the inhabitants of Phoenicia,[10] the extended connotations of the term cannot be ignored. Given the evangelist's interest in connecting Jesus with the events in Jewish history, the shift from Mark's terminology recalls the biblical contrasts between the Israelites and the indigenous population of the Promised Land.[11] Just as the Jews had priority over the Canaanites in the past, so too they retain this priority in the present. This conclusion mitigates Meier's suggestion that the opposition between ancient Canaan and ancient Israel is "transcended in Christ" when Jesus heals the

---

[9]Held, "Matthew as Interpreter," p. 226.

[10]Kilpatrick, *Origins of the Gospel*, p. 132.

[11]Manson, *Sayings of Jesus*, p. 200; Argyle, *The Gospel*, p. 119; Senior, *Invitation to Matthew*, p. 154.

woman's daughter.[12] The temporal subordination of the gentiles is not transcended but legitimized by the reference to the "Canaanite" and by the dialogue that follows.

The use of "Canaanite" may also reflect the social axis of Matthean salvation history. Kilpatrick suggests that the shift from Mk 7:26 to Matt 15:22 "seems to divert the reference of the story from the inhabitants of the great ports with their Hellenic pretensions...to the villagers who were relatively untouched by Hellenism and remained Semitic in speech and outlook."[13] Morover, the woman is identified as coming "from a region" (ἀπὸ τῶν ὁρίων, 15:22) rather than from one of the cities themselves.

The first line of dialogue reinforces the narrator's interest in paradigms derived from the Hebrew scriptures. While Mk 7:26 employs no titles, in Matthew 15:22b the woman addresses Jesus as "son of David" (15:22b; cf. 9:27; 20:30). She thus immediately evokes images of the ancient Israelite monarchy first introduced in the genealogy (1:1, 6)[14] and so confirms Israel's temporal priority over the native population of Palestine. "Son of David" also connects the woman with the faithful Jewish crowds who will later acclaim Jesus with this title (21:9, 15) and so distances her from the political leaders who will not (cf. 22:41-45). However, this is no more a "confession of discipleship" as J. M. Gibbs asserts[15] than is the

---

[12] *Vision of Matthew*, p. 104 n. 98. For additional counter-arguments see Schweizer, *Good News*, p. 330; and Tagawa, "People and Community," p. 153.

[13] *Origins of the Gospel*, p. 133.

[14] Gundry, *Matthew*, p. 311; Hooker, "Uncomfortable Words," p. 362: "The woman herself...acknowledges from the outset the sphere of Jesus' mission when she addresses him as 'Son of David.'"

[15] "Purpose and Pattern in Matthew's Use of the Title 'Son of

reference to "Lord" (κύριε) in 15:22. Jesus does not call the woman to follow him, nor does she seek to do so. Also arguing against Gibbs's point is the contrast provided by Matt 20:29-34, the next confession of Jesus as "son of David." In this case, the two blind men "followed him" (ἠκολούησαν αὐτῷ, 20:34).

The theme of Jewish privilege continues in the next three verses, all of which are redactional. In Matt 15:23a, Jesus meets the woman's request with silence (ὁ δὲ οὐκ ἀπεκρίθη αὐτῇ λόγον), a reaction consistent with his unwillingness to bestow proleptic blessings of the *Basileia* on non-Jews (cf. 8:7). Fenton even suggests that the delay between the request and its answer corresponds to the interval between the mission to the Jews and the admission of gentiles to the church.[16]

The disciples' response in 15:23b, "Send her away (Ἀπόλυσον αὐτήν) for she is crying after us," is also in accord with Matthew's agenda. The twelve are acting in harmony both with the injunctions concerning the mission previously issued by Jesus (10:5b-6) and with his own behavior: his silence after the woman's first request must be taken as a refusal. By adding v. 23, the first evangelist emphasizes that the earthly mission of Jesus and his followers is to the Jews alone. Thus the statement conveys Matthew's lesson in temporal priority which the disciples have now learned. The twelve do not, consequently, "represent the Jewish-Christians who are

---

David'," *NTS* 10 (1963/64): 450 (following Bornkamm).

[16]*Saint Matthew*, p. 255. Kilpatrick, *Origins of the Gospel*, p. 50, inexplicably states that the motivation for 15:22-24 is obscure; and Gundry, *Matthew*, p. 312, suggests it emphasizes the woman's faith. The connection with rabbinic warnings against engaging in conversations with women, e.g., *Pirke Aboth* 1.5, is not implied in the text. Jesus has no qualms about talking with other women in the gospel, nor do they show hesitancy in addressing him.

opposed to (or who do not understand) the entry of the Gentiles to the church."[17] According to the pericope, Jesus is the one "opposed to" fulfilling the request of the gentile.

Undaunted by Jesus' silence and the disciples' complaint, the woman persists. Consequently, Jesus must make explicit the implications of his silence: his mission is only to the Jews, he was "sent only to the lost sheep of the house of Israel" (Οὐκ ἀπεστάλην εἰ μὴ εἰς τὰ πρόβατα τὰ ἀπολωλότα οἴκου Ἰσραήλ). This problematic verse summarizes and secures the gospel's temporal axis. As a reexpression of 10:6, the restriction is now specifically related to Jesus' own mission rather than cast as instructions to the disciples. Further, it is now addressed to a gentile rather than to Jews.[18] The shift in context accounts for some differences in grammar and vocabulary between 10:6 and 15:24 (e.g., the change from second person plural imperative to first person singular passive), as well as minor changes in emphasis. While "the lost sheep of the house of Israel" appears in both versions, 10:6 implies rather than explicitly mentions the "only" (εἰ μή). The explicit limitation is required in the second version for at least two reasons. First, 15:24 is presented without the complementary limitation given in the second discourse; only 10:5b presents the mandate to *avoid* gentile areas. Second, the

---

[17]Hill, *The Gospel*, p. 254. He does however note that ἀπόλυσον could be translated "give her what she wants and let her go." Against Hill, see Gundry, *Matthew*, p. 312.

[18]Gundry, *Matthew*, pp. 312-13, states that because the logion contrasts with Jesus' initial silence and follows the disciples' comment, it is addressed to the disciples (cf. 10:5b-6). The statement is better read as an intensification of Jesus' initial refusal (silence) and not as a contrast. Further, Matthew frequently notes changes in audience: see in particular the shift in the parallel pericope (8:5-13) from the centurion to the crowd.

harsher wording to the woman is a necessary response to her persistence. While the Jewish disciples accept the restrictions in 10:5b-6 without comment, the woman argues.

Although Matt 15:24 is consistent with Jesus' earlier actions and instructions, and although even the Canaanite woman agrees with its premise, the restriction is nevertheless interpreted by many scholars as a piece of Jewish exclusivism which the evangelist received from a source and felt constrained to repeat. This conclusion misses the gospel's ultimate cross-ethnic, social concern; it ignores the intensification of 10:6 in 15:24 and so suggests Matthew is not only inconsistent but foolishly so; and it disturbingly sounds like Christian apologetic. The conclusion that a verse is repellent because it has a focus on the Jews might well be perceived by the reader sensitive to Jewish interests as prejudicial. A positive focus on Jews does not necessarily imply a negative view of gentiles. Ironically, exegetes rarely classify Christian excoriations of Jews or, more comparably, Jesus' interest specifically in gentiles, as "repellent" or even "restrictive." While of course it would be dishonest for any historian to claim that all Jews who accepted Jesus' message welcomed gentiles -- particularly those not in conformity to the ritual Law -- wholeheartedly into the church, it is equally sloppy to claim that all verses which suggest Jewish priority are abhorrent, un-Christian, anti-gentile, or even from a Jewish source. Every such instance must be analyzed within its overall context to determine its contextual connotations and functions and, based on this information, to propose the likely social matrix that would give rise to its appearance.

A helpful first step is to ask whether, both in and of itself and in the context of the first gospel, the instance in question is in any way abhorrent. When applied to Matt 15:24, the question yields negative results. The verse itself contains no ethnic slurs or even hints that the gentiles are perceived by Jesus to be unworthy of his attention. The focus is entirely on the Jews, and the exclusivity statement in this chapter does not even mention the gentiles. While Jeremias suggests the restriction is unwelcome in a messiah who is supposed to redeem all humanity, Matt 15:21-28 clearly indicates that the logion is consistent with themes established in the Hebrew scriptures: it confirms the doctrine of election and the supersession of Israel over Canaan.[19] Nor are these concepts incompatible with universal salvation. For example, while Israel may be the "chosen people," conversion into this nation had become both possible and not infrequent. Attacking the question of repellent exclusivity from a different perspective, one might argue that the replacement of Canaanite hegemony with the Israelite monarchy is also repellent: the deity granted the Hebrews an exclusive claim. While a case could be made against Yahwistic imperialism, this is neither Jeremias's nor the Bible's line of argument. Consequently, Jeremias makes a value judgment on 15:24, but he fails to support it. Indeed, if Matthew found the logion uncongenial, then its anticipation in 8:7, its presence in 10:6, and its intensification in 15:24 are difficult to explain. Even if the evangelist were a slave to sources, which is not the case,[20] such consistency suggests a positive reception of this motif.

Jeremias attempts to bolster his conclusion that Matt

---

[19]Blauw, *Missionary Nature*, p. 67. Agreeing with Jeremias's description but assigning the verse to the proverbial "Jewish-Christian source" are, among others, Tagawa, "People and Community," p. 154; and Manson, *Sayings of Jesus*, p. 201.

[20]See the perceptive comments on the consistency of the theme of exclusivity in W. Trilling, *Das Wahre Israel*, p. 84; as well as J. Reumann's review of *Das Wahre Israel*, 2d ed., *JBL* 79 (1960): 377; and Hare, *Jewish Persecution*, p. 146 and n. 1.

15:24 has a claim to authenticity by reconstructing an Aramaic original: (a) οὐκ...εἰ μή is a translation of לא...אלא ("not...but", or "only"); (b) ἀπεστάλην is a divine passive, perhaps derived from the Aramaic present perfect ("has sent," אשתדרית);[21] (c) ἀποστέλλειν εἰς plus the group concerned is not classical Greek but a Septuagintal formulation (LXX Jer 30:8; II Kgs 18:20; Acts 26:17), and εἰς is the equivalent of the Hebrew/Aramaic בי; (d) the interchange between πρός in 10:6 and εἰς in 15:24 indicates a translation variant based on the original בי; and (e) ἀποστελλειν εἴς τινα in 15:24 is a pre-Matthean formulation since the first gospel favors προς τίνα (21:34, 37; 23:34, 37; 27:19).[22] These reconstructions are beset with problems. First, the burden of proof remains on the one who posits an underlying tradition. Jeremias not only lacks an original, but also any argument based on an alleged Semitic Urtext, especially in cases where the Greek is comprehensible, is weak. The inconclusive nature of Jeremias's appeal is demonstrated as well by different reconstructions of the hypothetical original. Using his own method one could argue for two Aramaic originals, one using ב to correspond with πρός, and the other reading ל and so corresponding to εἰς. On the other hand, the

---

[21]*Jesus' Promise*, p. 27, arguing against Bultmann, *History of the Synoptic Tradition*, p. 163, who locates the saying in the early church's concern with the gentile mission.

[22]*Jesus' Promise*, pp. 26-27 and n. 2. Kilpatrick, *Origins of the Gospel*, p. 50, claims the composite nature of 15:22-24 and the parallel to 10:5b-6 indicate that the exclusivity logion "is not derived from a written source other than Mk and M." This indirectly argues against an Aramaic original but is itself based on two false premises: it ignores the possibility that Matthew had additional sources, either oral or written; and it eliminates the redactional role of the evangelist. For a detailed criticism of Jeremias's reconstruction, see Gundry, *Matthew*, p. 313.

appeal to a translation variant to explain the change from πρός in 10:6 to εἰς in 15:24 is unnecessary. Because εἰς appears twice in 10:5b, the use of πρός in 10:6 is both stylistically pleasing and symbolically representative of the difference between the prohibited mission to the gentiles and the enjoined mission to the Jews. Finally, some scholars claim that 10:5b-6 is the original expression, 15:24 is secondary.[23] The various arguments that support Matthew's agreement with the thrust of two exclusivity logia combined both with the evangelist's freedom to redact received sources and with the difficulties in reconstructing an Aramaic original commend the conclusion that at the very least 15:24 is consistent with Matthew's revision of Mark 7:24-30 and strongly suggest that the verse is a Matthean creation.

Jesus' explicit refusal to aid the Canaanite woman is followed by the final verse peculiar to the Matthean account. The woman responds by prostrating herself before Jesus and addressing him for the second time as "Lord" (Κύριε). The title reiterates the privileged position of the Jew, both of Jesus as the Jewish miracle worker and of the Jewish community as the rulers of the Canaanites. It also allows the problematic statement in 15:26 (Mk 7:27) to serve as a commentary on the exclusivity pronouncement.

Mark 7:27-28 reads: "And he said to her, 'Let the children first (πρῶτον) be fed, for it is not good (οὐ ἐστιν καλόν) to take the children's bread and throw it to the dogs' (κυναρίοις). But she answered him, 'Yes, Lord, but (καί) even the dogs under the table eat the children's (παιδίων) crumbs.'" Through changes in syntax and vocabulary, Matthew shifts Mark's emphasis on the gentile mission to a focus on the present priority of the Jews. The first gospel omits the temporal indicator "first" (πρῶτον),

---

23Trilling, *Das Wahre Israel*, p. 82; Munck, *Paul and the Salvation of Mankind*, p. 201 (with hesitancy).

includes the confessional title "Lord" (κύριε), and adds a reference to "their master's" (τῶν κυρίων αὐτῶν) table.

By stating that the bread must *first* (πρῶτον) be given to the children, Mk 7:27a implies a "next" or "second" time when the dogs will eventually get their share.[24] Because Matthew lacks this temporal signifier, those scholars who see the gospel as expressing a similar development with the mission going first to the Jews and, following their failure to receive the good news, to the gentiles, have a problem: why would the redactor remove a term consistent with the text's overall soteriology? The most frequent explanation by those who support the theory of Markan priority, that πρῶτον is a later insertion into Mark's gospel,[25] is not supported by the ancient manuscripts. It is consequently more helpful to seek the reasons for Matthew's omission of the term in the different emphases of the first two gospels.

Mark depicts both an increasingly close association between Jesus and the gentiles (7:24, 31; 8:27; etc.) and a widening separation between Jesus and the Jews (esp. 7:19b). Given this reorientation of the mission, πρῶτον for Mark implies a distinction rather than a continuation. Mark 7:27a signals the end of the mission to the Jews: the children are finished; now the dogs can eat. Matthew, however, explicitly indicates that Jesus' mission is to the Jews alone; there is no

---

[24]Jeremias, *Jesus' Promise*, p. 29 n. 2, observes that πρῶτον implies "an eschatological ὕστερον," and thus the privilege of Israel is a "temporary right." Gundry, *Matthew*, p. 314, notes that, although unlikely, πρῶτον might have been used by "narrow-minded Jewish Christians" who expected all Israel to be saved before the eschatological mission to the gentiles.

[25]Held, "Matthew as Interpreter," p. 198 (following Bultmann); Wilson, *Gentiles*, pp. 9-10 (following Klostermann, Lohmeyer, Jeremias, Munck, and Cranfield).

need for a "first" since for Jesus' earthly charge there can be no "next."[26] And because the commission in Matt 28:16-20 does not abrogate the mission to the Jews, the second connotation of πρῶτον is also inapplicable. The Jews will not have finished with the meal of the gospel; they will continue to be fed the word while the invitation to dine is extended to the gentiles. Thus the evangelist had at least two reasons for eliminating the problematic term.

Following Jesus' third attempt at discouragement, the woman responds using his terminology and so indicating her assent to the divine plan behind the restriction. Both participants in the conversation share a common metaphoric vocabulary: the dogs are the gentiles, the children Jews.[27] Modern scholars also accept this interpretation, but they disagree on its extended connotations in the first gospel. The focus of the debate is on the relationship between 15:26-27 and 7:6, "Do not give to dogs (τοῖς κυσίν) what is holy and do not throw your pearls before swine, lest they trample them under foot and turn to attack you." At issue is the extent to which Matthew manifests anti-gentile prejudice.

Commenting on Matt 7:6, Argyle observes: "The Gentiles were called 'dogs' or 'swine' because they were enemies of

---

[26]Munck, *Paul and the Salvation of Mankind*, pp. 262-63, notes that for Mark, the issue is "how far the time has come for the gentiles to be helped, and not, as in Matthew, how far Jesus is to help them at all." See also Hill, *The Gospel*, p. 254.

[27]Hill, *The Gospel*, p. 254; Wilson, *Gentiles,* p. 11 (citing Strack-Billerbeck and following Jeremias and Michel). Debate remains over the diminutive κυνάρια ("puppies"). Jeremias, *Jesus' Promise*, p. 29; Gundry, *Matthew*, p. 314; and Bosch (cited in Wilson, *The Gentiles*, p. 11) suggest it may mitigate the harshness of the saying. Green, *The Gospel*, p. 147, claims that by the first century the term had lost its diminutive force.

Israel. This verse, therefore, looks like a bit of Jewish exclusiveness and may be ascribed to the Judaistic and anti-Gentile tone of much of the matter peculiar to Matthew."[28] Counter arguments are, however, easily mustered. First, no conclusive evidence that rabbis employed either term as a common metaphor for gentiles exists.[29] While Fiorenza

---

[28]Argyle, *The Gospel*, p. 61; Senior, *Invitation to Matthew*, pp. 82-83 ("may have originally been used in the context of Jewish-Gentile tensions"); Carlston, "Interpreting the Gospel," p. 5 ("probably reflects the author's Jewish-Christian background"); Green, *The Gospel*, p. 94 ("an epigram with a strong anti-Gentile bias"); Brandon, *Jesus and the Zealots*, p. 174 (identifies swine as a rabbinic term for Rome or the non-Israelite world and dogs as "a Jewish-Christian appellation for Gentiles"); Manson, *Sayings of Jesus*, p. 174 ("a bit of apocalyptic Jewish exclusiveness, adopted by extreme Jewish Christians"); and see idem, *Jesus and the Non-Jews*, p. 3; Abel, "Who Wrote Matthew?" p.144 ("characteristic of Matthew's Judaistic background"); Allen, *Critical and Exegetical Commentary*, pp. 66-67. Schweizer, *Good News*, pp. 168-70, notes that in the Pseudo-Clementines 3.1 the saying is used by Jewish Christians to attack members of the Catholic church. The Clementine passage however concerns a religious orientation rather than an ethnic distinction.

[29]Abrahams, *Studies in Pharisaism*, vol. 2, pp. 194-95, esp. on *Mid. Ps* 4:8: "Although here heathens are described as dogs, the association is not familiar, as it is explained exegetically." Abrahams also indicates that *T. B. Nidda* 77a is not relevant to the discussion, and that frequently "dogs" refers to slaves, not gentiles per se. See also J. S. Bloch, *Israel and the Nations* (Berlin and Vienna: Benj. Harz: 1927), pp. 211-20. Manson, *Sayings of Jesus*, p. 174, notes that in I En 89:42, Philistines are called "dogs," and Edomites "boars." However, he also suggests that "if there is a tendency in Judaism to speak of Gentile nations as 'dogs' or 'swine,' it is not merely because they are Gentiles, but because they are enemies of Israel." His employ of "if" is telling, and the distinction between gentiles as enemies of Israel and gentiles as specifically and simply an

observes that "since dogs and swine were considered unclean animals, they could be used figuratively to characterize pagans,"[30] she omits from the referent those among the Jewish population who might be seen as unworthy. For Matthew's purposes, the verse may be better interpreted as a warning against the Jewish leadership who, according to the mission discourse, will "turn to attack" (cf. 10:17).[31] The association is specifically implied in the preceding verse, where the charge of "hypocrisy" (cf. 23:13ff.) is made.[32] Second, near-contemporary Christian references to "dogs" such as II Pet 2:22 suggest not ethnic gentiles but general evil-doers and apostates. Philippians 3:2 places "dogs" in the same context as "those who mutilate the flesh," which in context suggests Jews and/or Judaizers rather than ethnic gentiles per se. In Rev 22:15 dogs are associated with sorcerers, fornicators, murderers, idolators, and liars. Neither Jews nor gentiles have cornered the market on these activities. The Didache 9:5 even applies Matt 7:6 to the distribution of the Eucharist to unbelievers, who may be Jews. Third, because the context of the couplet does not suggest a reference to gentiles -- indeed, as Davies notes, "Generally where the Gentiles are in mind this is explictly stated" (cf. 6:7)[33] -- some commentators are

---

ethnic category is relevant to the present discussion.

[30]E. S. Fiorenza, *In Memory of Her* (New York: Crossroad, 1983), p. 137.

[31]Hare, *Jewish Persecution*, p. 123, suggests that 'dogs' and 'swine' probably refer to gentiles but notes the allusion is "far too vague...to be taken as evidence that Gentile persecution of Christians was a matter of serious concern to the author of this gospel."

[32]On the possible break between 7:1-5 and 7:6 see Kilpatrick, *Origins of the Gospel*, p. 76.

[33]*Setting*, p. 196. Thus the logion also does not deal with the

forced to surmise that the redactor modified the "original anti-gentile connotation" of 7:6 to indicate merely that the Christian message should not be shared with those who would neither understand nor respect it.[34] Others conclude that even if the equation of dogs with gentiles is present in the received text of the gospel, "it is unlikely to have been part of the meaning of the original Aramaic sayings, which simply warned against lack of discrimination (in teaching?)."[35] Although "dogs" does refer to gentiles in 15:26-27, there a different, distinctive term ("puppies") is employed. Thus, Matt 7:6 has no immediate connection with the Matthean attitude toward or depiction of non-Jews. It is more likely that 7:6 is a cross-ethnic warning against preaching the gospel to anyone -- Jew or gentile -- who is not prepared to receive it. Given the parallel structure of the verse; its juxtaposition to the reference to hypocrites in 7:5, and the more common connection between gentiles and pigs, Matthew may well be exhorting the church to avoid members of the establishment, be they *Jewish* dogs or gentile pigs.

Nevertheless, the association of gentiles with dogs, puppies or not, in Matt 15:26 is an ethnic insult. Its presence is initially surprising, since the redactor has repeatedly indicated that the word will go out to the gentiles and many among the nations will receive it. To argue simply that Matthew felt constrained to copy Mark here is unacceptable, but the appeal to Mark's version offers a clue to Matthew's agenda. The first evangelist may have repeated the difficult

---

directives in 10:5b-6 and 15:24, as Manson, *Jesus and the Non-Jews*, p. 1, argues; on this see Fenton, *Saint Matthew*, p. 110.

[34]Senior, *Invitation to Matthew*, pp. 82-83; and particularly Green, *The Gospel*, p. 94.

[35]Hill, *The Gospel*, pp. 147-48; cf. Cox, *The Gospel*, pp. 60-61; Fenton, *Saint Matthew*, p. 110.

verse in order to modify its disparaging connotations. The insult becomes a form of instruction presented by the response to Jesus' comment.

Rather than take offense, the woman adopts his metaphor. She acknowledges that, as a Canaanite, she is not entitled to the privileges of her historical and theological "masters," the Jewish community.[36] There may even be a word play on the terms for "Canaanite" (Χαναναία) and dogs (κυνάρια).[37] The temporal and social interests of the gospel are highlighted through three redactional modifications of Mk 7:28. The confessonal title κύριε is inserted for the third time, again indicating her faith and her recognition of proper authority. More intriguingly, Mark's "children" (τῶν παιδίων) have become, in the Matthean version, "their masters" or, literally, "their lords" (τῶν κυρίων αὐτῶν). Since the "masters" have power over both the Jewish children and the gentile dogs, Jews and gentile have been metaphorically united. Neither rules, and both are dependent for food on the "Lords". Moreover, since ethnic Jews are associated metaphorically with the children, the "masters" need not represent the Jewish community. Because it has no antecedent, the "masters" may well be Matthew's reintroduction of social categories. The woman notes that both the people at the apex of society, the masters, and those on the lowest rung, the Canaanites or "dogs," share the same food. Finally, the dogs have been moved from "under the table" (ὑποκάτω τῆς τραπέζης), where they were located in Mk 7:28. Thus they are on the same level as the children, rather than in a

---

[36]Manson, *Jesus and the Non-Jews*, p. 23; cf. Jeremias, *Jesus' Promise*, p. 30 (following Schlatter); and Munck, *Paul and the Salvation of Mankind*, p. 263. Munck, p. 262 n. 1, also suggests that the response may be a commonplace (cf. Philostratus *Life of Apollonius* 1.19); as does Gundry, *Matthew*, p. 314.

[37]Suggested by Dale C. Allison, Jr.

perpetual state of denigration. However, they remain spatially as well as temporally removed from the children and the masters, since their time has not yet come. It would be inappropriate ("it is not fair," Οὐκ ἔστιν καλόν) for the dogs, who eat later, to be given the food of the gospel before the children of Israel receive their nourishment. The distinction between dogs and children conforms to the temporal axis; their association, cast in terms of necessary fulfillment -- "even the dogs eat the crumbs that fall from their masters' table" -- anticipates the social axis when all will have equal access to the mission.

Ultimately, the woman is able to demonstrate her faith not by arguing against the insult to her ethnic group, but by indicating that both the gentile dogs and the Jewish children are under the same authority. In Mk 7:29, the woman simply outwits Jesus (διὰ τοῦτον τὸν λόγον); in Matthew, she indicates her faith and her conformity to the heavenly plan of salvation history. She is able to obtain a miracle because she accepts her marginal position as a gentile.

The Broader Narrative Context: Matthew's Response to Judaism

Most scholarly analysis of the contribution Matt 15:21-28 makes to the gospel's view of Jews and gentiles follows one of two methods. The first seeks to reconstruct the church setting, the background, of the scene. Here both presupposition and conclusion most often suggest that the pericope reflects a pre-Matthean Jewish-Christianity reluctant to evangelize among the gentiles. The second approach analyzes the account within its literary context, and it addresses such questions as how the exclusivity logion is related to the Great Commission, whether the context of the pericope depicts the rejection of the Jews, and if so, whether this rejection is the prerequisite for the gentile mission. The usual conclusion is that the narrative smacks of Jewish exclusivity, but this prejudicial attitude is superseded by the evangelist's universalistic pronouncements.

Of these two approaches, situating the account within the context of pre-Matthean debates over the mission to the gentiles is not only more speculative, it is less helpful. The search for the story's origins involves both a reconstruction of the Matthean community and a classification of that community within ill-defined categories of "Jewish-Christianity" and "gentile-Christianity." While almost all of the conclusions reached are plausible, some are mutually exclusive and none is verifiable. The chaotic state of scholarship is one indication of the drawbacks of this approach. For example, Hill proposes that Matt 15:21-28 "was employed for the guidance of the Matthean church in its relations with Gentiles."[38] But it is not clear what this lesson is. The idea that the Matthean church is to continue to view gentiles as dogs is surely barking up the wrong tree. Is the church to accept Jesus' words that the mission is just to Israel or to agree with the woman that gentiles too should receive the benefits of the *Basileia*? According to Munck, the pericope indicates that Jewish-Christianity did not carry on a mission to the gentiles, but it nevertheless recognized that such a mission was authorized. This argument follows from his twin conclusions that "the view must have existed from the

[38] *The Gospel*, p. 253; cf. Held, "Matthew as Interpreter," pp. 198 ("It is significant that the strict Jewish-Christian standpoint is acknowledged by the Matthean narrative and yet is overcome by the great faith of the Gentile woman"), 267; Brandon, *Jesus and the Zealots*, pp. 172-73; Albright and Mann, *Matthew*, p. xxiii; Munck, *Paul and the Salvation of Mankind*, pp. 259-60.

first that the Gospel concerned everyone; and so it had to be laid down that the sending of the twelve disciples concerned no one but the Jews" and that "the salvation of Israel is presumably always regarded as the way that is to lead the Gentiles to share in the salvation that is to come."[39] Yet if this pericope is taken as a practical lesson, then the Great Commission can have no bearing on the activities of the congregation. It becomes unclear which material is relevant to the readers, and which concerns some other group.

Proponents of the reconstruction of the community underlying the pericope are, moreover, frequently forced to invent Aramaic originals or to appeal to the hypothetical Jewish-Christian (M) source to support their conclusions. The latter step in particular displays a myopic view of those Jews who did accept Jesus to be the messiah by implying that "Jewish-Christianity" was exclusivistic at the very least and, likely, anti-gentile. Finally, such reconstruction of the situations underlying the "received material" usually slights the creative capacities of the evangelists.

The better approach to the interpretation of a pericope or of any verse within it is to look first at the literary context, both immediate and general, and so determine if it is consistent or antithetical to the rest of the text. However, this method also presents problems: although less speculative than reconstructing the community behind the text, contextual analysis has also failed to yield critical consensus. Indeed, unlike the context of Matt 8:5-13, the general narrative section in which 15:21-28 is embedded cannot be easily determined. The starting point is generally agreed to be 13:53, the end of the Parables of the *Basileia* and the accompanying shift in Jesus' location. The next section may begin at 19:1

---

[39] *Paul and the Salvation of Mankind*, pp. 263-64.

(following the end of the Galilean tour), 17:1 (the transfiguration "after six days"), 16:21 (the first passion prediction), 16:13 (the entry into Caesarea Philippi), 15:29 (the departure from gentile borders), or one of several other points. Of these various options, Matt 16:12, the conclusion of the miraculous feedings, seems the best choice for the final verse of the general context. The next verse depicts a change in location, a change in theme ("who is Jesus"), and a change in tone (it introduces the passion).

Some scholars claim that the various narratives in Matt 13:53-16:12 depict an increasing separation between Jesus and Judaism and thus, either implicitly or explicitly, a closer connection between Jesus and the gentile world. Franzmann offers an extreme example of this process. Commenting on Matt 14:13, he concludes that Jesus "separated and freed his disciples...inwardly from Judaism -- from its tradition, with its inadequate and false conception of purity, from its rebellious sign-seeking, from its perilously pervasive teaching in every form...."[40] Others argue for a continuation of the policy set forth in the mission discourse: the Jews remain the target of Jesus' message, and any contact he has with gentiles only foreshadows the Great Commission. If hypothetical reconstructions of Matthew's sources are tabled, if Matthean divergences from Mark are emphasized, and if Matthew is viewed as a consistent, competent author -- three quite legitimate steps -- the latter argument receives substantial support from contextual analysis.

Matthew 13:53-16:12 highlights the temporal axis by depicting a typological association between Jesus and Israelite history. The various pericopes within this section

---

[40]*Discipleship*, p. 129. See also the kinder comments by Meier, *Vision of Matthew*, p. 94, who entitles his section on 13:53-16:12 "Christ withdraws His Church from Judaism."

reinforce both Jesus' connection with the Jews and the privileges of the Jewish community in salvation history. But, by setting up comparisons between cities and the wilderness, between the Jewish leaders and the faithful crowds, between the believing gentile and the obtuse disciples, Matthew also emphasizes the cross-ethnic dimensions that give shape to the social axis. The following pericope-by-pericope analysis of the entire section demonstrates these conclusions.

Although Matt 13:53-58 (Mk 6:1-6a//Lk 4:16-30) depicts the rejection of Jesus by his home town and 14:1-12 concerns the execution of John the Baptist by Herod Antipas, in neither instance are the Jewish people as a whole condemned. The people of Nazareth take offense (ἐσκανδαλίζοντο ἐν αὐτῷ, 13:57) because they wrongly perceive Jesus to be an upstart. His authority, manifested by wisdom and mighty works, competes with their self-given authority to judge. But these people do not "typify Israel as a whole."[41] They are best contrasted not with the faithful gentile of 15:21-28 but with the crowds who follow Jesus in 14:13-21. The people in the town are characterized by stasis and faithlessness; the people in the wilderness are mobile and faithful. Matthew's social interests also explain the addition of the pronoun αὐτῶν, "their," to "synagogue" in 13:54. This redactional insertion does not, contrary to much Matthean scholarship,[42] indicate the separation of the Matthean church from the Jewish people. Rather, it signals that the synagogue is the place of worship of

---

[41] Meier, *Vision of Matthew*, p. 96, cf. p. 95 and n. 81 connecting the appearance of ἀπιστία (RSV: "unbelief") in 13:58 with ἄπιστος (RSV: "faithless") in 17:17. The direct reference to the "faithless and perverse generation" in 17:17 is unclear, and "no faith" or "unbelief" is not far from the "little faith" that often describes the disciples.

[42] See Green, *The Gospel*, p. 138.

the immobile townspeople, not of the wandering Jesus. Again, the evangelist has severed the connection between the new community of disciples and the existent institutional structures of power.

Matthew 14:1-12, the companion to 13:53-58, reasserts the cross-ethnic motifs of the social axis. The parallels between the two narratives are extensive: Jesus' powers are observed but overlooked; John's powers are recognized (14:5) but ignored. Jesus is denounced because the people claim to know his family, but they are ignorant of his true origins as related in the infancy accounts; Herod is denounced, correctly, because the Baptist knows the true state of his domestic affairs. The people from Jesus' home focus on outside appearances and social norms; Herod's power is limited by pride and social conventions ("because of his oaths and his guests"). These connections attenuate the assertion that the population of Jesus' home town typifies all of Israel. Matthew 14:1-12, like chapter 2, specifically distinguishes the leadership, in this case another Herod, from the people who "hold John to be a prophet" and from the disciples of the Baptist -- who, again, are Jews.

In 14:13 Jesus withdraws (ἀνεχώρησεν), not to separate himself from Judaism but because of the execution of John. Nevertheless, the crowds follow him, and he in turn has compassion for them and cures their sick (14:14; contrast 13:58). The miracle that follows (14:13-21) reinforces Jesus' commitment to the Jewish people. The feeding of the five thousand in a "lonely" or "uninhabited place" (εἰς ἔρημον) recapitulates one prominent theme in the gospel and introduces another. First, the evangelist again establishes a distinction between urban areas and centers (Jesus' home town, the palace of Herod Antipas) and undefined locations where the faithful congregate. But the notice of the ἔρημος also reinforces the temporal axis by recalling the journey of the Hebrews in the wilderness and so providing a clear indication that Jesus is recreating Israelite history: the escape from the murderous political authority (14:1-12) to the wilderness where the people are miraculously fed (14:13-21), the doubt experienced by some in the desert (14:22-28), the giving and interpreting of the Torah (15:1-20), the encounter, subjection, and ultimate coexistence with the Canaanites (15:21-28), the recollection of the wilderness years as an ideal time (15:32-38), and the ultimate division of the united people into elite groups each claiming authority (16:1-12). Individual elements mentioned in 14:13-21 suggest further scriptural motifs. For example, Hill proposes that the twelve baskets may symbolize twelve tribes as well as twelve disciples.[43] This typology reinforces the connection between Jesus and the Jews. Rather than replace Israel or proclaim Jewish history no longer of value, Jesus' activities support the privileged position the Jews have in the divine program.

This recapitulation of Jewish history also serves to connect the second half of Jesus' mission with the first. The first seven chapters of the gospel have often been read as a retelling of the Torah, from the Genesis (γενέσεως) of Jesus in 1:1 through the history implied by the genealogy to the allusions to the slavery in Egypt, the role of Moses, the journey and temptation in the wilderness, to the giving of the Law on a mountain, etc. Matthew takes the Torah as the paradigm for Jesus' message, and so again the first gospel connects rather

---

[43] *The Gospel*, p. 247; cf. Gundry, *Matthew*, p. 295. Argyle, *The Gospel*, p. 113, suggests that the five loaves given to the five thousand plus the seven loaves given to the four thousand symbolize the twelve tribes. If so, then the evangelist has undercut Mark's gentile connotations of the second feeding, although Argyle may have counted too much on too little.

than divorces the Jewish messiah from the Jewish community.

Ironically, the figures paralleling those among the twelve tribes who doubted in the wilderness are not Pharisees and Sadducees but the twelve disciples. Just as the followers of both Jesus and John manifest doubt after the Sermon on the Mount, so they fail again when given a second chance to prove their faith. Matthew 14:22-28, Jesus' walking on the water, recalls the depiction of the storm at sea in 8:23-28. Both instances occur at evening, on the water, and following a miracle, and in both the disciples are classified as having "little faith" (8:26; 14:31). The faith of the gentiles in chapters 8 and 15 is thus not directly contrasted with the unbelief of the Jews -- the crowds in the wilderness certainly display their faith -- but with the "little faith" of those who should know Jesus best, his disciples. Consistently, Matthew emphasizes that positions of authority should be neither abused nor viewed as sacrosanct.

The description of Jesus' walking on the water is followed by a pericope riding a sea of controversy. Although in 15:1-20 Matthew limits Jesus' concern to the specific injunction concerning "eating with unwashed hands," scholars nevertheless have asserted that the pericope indicates Jesus' rejection of the Jewish people or, at the very least, of Jewish Law.[44] While Jesus' own opinion of Torah may be beyond recovery and the Matthean attitude toward *Halachah* already the subject of several lengthy studies, a few comments about

---

[44]R. Walker, *Die Heilsgeschichte im ersten Evangelium* (Göttingen: Vandenhoeck and Ruprecht, 1967), esp. pp. 140-42; Franzmann, *Discipleship*, p. 131; Argyle, *The Gospel*, p. 117; Carlston, "Interpreting the Gospel," p. 95, cf. pp. 76-77; Blair, *Jesus in the Gospel of Matthew*, p. 308, who states that the first gospel "is not meant to shackle men with an ethical code more rigorous and frustrating than that of the Pharisees."

these conclusions are warranted.

In part, these theories depend more upon the preconceived notions of the commentators than upon the pericope under analysis. Either they are reading the first gospel through Marcan glasses, or they project later church history onto the first-century text, or they see first-century Judaism as rigid and monolithic. They must also either overlook or strain the meaning of other statements recorded in the first gospel, from 5:17, "Think not that I have come to abolish the law and the prophets..." to 23:2-3, "The scribes and the Pharisees sit on Moses' seat, so practice and observe whatever they tell you...." While Mark's Syrophoenician woman may signal the extension of the mission to gentiles and the possibly related abrogation of Jewish *Halachah*, the first gospel emphasizes Jesus' faithfulness to Mosaic law and (the majority of) Pharisaic traditions as well as his connection to, not his rejection of, the Jewish community.

Matthew first eliminates Mk 7:3-4, which mentions the traditions of "all the Jews" (πάντες οἱ Ἰουδαῖοι). The omission indicates more than the evangelist's familiarity with Judaism; it produces a limiting effect by focusing attention on one particular group -- the religious authorities[45] -- rather than on the entire Jewish community. This limitation reappears in the redactional comment that the Pharisees took offense (ἐσκανδαλίσθησαν) at Jesus' words (15:12). The tightening of the section as well as the addition of "but to eat with unwashed hands does not defile a person" (Matt 15:20b) at the conclusion

[45]Carlston, "Interpreting the Gospel," p. 75; Tilborg, *Jewish Leaders*, pp. 14, 101: "The Pharisees represent the negative aspects of the divine salvation-economy." Strecker, *Der Weg*, pp. 30-31; and following him Tilborg, *Jewish Leaders*, p. 103, also see the Pharisees as representatives of the entire Jewish community.

of the pericope focuses on handwashing and away from Mark's rehearsal of other implicitly condemned traditions.[46] Because of its connection with Pilate's famous attempt at personal exoneration (Matt 27:24), the addition further deflects attention away from the Jewish people and onto their leaders. Both Jewish and gentile rulers are shown to place their own interpretations of legal procedure over the various laws themselves. Yet Jesus appeals directly to the legal corpus: Matthew's substitution of θεός (15:4) for Μωυσῆς (Mk 7:10) demonstrates that Jesus upholds rather than opposes the validity of the Torah. Most significant, Matthew omits Mk 7:19b, "he declared all foods clean" (καθαρίζων πάντα τὰ βρώματα).[47] Thus the Jewish Law and the Jewish people are reaffirmed during Jesus' mission.

The account of the Canaanite woman in 15:21-28 prevents any possible conclusion that 15:1-20 demonstrates either the rejection of Levitical law or the extension of the mission to gentiles. Its fidelity to Jewish tradition and to the Jewish community, indicated most strongly by the repetition

---

[46]G. Barth, "Matthew's Understanding," p. 87; Tilborg, *Jewish Leaders*, p. 16; R. Banks, *Jesus and the Law in the Synoptic Tradition* (Cambridge: University Press, 1975), p. 137; Argyle, *The Gospel*, p. 118; Hill, *The Gospel*, p. 250.

[47]G. Barth,"Matthew's Understanding," p. 89, noting that while Mk 7:15 is directed against Levitical law, Matt 15:11 is concerned with words, cf. pp. 94-95, 158, 162-64; Rohde, *Rediscovering*, p. 58; Hummel, *Auseinandersetzung*, pp. 46-49; Fenton, *Saint Matthew*, pp. 251-52. Meier, *Vision of Matthew*, p. 103 and n. 95, claims that "nothing substantial is altered by the omission" of Mk 7:19b. Gundry, *Matthew*, pp. 305-6, suggests that Matthew's reading "into the mouth" (15:11) in place of Mark's "into him" is "*Matthew's way of advancing for emphasis Mark's editorial comment that Jesus was 'cleansing all foods'*" (emphasis his).

of the exclusivity logion, in turn provides a contextual standard against which the following pericope, the feeding of the four thousand (Matt 15:29-39), is best understood. Contextual analysis indicates that the restriction of the mission and its accompanying motif of fulfilling the promises made to Israel according to the Torah, two dominant themes in the first gospel, are recapitulated here.

Like 15:1-20, 15:29-39 addresses Jesus' interest in providing food for the hungry. And like 15:1-20, this pericope has also been interpreted in terms of the universal mission. That this second miraculous feeding concerns a gentile crowd -- even though the ethnic background of the people is never specified in this gospel known for making such specifications -- is a prevailing conclusion in New Testament analysis.[48] Matthew 14:13-21, the feeding of the five thousand, is often viewed as symbolizing the mission to the Jews; the doublet in 15:29-39 must, therefore, represent an outreach to the gentiles. The arguments used to support this theory are, however, not without problems. Against the claim that the setting of the pericope, the area around the Sea of Galilee (15:29), is home to a largely gentile population, two factors might be adduced. First is the demographic evidence that the area also supported a substantial Jewish population on the western shore. Second, while Gaulonitis on the east did have a heavy gentile population, Matthew has not indicated the specific location of the event -- perhaps because of the

[48]Giblin, "Theological Perspective," p. 657 n. 44; Argyle, *The Gospel*, p. 122; Cox, *The Gospel*, pp. 103, 108; Hill, *The Gospel*, pp. 255-56; Fenton, *Saint Matthew*, p. 257; Green, *The Gospel*, pp. 147-48; et al.; and the extreme view of F. Spitta, *Jesus und die Heidenmission* (cited and discussed in Jeremias, *Jesus' Promise*, p. 29 and n. 1), who asserts that Jesus not only preached to the gentiles but also inaugurated the gentile mission.

thematic interest in lonely regions rather than cities. The only other mention of the Sea of Galilee in the gospel, at 4:18 following the prophecy from Isaiah concerning the "Galilee of the gentiles," is less influential in interpreting the passage in chapter 15 than is its immediate juxtaposition to 15:24. Indeed, the evangelist undercuts the gentile connotations of the geography by omitting Mark's note in 7:31 that Jesus went "through the region of the Decapolis." Nor is the claim that Jews would not have used the expression "the God of Israel" (15:31) convincing; the same expression is used by the Jewish priest Zechariah in Lk 1:68. The ethnic connotations of the expression function instead to reinforce the restricted mission -- Jesus is sent only to the lost sheep of Israel, and it is Israel's deity who determines both miracles and mission. Lohmeyer suggests that the seven baskets collected by the disciples in 15:34 may symbolize the seven deacons of Acts 6.[49] Even if the question of the relationship between the first gospel and the Lucan material is dismissed, an argument based on the number seven is weak. Finally, Rawlinson's claim that the employ of σπυρίς for "baskets" (Mk 8:8; Matt 15:37) instead of κόφινος (Mk 6:43; Matt 14:20) indicates the supra-Palestinian or universal nature of the pericope is unhelpful.[50] The argument is overly subtle, and it does not refer directly to the Matthean text.

Analysis of Matt 13:53-16:12 supports the conclusions made in the study of 15:21-28. The exclusivity logion is strategically located in the account of the Canaanite woman, and it is programmatic for the first evangelist's redactional concerns. While Mark's presentation of the various stories in this section emphasizes the gentile mission and the separation

---

[49]"Das Abendmahl in der Urgemeinde," *JBL* 56 (1937): 236.

[50]Discussed in Hill, *The Gospel*, p. 256.

of Jesus from Judaism and Jews, Matthew modifies each account to reinforce both temporal and social axes. The privileged position of the Jews is retained during Jesus' ministry; "the Gospel belongs to them first of all."[51] But Matthew refrains from making the simple distinction between faithful gentiles and evil Jews. The several pericopes recounted in 13:53-16:12 depict divisions not between Jews and gentiles, but between the static and the mobile, the urban centers and the deserted peripheries, leaders who misuse their own authority and followers who place their trust in Jesus.

[51] G. Barth, "Matthew's Understanding," p. 101 n. 4.

VI

The Great Commission

Although gentile characters appear in the genealogy, the infancy narrative, and the miracle stories of chapters 8 and 15, they are not among Jesus' disciples. They do not receive instruction as do the Jewish crowds, they do not follow Jesus on his preaching tour, and they are specifically eliminated from the missionary focus of both Jesus and the twelve. Ruth and Rahab, the Magi, the centurion and the Canaanite woman all anticipate the extension of the mission to the gentiles, but the inauguration of this universal program only occurs in the last four verses of the gospel.

Matthew 28:16-20, the Great Commission, is no doubt a key to understanding the gospel.[1] In these four verses such

---

[1]G. Bornkamm, "The Risen Lord and the Earthly Jesus: Matthew 28:16-20," in J. M. Robinson (ed.), *The Future of Our Religious Past* (London: SCM, 1971), p. 205 (cf. Rohde, *Rediscovering*, pp. 47-54, 78); Carlston, "Interpreting the Gospel," p. 8; Garland, *Intention*, p. 46; J. D. Kingsbury, "The Composition and Christology of Matt 28:16-20," *JBL* 93 (1974): 573; E. Lohmeyer, "'Mir ist gegeben alle Gewalt!' Eine Exegese von Mt 28.16-20," in W. Schmauch (ed.), *In Memoriam Ernst Lohmeyer* (Stuttgart: Evangelisches Verlagswerk, 1951), pp. 42, 46, 49; B. Malina, "The Literary Structure and Form of Matt. xxviii.16-20," *NTS* 17 (1970): 87; O. Michel, "Der Abschluss des Matthäusevangeliums," *Evangelische Theologie* 10 (1950/51): 21; J. Schaberg, *The Father, the Son and the Holy Spirit: The Triadic Phrase in Matthew 28:19b* (Chico: Scholars, 1982), pp. 3, 60 n. 12; G. Schille, "Bemerkungen zur Formgeschichte des Evangeliums II. Das Evangelium des Matthäus als Katechismus," *NTS* 4 (1957/58): 113; Strecker, *Der Weg*, p. 213; Trilling, *Das*

major concerns as the extent of Jesus' authority, the validity of the Mosaic Law in the Matthean church, the role of the Jew in the new community of faith, and the relationship between Matthean universalism and the exclusivity logia of 10:5b-6 and 15:24 are recapitulated and developed. For Matthew, a new period in salvation history begins with the resurrection. The mission of the church is marked by extension -- the disciples now turn toward the gentiles -- and by continuity -- the mission to the Jews and the promises to them made in the scriptures remain in place.

Die Wende der Zeit [2]

While the importance of the Easter event for the first gospel is not questioned, the interpretation of the resurrection is. Taking its cue from Conzelmann's analysis of the third gospel, one school of thought concludes that Matthew depicts three successive eras of salvation history: they are most often categorized as of Israel, of Jesus, and of the church.[3] The

---

Wahre Israel, pp. 12-14, 21-28.

[2]The term is Meier's in "Salvation-History," p. 209. Meier combines the death and resurrection into one event signaling the turn of the age, but the two are best kept separate: the new age is foreshadowed by the crucifixion although it does not break in until the commission itself.

[3]H. Conzelmann, *The Theology of Saint Luke* (New York: Harper and Row, 1960), originally titled *Die Mitte der Zeit.* See Meier, *Antioch and Rome*, p. 60; Walker, *Heilsgeschichte*, pp. 114-118; Strecker, *Der Weg*, pp. 86-93; and "Concept of History," p. 73; Trilling, *Das Wahre Israel*, e.g., p. 215, on the guilt of the Jews; and perhaps Hummel, *Auseinandersetzung*, pp. 268-69 (but cf. p. 168; and the commentary by Meier, "Salvation-History," p. 203 and n. 3). See also Rohde, *Rediscovering*, pp.

restriction of the mission to ethnic Israel is viewed as applicable only to the second stage[4] during which, depending upon the emphasis of the commentator, either the soteriological privilege of the Jews is fulfilled (frequently with the implication that it is also ended) or their guilt is established. Others argue that Matthew "presupposes the homogeneity of the time of Jesus and that of the church, and he never considers Jesus' words as applicable only to his lifetime."[5]

Analysis of the narrative context of the Great Commission, its geographical setting, and the three principal themes it addresses -- the authority of Jesus, the initiatory rites of the church, and the extent of the mission -- leads to a compromise interpretation. With the resurrection a new era

---

131-32 n. 38; Carlston, "Interpreting the Gospel," p. 9. J. Kingsbury offers a two-part division: the time of Israel and the time of Jesus (which is combined with the time of the church) in "Structure of Matthew's Gospel," p. 471; cf. his "Form and Message of Matthew," *Int* 29 (1975): 16. Terence L. Donaldson, *Jesus on the Mountain: A Study in Matthean Theology* (Sheffield: JSOT, 1986), p. 211, discusses a two-stage salvation history in which material up to and including John the Baptist (cf. 11:11-13) concerns the promise and history from Jesus on concerns its fulfillment. Tagawa, "People and Community," p. 156, comments on the "heilsgeschichtliche interpretation."

[4]Meier, *Antioch and Rome*, p. 60; cf. Schweizer, "Observance of the Law," p. 227; and Strecker, "Concept of History," p. 73.

[5]Tagawa, "People and Community," p. 157. Gaston, "Messiah of Israel," p. 33, argues directly against Strecker and Walker by claiming Matthew does not contrast historical periods but "two different christologies, that of the Messiah of Israel and that of the Lord of the Gentiles. The Gospel contains both simultaneously." See also G. Barth, "Matthew's Understanding," pp. 100-101 n. 4.

begins, but here as well as throughout the rest of the gospel continuity rather than change is the dominant motif. The social axis is reinforced, and the temporal axis is modified simply to indicate that the gentiles now share in the privileges previously held only by the Jews.

The immediate narrative context of the Great Commission, the crucifixion, is accompanied by harbingers of the new era: the tearing of the temple veil (27:51; cf. Heb 6:19; 9:3; 10:20); the anticipation of the resurrection of the saints (27:52-53); and the miraculous natural signs (27:45, 51, 54). However, neither the apocalyptic portents nor the confessions of the centurion and those with him indicate the present arrival of the next stage in salvation history; the new era breaks in only at the resurrection, when "all authority" is given to Jesus. Consequently, the crucifixion is not the "moment when the Gentiles first come to full faith in the Son of God,"[6] and the soldiers do not symbolize "the whole Gentile community."[7] Indeed, the role of the other non-Jews in the passion narrative (e.g., 27:27-31) prevents this latter interpretation. Thus the temporal axis is buttressed rather than undercut by the future thrust of the events at the cross.

The tearing of the veil indicates that the Jewish cultus will cede its authority to the noncentralized, nonhierarchical church: it portends the ultimate demolition of spatial boundaries. It also anticipates the burning of the Temple in 70 C.E. and, along with the earthquake, symbolizes the punishment of the Jewish leadership for contributing to the death of Jesus. Yet these signs of upheaval have still more wide-ranging

---

[6]Meier, "Salvation-History," pp. 207-8; and *Law and History*, pp. 31-32; cf. Senior, *Passion Narrative*, p. 311; and "Death of Jesus," pp. 325-26.

[7]Meier, *Antioch and Rome*, pp. 61-62; cf. idem, *Vision of Matthew*, p. 35.

implications. By rending the fabric of the religious institution as well as of the earth itself, the evangelist highlights the ultimate worthlessness of earthly centers. One can never rest assured; one is never firmly grounded in anything except faith manifested in action. Thus the religious leadership is punished for failing to repair their hierarchical, marginalizing system of control, and the people in Jerusalem are shaken out of their complacency by the appearances of their dead.

But the Jerusalemites do receive a second chance at redemption during the new era. The resurrected saints reinforce the continuing mission to Israel both by the missionary aspect of their travels and by the word play the evangelist employs in the pericope. By connecting Jerusalem's inhabitants with the representatives of their righteous past, Matthew indicates that the people have the potential to repent. And by calling Jerusalem the "holy city" (τὴν ἁγίαν πόλιν, 27:53) populated by both the saints or "holy ones" (σώματα...ἁγίων) and the many to whom they appeared, the evangelist resanctifies the city through the repetition of the key term "holy."

This resanctification does not, however, signal the retention of Jewish priority. The resurrected saints remain primarily symbols of the past. Although they do not appear until after the resurrection (μετὰ τὴν ἔγερσιν αὐτοῦ, 27:53), the evangelist breaks narrative continuity to describe this portent in the context of the signs at the cross. The anachronistic mention also preserves the temporal priority of the Jews until "the dawn of the first day of the week" (28:1). Their special privileges are all in the context of pre-resurrection material. Thus the appearance of the saints structurally anticipates both the Easter event and the general resurrection at the eschaton, and it is part of the fulfillment of the promises made to the Jews: their holy dead receive the first opportunity for the benefits of the *Basileia*. Finally, the shifts in narrative time caused by the anachronistic mention of the miracle serve to unite Jewish present, past, and future. The saints thereby reinforce the continuing availablility of heavenly promises to the Jewish people. In the new era of the church, everyone starts over. Both Jews and gentiles will be on an equal, and for the purposes of the church, mobile footing. Even the dead cannot stay put in the new era.

The changes the first gospel makes to Mark's description of the cleansing (Matt 21:12-17; cf. Lk 19:45-46; Mk 11:17) continue to enhance Matthean themes. In Mark, Jesus quotes from Isa 56:7 in stating that his house "shall be called a house of prayer for all the nations" (πᾶσιν τοῖς ἔθνεσιν); he thus connects the Temple with the gentile mission. Matthew, not surprisingly, omits the last three words of the prophecy. "Jesus' parabolic action...excludes any notion of a historical gentile mission."[8] Concentrating on the social rather than temporal implications of the omission, Tilborg observes that "if καὶ τοῖς ἔθνεσιν ['and for the gentiles'] has been left out on

---

[8]Wilson, *Gentiles*, p. 13 n. 3. See also W. G. Kümmel, *Promise and Fulfillment*, pp. 118-19 n. 53. Wilson and Kümmel argue against, respectively, Manson, *Jesus and the Non-Jews*, pp. 12, 15, who suggests that Luke and Matthew both omit the phrase because the gentiles had already destroyed the Temple; and E. Lohmeyer, *Kultus und Evangelium* (Göttingen: Vandehoeck and Ruprecht, 1942), pp. 44-45 (cited in Kümmel), who interprets the "cleansing" of the Temple (particularly in Mark) as indicative of the preparation for the eschatological worship by the gentiles in their court. Jeremias, *Jesus' Promise*, p. 65 n. 4, offers a third view: the omission "may simply represent an abbreviated quotation"; and Stendahl, *School of St. Matthew*, p. 67, adds that because Matthew 21:16 also omits the attribute ἕνεκα τῶν ἐχθρῶν σου from Psalm 8:2, "one should therefore be cautious in repeating the common statement that Matthew's manner of abbreviating Mark's text reveals his views on missions to the heathen."

purpose, it should be seen within the framework of an anti-Israel theology, which refuses to see the religious center of Israel as the religious center of all mankind."[9] While the Jewish leadership is rejected, the gospel neither depicts a rejection of Israel per se nor an "anti-Israel" theology. The first evangelist is not "anti-Israel" but anti-positions of power, as a comparison of Matt 27:51-54 with Mk 15:39 shows.

According to Mark, the centurion's climactic confession, the first accurate christological perception that the Son of Man is one who suffers and dies, is motivated by the death of Jesus: "And when the centurion, who stood facing him, saw that he thus breathed his last, he said, 'Truly this man was the son of God'" (Mk 15:39). For Matthew the soldiers are moved by the apocalyptic signs, not by the passion of the man on the cross: when they "saw the earthquake and what took place, they were filled with awe" and made their confession (Matt 27:54). This shift directly connects the gentile soldiers and the resurrected Jewish saints and so prefigures a post-Easter church comprised of both ethnic groups.

Matthew's soldiers are also connected explicitly and implicitly to the other gentiles who appear in the text. The Magi, like the men at the cross, make their confession because of a natural portent. But to undercut any conclusion that all gentiles will receive the gospel, the evangelist also parallels the soldiers at the cross who acknowledge "Truly this was the Son of God" (27:54) with the soldiers who torture Jesus and mock him as "King of the Jews" (27:29). Here the royal title used as a sign of faith by the Magi in 2:2 indicates scorn. Gentile background -- perhaps emphasized by the evangelist's specifying that the soldiers who mocked Jesus were "of the governor" (τοῦ ἡγεμόνος, 27:27) -- signifies neither

---

[9]*Jewish Leaders*, p. 146.

righteousness nor infidelity. The actions of the governor's soldiers also ironically reveal the ultimate powerlessness of earthly positions of authority. The title "King of the Jews," while correct on the lips of the Magi, is ultimately tainted not only by Herod's desire for the same title but also by its appropriation by the soldiers and its appearance on the cross. The better title is one that deemphasizes positions of authority and stresses relationships, such as "Son" (27:54). It is this familial image, one that suggests service rather than domination, that frames the gospel (1:1; 28:19).

Like the guard at the cross, the soldier in 8:5-13 too is explicitly identified as a centurion, but in neither case is their ethnic ancestry mentioned. Thus Matthew avoids an emphasis on the gentile background of the confessors while at the same time reinforcing through analogy and juxtaposition the temporal distinctions between Jews and non-Jews. The temporal axis is again superseded by the evangelist's concern with social dichotomies. The centurions thereby fill dual roles: they are both gentiles and "men under authority."

The soldiers in 27:54 may also be associated with the Canaanite woman of 15:21-28 through more than gentile ancestry. The juxtaposition of the guards at the cross to the "many women there, looking on from a distance" (27:55) recalls this earlier supplicant. Both the Canaanite woman and the governor's soldiers had to overcome a distance from Jesus; for the former the problem was ethnic and geographical boundaries; for the latter it was the inexorable workings of the Roman political machine and Jesus' death. Thus the soldiers at the cross have an overdetermined symbolic value: they are reminders of the faithful centurion, the Canaanite woman, and the Magi as well as of the soldiers who torture Jesus and the Roman procurator who orders his execution. Further, their appearance confirms the observation that the gospel is a narrative whole relating past to present and future, infancy to passion, the age of Israel to the age of the church.

Continuity with the past, both narrative and world historical, is re-established by the geographical notice which begins the more immediate context of the Great Commission. In this final pericope, the disciples and Jesus come full circle, back to the Galilee where the original commission occurred and where Jesus predicted he would return (26:32; Mk 14:28).[10] And here again the exact location of the commission is not specified. The mountain, the meeting place between heaven and earth, is a displaced center without inherent authority, without peripheries; like the unidentified place of Moses' burial (Dt 34:6), the location of the Great Commission cannot become a new cultic site, a new Jerusalem. Nor are the disciples entrusted with positions of permanent authority. Although continuity among characters is preserved from the original mission discourse to the resurrection appearance, the notice of only "eleven disciples" in 28:16 confirms both that the new era is more than a recreation of the old and that elite positions -- in this case a leader in the church -- can lead to corruption.

Those who argue that the Great Commission does not inaugurate a new era minimize the shift in setting from Jerusalem to Galilee and the change in the number of disciples. For example, Kingsbury uses a christological model to construct the Matthean program of salvation history and concludes that the time of Jesus is continuous with the time

---

[10]Thompson, *Matthew's Advice*, p. 21, cf. pp. 25, 39; Schaberg, *The Father*, p. 38, following Kingsbury, "Composition and Christology," pp. 580-82. See the possible symbolic interpretations of the setting in Schaberg, *The Father*, pp. 1, 59, 89 and, esp. Donaldson, *Mountain*, pp. 170-90.

of the church rather than with the time of Israel.[11] Similarly, Lloyd Gaston states that "nothing has really changed in Matthew's Jesus by his exaltation" because "the authority he now has, he always had....Jesus for Matthew is the Lord who has authority over the Gentiles, an authority which he did not acquire at a certain point in time, but an authority which he has only because he was the rejected Messiah of Israel."[12] Yet the gospel does not present him as rejected by all Israel, nor can the membership in "Israel" of the Galilean women at the cross and the tomb be questioned. Indeed, the resurrected saints are part of "all Israel."

Gaston and others support their position with references to such passages as Matt 11:27, which states that Jesus and the Father share "all things" (Πάντα μοι παρεδόθη ὑπὸ τῷ πατρός μου, 7:29; 9:8; 21:23c; and 26:53).[13] This argument too

---

[11]See above, n. 3.

[12]"Messiah of Israel," pp. 27, 38; cf. C. E. Carlston, "Things That Defile," p. 84; S. Brown, "The Two-Fold Representation of the Mission in Matthew's Gospel," *StTh* 31 (1977): 24, in dialogue with H. Kasting, *Die Anfänge der urchristlichen Mission* (Munich: Kaiser-Verlag, 1969). K. Barth, "Exegetical Study," pp. 62-63, offers a variation of this conclusion: Jesus' authority remains constant, but during his earthly tenure it is "implicit and hidden." K. Stendahl, "The First Gospel and the Authority of Jesus," *Int* 16 (1962): 462, in a review of E. P. Blair's *Jesus in the Gospel of Matthew*, agrees with Blair (p. 140) that Matthew attributes divine authority to the earthly Jesus. However, he goes on to question "Is Matthew not aware of a difference between Jesus' earthly ministry and the post-resurrection situation?...only the glorified Lord can speak such language" (pp. 462-63).

[13]On 28:18-20 and 11:25-30 see M. J. Suggs, *Wisdom, Christology, and Law in Matthew's Gospel* (Cambridge: Harvard University, 1970), p. 120; Kingsbury, "Composition and Christology," pp. 576, 581; Hill, *The Gospel*, p. 206.

overlooks the significant terms modifying Jesus' post-resurrection position; now "*all* authority (πᾶσα ἐξουσία) in heaven and earth" is his. No longer simply Lord of the earth, Jesus has become the cosmocrator empowered to proclaim a universal mission.[14] The redactional summary of Matt 7:28-29 does not concern the extent of Jesus' authority so much as the comparison made between it and that of the scribes (cf. 21:23c).[15] The authority noted in 9:8 is limited to one albeit a highly significant action, and although 26:53 states that Jesus has "more than twelve legions of angels" at his disposal, he is not in direct control over them. Rather, he prefaces this notice with the question "Do you think that I cannot appeal to my Father...?" Finally, since the evangelist has already equated soldiers with subordination as well as with ruling (cf. 8:5-10), Jesus' military capabilities cannot be used to indicate complete authority. For the first gospel, it is unlikely that any appeal to military power would suggest permanent authority. The theory that nothing substantial has changed because of the resurrection is attenuated even more by the particle οὖν,

---

[14]Malina, "Literary Structure," p. 120; Thompson, "Historical Perspective," p. 259; J. D. Kingsbury, *Matthew: Structure, Christology, Kingdom* (Philadelphia: Fortress, 1975), p. 77; and "Composition and Christology," p. 576 (on "in heaven and earth") Blauw, *Missionary Nature*, pp. 78, 83; R. A. Guelich, "Not to Annul the Law Rather to Fulfill the Law and the Prophets: An Exegetical Study of Jesus and the Law in Matthew with Emphasis on 5:17-48" (Ph.D. diss., University of Hamburg, 1967), p. 270. Meier, "Salvation-History," p. 212, objects to the "complete paralleling" of 11:27 with 28:19 because the former concerns the "revelation of apocalyptic secrets by the Son" and the latter depicts "the royal power of the enthroned Kyrios"; cf. his *Vision of Matthew*, pp. 81-82; and *Law and History*, p. 37.

[15]See Tilborg, *Jewish Leaders*, pp. 142-43.

"therefore," which opens 28:19. It is "on the basis of his universal authority" that Jesus extends both the duties and the missionary focus of the disciples.[16]

Although not definitive, evidence from outside the first gospel also strongly suggests that Jesus' christological position has changed. Both Pauline and Marcan emphasis on the passion indicates it was a possible commonplace in the early church to see a shift in power occasioned by the resurrection.[17] Also supportive are several studies of the *Gattung* of Matt 28:16-20. If the pericope could be classified as a "royal commission" like that in II Chron 36:23,[18] or as an enthronement ritual,[19] or as a "throne-theophany commission" like Daniel 7,[20] then one could argue that Jesus has received a

---

[16]Donaldson, *Mountain*, p. 210; cf. Schaberg, *The Father*, p. 90; Plummer, *Exegetical Commentary*, p. 429; Hooker, "Uncomfortable Words," p. 363. On Matthew's editorial use of the particle see Kingsbury, "Composition and Christology," pp. 576-77.

[17]C. H. Dodd, "Matthew and Paul," p. 294, on Paul; Hooker, "Uncomfortable Words," p. 364, on Mark.

[18]Green, *The Gospel*, p. 14; Malina, "Literary Structure," pp. 86-103; and esp. B. J. Hubbard, *The Matthean Redaction of a Primitive Apostolic Commissioning: An Exegesis of Matthew 28:16-20* (Missoula, MT: Scholars, 1974). Against this theory see Gundry, *Matthew*, p. 597.

[19]So Michel, "Der Abschluss," pp. 22-23; and following him, Jeremias, *Jesus' Promise*, p. 39. Against this theory see Trilling, *Das Wahre Israel*, pp. 32-33, 46; De Ridder, *Dispersion*, pp. 172-75 (offering the alternative that 28:16-20 is the "throne-speech" of the new ruler and not the proclamation of enthronement); Malina, "Literary Structure," p. 89.

[20]Schaberg, *The Father*, pp. 189, 229, 238, etc., but cf. Luise Abramowski, "Die Entstehung der dreigliedrigen Taufformel -- ein Versuch," *ZTK* 81 (1984): esp. 427-28 (responding directly

new authority. However, the Matthean Great Commission fails to conform perfectly to any established literary pattern, and the differences ultimately outweigh the similarities. The evangelist may even have deliberately avoided substantial connections to the enthronement ritual or royal commission in order to decrease a possible emphasis on centers or elite positions; that the pericope is heavily redacted if not an original composition of the evangelist is not in doubt.[21] Malina claims that because the gospel was intended to be read aloud -- which itself is speculation -- the determination of the literary form would be "a necessary prerequisite for the general and specific interpretation and determination of the parts of the text."[22] However, there is no necessary connection between oral presentation and the determination of literary form. The question of form itself may, finally, be inapplicable. Even if some implied connection to an established *Gattung* could be recovered, it is not clear how to determine if the evangelist is being evocative of an earlier genre or subversive of it. Whatever conclusion is drawn must therefore be supported first by what is said and not by the form in which it is placed. While the form of the Great Commission, with its

---

to Schaberg); and the discussion in Donaldson, *Mountain*, pp. 176-77. Meier, "Salvation-History," pp. 210-11 and n. 15 concludes that the passage is "so *sui generis* that a form-critical category (dealing with the *typical*) can hardly be assigned to it"; cf. his "Two Disputed Questions in Matthew 28:16-20," *JBL* 96 (1977): 424.

[21]Meier, "Salvation-History," pp. 210-11; and "Two Disputed Questions," p. 410; G. Barth, "Matthew's Understanding," p. 131; Kilpatrick, *Origins of the Gospel*, pp. 48-49; Kingsbury, "Composition and Christology," pp. 573-77; Michel, "Der Abschluss," pp. 19-21; Schaberg, *The Father*, pp. 43-44 and notes.

[22]"Literary Structure," p. 87 n. 4.

possible implications of enthronement, may highlight Jesus' power, the words describing the scene as well as Jesus' own mandate to his disciples clearly indicate that he has a new type of power. And, since his status is both continuous with his earthly existence and extended beyond it, so too the mission of the church will be both in continuity with and extended beyond the place of Israel.

The Injunctions

Accompanying the change in Jesus' status are several modifications of the original mission charge. In Matt 10:1 the twelve are empowered to perform exorcisms and healings; in 10:8 the command to perform resurrections is given. But although they are exhorted in 10:7 to "preach, proclaiming the Kingdom of Heaven is at hand," the disciples are not, in contrast to Mk 6:30, authorized to teach. During Jesus' mission to the Jews, this activity is reserved for him alone (cf. 4:23; 11:1).[23] Only in the new era signaled by the Great Commission is the responsibility of the disciples, like the authority of their master, extended.

The content of the new teaching (διδάσκοντες αὐτούς), "to observe all that I have commanded you" (τηρεῖν πάντα ὅσα ἐνετειλάμην ὑμῖν, 28:20a), as well as the new initiation rite of baptism "in the name of the Father, Son, and Holy Spirit" with which it is associated have implications for Matthew's attitude toward the Law and the focus of the post-resurrectional missionary program. If this teaching signifies

---

[23]Schaberg, *The Father*, p. 2. S. Brown, "Mission to Israel," p. 76 n. 12, claims that preaching and teaching are "closely related." Among those who equate the two are Kingsbury, *Structure*, pp. 20-21; and Strecker, *Der Weg*, pp. 126-28.

an abrogation of Jewish Law and if baptism is offered as a *replacement* for circumcision, then the conclusion that the new mission is directed only to gentiles receives substantial support.

There are several factors which might suggest that the injunction to baptize "implicitly rescinds the command of circumcision and so rescinds that fidelity to the Mosaic Law which marked [the] public ministry."[24] The appearance of "implicitly" in Meier's statement is telling. It is methodologically questionable to make conclusions about an author's sources based on the *absence* of a reference, particularly in cases where the absence does not create a gap in the narrative. Garland proposes that the mandate to "teach all that I have commanded you" should be distinguished from the teachings of Moses, the scribes, and the Pharisees.[25] But this interpretation is forced to dismiss or overlook such passages as 23:2-3 and 5:17-18. With the exception of their apocalyptic emphases, Jesus' teachings are generally in accord with those of the Pharisees and Moses. The common counterargument -- that 23:2-3 comes from a time during which Matthew's community was still connected with the synagogue and that therefore it does not represent the evangelist's own theological position[26] -- is also not helpful. Matthew 23:2-3 appears in the opening position of the "woes" against the scribes and Pharisees: writers rarely give prominence to an idea with which they do not agree; nor do

[24]Meier,"Salvation-History," pp. 205-7; *Law and History*, pp. 28-30; *Vision of Matthew*, pp. 13, 212-13; cf. Baum, *Is the New Testament Anti-Semitic*, p. 64; Carlston, "Things That Defile," p. 84; Hare, *Jewish Persecution*, p. 130 n. 1.

[25]*Intention*, p. 46, cf. p. 131 n. 25.

[26]Meier, *Vision of Matthew*, pp. 160, 163; cf. G. Barth, "Matthew's Understanding," p. 86.

they emphasize such points with similar statements elsewhere in the gospel. Tilborg proposes that πάντα ("all") in 23:3 might be taken in a limited sense,[27] but there is no reason to move away from the plain meaning of the word. Again, the emphatic placement of this term at the beginning of the sentence suggests not a limiting but a heightening of the meaning. And, at no point does Matthew, unlike Mark 7:19, explicitly rescind the Law.

Based on 5:17-18, the conclusion that Jesus has "fulfilled" (πληρόω) and so made obsolete the Law through his death and resurrection[28] is also an overreading of the text. G. Barth suggests that "to fulfill" (πληρῶσαι) "signifies a more comprehensive event: The teaching of Jesus is concerned with the establishment of the law....Hence it is unthinkable for Matthew that the law should be abolished by the death of Jesus."[29] Supporting this christological observation is the evangelist's style of repeating details. Not only have heaven and earth not passed away, their presence is reinforced by the emphasized Galilean and mountaintop settings of the resurrection scene. Indeed, the explicit mention of "heaven and earth" in 28:18 indicates not their passing away but their perduring "to the close of the age" (28:20).

Finally, Carlston observes that "nothing in the Great Commission says anything about keeping the Law."[30] This is

---

[27]*Jewish Leaders*, pp. 134-37; cf. Allen, *Critical and Exegetical Commentary*, p. 244; E. Haenchen, "Matthäus 23," *ZTK* 48 (1951): 38-40; but see Garland, *Intention*, p. 48.

[28]Cf. Meier, *Law and History*, p. 123; Baum, *Is the New Testament Anti-Semitic*, p. 90; Douglas J. Moo, "Jesus and the Authority of the Mosaic Law," *JSNT* 20 (1984): 23-28.

[29]"Matthew's Understanding," p. 147; cf. Hill, *The Gospel*, pp. 117-18 (citing IV Ezra 9:36f; *Ex Rabbah* 1:6).

[30]"Things That Defile," p. 84. Such arguments from silence are

true, but nothing in Matt 28:16-20 or elsewhere in the gospel speaks of the Law's abrogation either. Further, according to the Great Commission a true disciple observes everything that Jesus commanded, and these injunctions include keeping the commandments of the Torah (5:19), having a righteousness that exceeds that of the Pharisees (5:20), observing what these leaders say (23:3), being perfect (5:48). These verses from the Sermon on the Mount and elsewhere in the text cannot be excised or relegated to the closet of legal dress out of fashion in the increasingly gentile church. They are intrinsic parts of the gospel, supported rather than contradicted by other passages within the text (e.g., Matt 15:1-20; cf. Mk 7). Since there is no specific evidence that the first gospel does not retain the Law, and since various statements within the text suggest not a tacit retention but an emphasis on the commandments,[31] there is no reason to see the command to baptize as a replacement for circumcision.

---

also attenuated by appeals to later sources, such as the Eusebian reading which omits the reference to the Father and Son as well as the command to baptize. See Lohmeyer, "Mir ist gegeben," p. 29; F. C. Conybeare, "Matthäus 28,9: The Eusebian Form of the Text," *ZNW* 2 (1901): 275-77; and the discussions in Allen, *Critical and Exegetical Commentary*, pp. 307-8; and F. W. Beare, "The Sayings of the Risen Jesus in the Gospel Tradition: An Inquiry into Their Origin and Significance," in W. F. Farmer et al., *Christian History and Interpretation* (Cambridge: University Press, 1967), p. 165 (accepting the longer reading); Green, *The Gospel*, pp. 230-31 (accepting the shorter).

[31]On the plausible although unnecessary conclusion that the emphasis was occasioned by a confrontation with antinomians, see Bornkamm, "End-Expectation," pp. 24-25; Hummel, *Auseinandersetzung*; following him, G. Barth, "Matthew's Understanding," p. 71; and following Barth, Moo, "Jesus and the Mosaic Law," p. 28.

Nevertheless, several explanations for the lack of reference to this Jewish ritual have been proposed. S. Brown suggests that Matthew's concern was not whether to circumcise gentiles but whether to preach the gospel to them in the face of local Jewish opposition.[32] For Trilling, since the primary division in the gospel is not between Jew and gentile but between Israel and the church comprised of a *corpus mixtum*, no specific prerequisites for the mission to the gentiles need be noted.[33] Yet it is likely that the issue of circumcision would have arisen in any church which had both Jewish and gentile members. G. Barth proposes that Matthew's sources did not mention circumcision,[34] but here the issue is merely displaced onto the question of sources. Munck concludes that the Jewish Christians did not regard circumcision as the "*sine qua non* of salvation."[35] But neither the silence of any hypothetical sources nor Matthew's own lack of reference to circumcision indicates that the ritual was unimportant to the evangelist or the members of the community. A comparable situation from the rabbinic sources is instructive. Commenting on Hannukah, phylacteries, tzitzit, and mezuzoth, G. Alon states: "The absence of tractates in the Mishna dealing with specific laws, and even the paucity of laws relative to a given subject in the Tannaitic tradition as a whole, has no bearing on these laws *themselves* or their importance in the time of the compilers of the traditions, or on the attitude of these scholars towards them."[36] As Schaberg notes, the silence

---

[32]"Matthean Community," pp. 218, 221.

[33]*Das Wahre Israel*, p. 214.

[34]"Matthew's Understanding," p. 163.

[35]*Paul and the Salvation of Mankind*, pp. 107, 228, 244; idem, "Jewish Christianity in Post-Apostolic Times," *NTS* 6 (1960): 103-16.

[36]*Jews, Judaism, and the Classical World* (Jerusalem: Magnes

might indicate *either* that the issue was already settled with the injunction to circumcise revoked, *or* that it was "composed to ground the authority of those who believed circumcision was not necessary," *or* that its validity was taken for granted.[37]

This last option is most consistent with both the actual words of the text and the motifs of continuity and extension. Because the first mission is only to the Jews, the circumcision of all potential male disciples is presupposed. The focus of the Easter mission requires a new initiation rite, which is baptism. For the Jews in the church, entry into the *Basileia* entails the practice of Judaism plus fidelity to the words of Jesus; therefore they are both circumcised and baptized. Because the mission to them has not ended, circumcision remains practiced.[38] And because in the age of the church Jews and gentiles are equal participants in salvation history, it is possible that both engaged in the same ritual practices. Gentile converts, who might have been expected to follow the dietary regulations, might also have accepted the practice of circumcision.

This conclusion is not inconsistent with Matthew's emphasis on the continuing validity of the Torah, and it may help to explain how the gospel distinguishes ethnic-gentile members of the church from those gentiles who, like the tax collectors, are to be shunned by the community (cf. 6:7; 18:17). Just as the era of the church is an extention of rather than a break with the era of Israel and Jesus, so the laws that

---

Press, 1977), p. 10.

[37] *The Father*, pp. 329, 345 nn. 42, 43.

[38] A similar argument based on Pauline material appears in Gager, *Origins of Anti-Semitism*, pp. 193-269. See also the comparison between Paul and Matthew in Meier, *Antioch and Rome*, pp. 62-63.

prevailed during the earlier time, unless explicitly changed, also mark the latter. Thus the evangelist had no need to mention circumcision. Nor would a reference be consistent with the gospel's themes. Given Matthew's interest in upending hierarchies, the absence may be explained in terms of the ritual's focus. Circumcision establishes a distinction with an accompanying potential for abuse of power between men and women within the church. Just as the gospel omits any mention of this male ritual, so too it does not comment on, for example, menstrual legislation. Both might have been preached by the Matthean disciples, but a mention of either would have undermined the evangelist's thematic emphases. Second, circumcision is for Jews a ritual done by a father or his proxy to a child and again therefore can be construed as a form of domination. Matthew is concerned with what people do rather than in what is done to them as infants.

It is also plausible that the question of circumcision was not a central issue to the members of the Matthean church. This conclusion is not based on the claim that diaspora Jews "offered the Gentile world a debased form of their ancestral religion, paganized to make it attractive to non-Jews."[39] It is methodologically and historically inappropriate to categorize all of Palestinian Judaism as strictly legalistic while the diaspora communities are viewed as emphasizing proselyte baptism rather than circumcision and so offering potential converts a watered-down version of the tradition. To avoid the reductive and often implicitly anti-Jewish division of

---

[39]And so denied by A. T. Kraabel, "The Roman Diaspora: Six Questionable Assumptions," in G. Vermes and J. Neusner (eds.), *Essays in Honour of Yigael Yadin* (=*JJS* 33 [1982]), p. 449. But cf. G. La Piana, "Foreign Groups in Rome during the First Centuries of the Empire," *HTR* 20 (1927): 392; S. Brown, "Matthean Community," p. 201.

accommodationist diaspora vs. fanatically conservative Palestine, commentators must also avoid the equally monolithic view that all first-century Jews saw circumcision as the most important aspect of their religion or insisted upon the circumcision of gentile sympathizers. A similar problem with reductionism arises in many scholarly classifications of early Christians according to ethnic categories. For example, while some Jewish followers of Jesus may have regarded the Torah as no longer binding, their gentile counterparts may have accepted circumcision along with the rest of the Law. This latter point is particularly significant given the hypothesis that Matthew addresses a community in Antioch, where evidence of gentiles practicing Jewish rituals repeatedly appears from Paul's letters to the epistles of Ignatius to the sermons of John Chrysostom.

Matthew emphasizes the retention of the Law and continuity between the age of Israel and the age of the church. In this second period of salvation history, the gospel will be preached to the gentiles as well as the Jews, and the rules for admission into the *Basileia* are extended rather than repealed. Thus it is likely that male gentile members of the church engaged in the rite of circumcision. However, given that the ritual itself is not mentioned in the text, and that the silence may well indicate that circumcision as well as the multitude of other practices not explicitly noted by the evangelist were presupposed, this "problem" may have no bearing on the reconstruction of the church's ethnic make-up, mission focus, or attitude toward the Law.

The Translation

Analyses of the Great Commission focus not only on the periodization of history and the retention of Jewish Law; a major crux concerns which peoples will be included in the new church. To solve this problem, a more comprehensive approach than that employed in the earlier analyses is required. While all translation is also an act of interpretation, for the most part the English equivalents of Matthew's Greek are not under debate. Critics remain concerned with questions of punctuation, emphasis, and tone but not with the words themselves. There is, however, a most intriguing problem of translation in Matt 28:19a which directly impinges upon the entire missionary program. On the one hand, D. R. A. Hare and D. J. Harrington best represent those who conclude both that πάντα τὰ ἔθνη should be translated "all the gentiles" and that consequently the phrase cannot include Israel.[40] "In the future converts from Israel will not be refused, but their conversion will not be sought. Henceforth the mission is not to Israel and the Gentiles but only to the Gentiles."[41] The reverse position, that the phrase reads "all the nations" or "all the peoples" and that the Jews remain included in the Christian mission, is most forcefully presented by J. P. Meier in his response to Hare and Harrington.[42]

---

[40]"Make Disciples," pp. 359-69, following, among others, Clark, "Gentile Bias," pp. 165-72; and Walker, *Heilsgeschichte*, pp. 11-13. See also Hare's "The Rejection of the Jews in the Synoptic Gospels and Acts," in A. Davies (ed.), *Anti-Semitism and the Foundations of Christianity* (New York: Paulist, 1979), pp. 39-40; J. H. Bavinck, *An Introduction to the Science of Missions* (Philadelphia: Presbyterian and Reformed, 1960), p. 118 (but cf. p. 70); Green, *The Gospel*, pp. 147, 199; Gager, *Origins of Anti-Semitism*, p. 147; Gaston, "Messiah of Israel," pp. 37-38.

[41]Hare, *Jewish Persecution*, p. 148.

[42]"Nations or Gentiles," pp. 94-102; cf., among others, the RSV; NEB, Plummer, *Exegetical Commentary*, pp. xxv, 429-30; K. L. Schmidt, "ETHNOS," *TDNT*, vol. 2, p. 359; F. V. Filson, *A*

This debate is complicated by methodological questions. Most discussions of both ἔθνος and πάντα τὰ ἔθνη are lexically oriented.[43] The first gospel along with the Septuagint, intertestamental and pseudepigraphical writings, and other Christian texts have been analyzed for connotations they accord to the terms. Because these various texts reveal the range of possible definitions, the philological explorations are helpful. However, especially for frequently occurring terms located in a variety of contexts, word studies must be supplemented with other approaches. In cases where multiple translations are viable, the context of the term is the primary determinant of its meaning. Therefore, while non-Matthean uses of ἔθνος and πάντα τὰ ἔθνη can be mustered to suppport particular translations of Matt 28:19a, that gospel itself -- and more specifically the immediate context of the term -- must remain the deciding factor in translation and

---

Commentary on the Gospel According to St. Matthew (New York: Harper and Bro., 1960), p. 267; Franzmann, *Discipleship*, pp. 220-22; J. P. Brown, "Form of 'Q'," p. 30; Albright and Mann, *Matthew*, pp. 361, 362; Trilling, *Das Wahre Israel*, pp. 12-14, 26-28; Hahn, *Mission*, p. 125; Thompson, *Matthew's Advice*, p. 21, cf. pp. 38-39; De Ridder, *Dispersion*, pp. 183-84, cf. p. 188; Hill, *The Gospel*, pp. 43, 72, 361; Hubbard, *Matthean Redaction*, pp. 84-87; Schweizer, *Good News*, p. 359; Garland, *Intention*, p. 208 (but in agreement with Hare and Harrington on pp. 213-14); Strecker, *Der Weg*, p. 117, and following him Rohde, *Rediscovering*, p. 83 (but cf. p. 132 n. 38); Schaberg, *The Father*, p. 118 (following Meier); K. Barth, "Exegetical Study," p. 64.

[43]Trilling, *Das Wahre Israel*, pp. 26-28, followed by Hubbard, *Matthean Redaction*, pp. 84-87, uses the same method but looks specifically at the combination of ἔθνος with πᾶς. Gaston, "Messiah of Israel," p. 35, connects Matt 28:19f. with the Didache: "The Teaching of the Lord through the Twelve Apostles to the Gentiles."

interpretation.

Moreover, separate uses of the same term within one text or by the same writer not only can sustain but indeed can require different translations.[44] For example, the Pauline term δικᾶιος has been rendered "upright," "righteous," "fair," "honest," and "innocent" depending upon the context. John Knox even applies this observation to Paul's uses of τὰ ἔθνη and πάντα τὰ ἔθνη. The ability of a word to assume multiple translations also should not be manipulated to support the preconceived agenda of the translator, as the famous examples of Phoebe the deacon in Rom 16:1 and Junia the apostle in Rom 16:7 indicate. This is a particular problem for investigations of ethnic and religious groups. As J. A. Goldstein notes, the presupposition of a sharp distinction beween Jews and Hellenism might lead to the conclusion that "the word 'Gentile', so frequently opposed to 'Jew', really means 'Greek'."[45] The context again, and not the pretext of a translation, must be the deciding factor. Finally, while a single term is most often translated by a single corresponding element, both the original expression and the

---

[44]John Knox, "Romans 15:14-33 and Paul's Conception of His Apostolic Mission," *JBL* 83 (1964): 1-11; cf. Munck, *Paul and the Salvation of Mankind*, p. 107 n. 1. A similar discussion based on the contextual interpretation of ἔθνος in Matt 21:43 appears in Cope, *Matthew, A Scribe*, p. 86.

[45]"Jewish Acceptance and Rejection of Hellenism," in Sanders et al. (eds.), *Self-Definition*, vol. 2, p. 71; cf. M. Goldstein, *Jesus in the Jewish Tradition*, p. 51, on translating גוים (*goyim*) as "gentile" or "Christian" in the rabbinic literature; and J. N. Sevenster, *The Roots of Pagan Anti-Semitism in the Ancient World* (Leiden: Brill, 1975), pp. 38-39: "Though Greeks and Latins refer to the Jews as an ἔθνος or a *natio* or a *gens*, i.e., a folk or tribe, there is no genuinely racial or racist connotation....The large mass of converts among other peoples prevented the racial idea from developing."

translation may sustain more than one appropriate interpretation. Otherwise, such common literary devices as paranomasia, metaphor, and simile could not exist.

If these various caveats are considered, then a consistently appropriate translation of one phrase throughout the majority of a document offers a strong case for applying the same translation to any passage left in question. This assumption determines Hare and Harrington's last approach: "When we come to Mt 28:19, the least we can say is that when Matthew uses *ethnos/ethne* he usually means 'Gentiles.' But we believe that we must go farther and say that he always means Gentiles."[46] The difficulty of supporting this claim is clearly indicated in Meier's response: of the fourteen uses of the terms in the first gospel, he firmly agrees with Hare and Harrington's translation in only seven cases (4:15; 6:32; 10:5, 18; 12:18, 21; 20:19). For the remaining half, including the Great Commission, he argues for the inclusive reading of "nations" or "peoples" (20:25; 21:43; 24:7, 9, 14; 25:32; 28:19).

The impasse created by this approach suggests that any solution to the problems of translation and interpretation requires at least a different method and probably an appeal to different supporting verses. Literary criticism can break the stalemate without losing the valuable points scored by practitioners of the lexical approach. On the question of translation, analysis of the integrity and structure of the gospel supports Hare and Harrington. But on the correct interpretation of Matt 28:19a, Meier's inclusive position is the more consistent with stylistic devices employed and themes established throughout the gospel.

Repetition and extension of thematic terms provide major clues to the best translation of πάντα τὰ ἔθνη in 28:19.

---

[46]"Make Disciples," p. 363.

That the gospel reveals a redactional tendency to repeat favorite themes is evident. For example, the phrase "I desire mercy and not sacrifice" (Hos 6:6) is inserted into both the discussion of table fellowship with tax collectors and sinners (9:13) and the controversy story of plucking grain on the Sabbath (12:7). Such duplication cannot be explained by a slavish dependence upon earlier material: in neither case does the verse appear in the Marcan (or Lucan) parallels upon which Matthew is dependent. Even those who claim Matthean priority would argue that the evangelist did not simply copy received material. The repetition is also consistent with the Matthean theme of grounding Jesus' teachings in the Jewish scriptures. Such repetitions as 3:2//4:17; 3:1//3:13; 4:23//9:35, 10:1; 10:6//15:24; and 19:30//20:16 reinforce particular motifs and therefore may be considered conscious literary designs. Nor need such statements have the same function in each context, as Stendahl observes regarding Matt 16:19 and 18:18.[47]

Since the entry of gentiles into the church is predicted in 24:14, the reappearance of this motif, like the mention of Galilee in 28:16 following the prediction in 26:32, would not be unexpected in the text's conclusion. A structural parallel reinforces this connection between the Great Commission and the explicitly gentile focus. While analogies between the infancy narratives and 28:16-20 are frequent subjects of critical discussion,[48] the most obvious parallel to the Great Commission -- the mission discourse in chapter 10 -- remains an unexplored territory. Rather than *compared* with the mission inaugurated at the conclusion of the gospel, the second discourse (as well as 15:24) is most often *contrasted* with it:

---

[47]*School of Saint Matthew*, p. 28; cf. E. von Dobschütz, "Matthäus als Rabbi," pp. 338-48.

[48]De Ridder, *Dispersion*, p. 184; Lohr, "Oral Techniques," p. 410, on 1:23 and 28:20; Malina, "Literary Structure," pp. 100-101.

Matt 28:16-20 and Matt 10:5b-6 are classified as contradictory and irreconcilable.[49]

In terms of subject matter as well as setting and characters the Great Commission is a recapitulation and extension of the original program of chapter 10. During Jesus' earthly career, the mission is restricted to Israel; in the new era, the mission is specifically extended to the gentiles. And this specific emphasis should be reflected in the translation. Just as 10:5b, Εἰς ὁδὸν ἐθνῶν μὴ ἀπέλθητε, is best translated "do not go into the road of the gentiles" or, more smoothly, "go nowhere among the gentiles," so 28:19a should be rendered "Therefore go, make disciples of all the gentiles."

Various grammatical observations support this conclusion. Hare and Harrington observe that ἔθνος cannot be used in the singular to describe gentile individuals; the standard form for this expression would be Ἕλλην, Ἑλληνίς (Acts 16:1; Rom 1:16; Gal 2:3; Mk 7:26). They further note that the term for disciple making, μαθητεύω, is most often used to refer to individuals rather than national groups. Third, like the command to make disciples, the injunction to baptize (βαπτίζω) requires an application to individuals.[50] Finally, the reference to individuals is reinforced by the grammatical shift present in both 28:19-20 and 25:32. The typical neuter formulation πάντα τὰ ἔθνη, which could connote countries, is redefined by

---

[49]E.g., Jeremias, *Jesus' Promise*, p. 27; Hill, *The Gospel*, pp. 70, 185; Cope, *Matthew, A Scribe*, p. 11; Manson, *Sayings of Jesus*, p. 180; Tagawa, "People and Community," pp. 152-53; S. Brown, "Two-Fold Representation," pp. 30-31.

[50]"Make Disciples," p. 368; Hare, *Jewish Persecution*, p. 148 n. 3; cf. Green, *The Gospel*, p. 231; Bavinck, *Science of Missions*, pp. 118-19; Malina, "Literary Structure," p. 102; and K. Barth, "Exegetical Study," p. 64, on the Nazis' ideological uses of the nationalistic interpretation.

the masculine plural object "them" (αὐτούς). [51] The (gendered) individual is the qualification of the neuter states. Because no ethnic or national entity is privileged in the age of the church, and because the mission is extended beyond the borders of Palestine to the whole world, it is more appropriate to translate 28:19 not as "all the nations" but as "all the gentiles" and so to reflect the gospel's cross-national interests.

---

[51] J. R. Michaels, "Apostolic Hardships and Righteous Gentiles: A Study of Matthew 25:31-46," *JBL* 84 (1965): 28 n. 6.

VII

The Rejection of the Jews

The Interpretation of the Great Commission

According to Hare and Harrington the translation of πάντα τὰ ἔθνη in Matt 28:19a as "all the gentiles" confirms the restriction of the Easter mission to non-Jews: "Matthew's universalism seems to be a universalism without Israel and over against Israel (ohne Israel, gegen Israel)"; thus "Israel's rejection of God and his Messiah has resulted in God's rejection of Israel."[1] Yet Meier concludes that the Jews are one of "all the nations" to be evangelized by the disciples and so by the Matthean church.[2]

Hare, Harrington, and Meier arrive at contrary conclusions while operating with the same presuppositions and approaches. All three describe the Matthean economy of salvation in the Pauline terminology of "to the Jew first and also to the Greek"; all reach this evaluation through contrasting rather than comparing Matt 28:19 with 10:5b-6.[3] Shared too is the conclusion that the Jews have lost their privileged position in salvation history. As Meier points out,

---

[1]"Make Disciples," pp. 363 n. 7 (citing Lange), 367; cf. Hare, *Jewish Persecution*, pp. 152, 155; and "Rejection of the Jews," pp. 38-39; Clark, "Gentile Bias," pp. 166-68.

[2]*Vision of Matthew*, p. 17, cf. pp. 55 n. 19, 210 n. 260; "Nations or Gentiles," p. 102; *Antioch and Rome*, p. 62 n. 137; cf. Trilling, *Das Wahre Israel*, p. 34; Fenton, *Saint Matthew*, p. 15; Hooker, "Uncomfortable Words," p. 363; B. F. Meyer, "Jesus and the Remnant of Israel," *JBL* 84 (1965): 126.

[3]Meier, *Law and History*, p. 27; Hare and Harrington, "Make Disciples," p. 366.

"It may be significant that Matthew himself in 28:15 no longer speaks of Israel but only of 'the Jews.' After the death-resurrection, there is no chosen people Israel, only Jews, one people or nation (cf. 24:7) among many."[4] The debate is consequently based on the question of degree: either the Jews have lost their privileged position in salvation history or they have lost everything; in either case, they have lost.

Compounding the problem of interpretation are the various subtleties of Hare and Harrington's thesis. Hare asserts that individual Jews may be evangelized and that they comprise the nucleus of the church; what is rejected is Israel as a nation or "corporate entity."[5] Yet the corporate community is comprised of individuals, and the commands to "make disciples" and "baptize" have individuals rather than national entities as their referents. To use the grammatical argument that Matt 28:19a should be translated "all the gentiles" because the verbs require a focus on individuals and then to speak of the rejection of the corporate community of Israel creates an inconsistency in the gospel that is not otherwise intratextually supported. Nor is it clear within the context of the Matthean missionary endeavor what the practical difference is between the corporate community and individual Jews who together comprise the Jewish people. Moreover,

---

[4]Meier, *Antioch and Rome*, p. 62 n. 137; cf. *Vision of Matthew*, pp. 17, 55 n. 19, 165-66, and esp. 210 n. 260; "Nations or Gentiles," p. 102; and the more forceful statement on Matt 28:15 by Dahl, "Passion Narrative," p. 51. Hare's comments appear in *Jewish Persecution*, pp. 15, 153-54. Also instructive are Hill, *The Gospel*, p. 43, cf. p. 72 in direct dialogue with Hare; Tilborg, *Jewish Leaders*, pp. 71-72; Senior, "Death of Jesus," p. 325; Garland, *Intention*, pp. 208, 214 n. 14; and Strecker, "Concept of History," p. 73.

[5]*Jewish Persecution*, pp. 153-54; Hare and Harrington, "Make Disciples," p. 363 and n. 7, following Lange.

from an ideological perspective, the first evangelist has eliminated all "corporate communities" except for the universal *Basileia*. In the new era, all patriarchal systems, including the notion of corporate communities, are no longer meaningful. Since Hare states that individual Jews may present themselves for baptism, the church appears to have no restrictions on entry; the segregation model does not apply. Finally, Hare's appeals to the prophetic tradition of the rejection of faithless Israel (Jer 6:19, 30; Isa 5:24f.; Amos 9:7-8a; Hos 13:4-16) are countered by other passages that indicate the continued priority of the people. Since Matthew does not support Israel's rejection/destruction by reference to these passages, Hare's appeal is further attenuated.[6] If Matthew's church still follows the Jewish Law, uses the Jewish Bible as its anchor, has a nucleus of ethnic Jews, and accepts Jewish converts, then it is difficult to see in what way the first gospel depicts the rejection of the Jews.

Yet Hare and Harrington's theory is not without support. For example, Matthew's church would have had several good reasons for stopping the mission to the Jews: the synagogue was in competition with the church for gentile approval if not for membership (cf. 23:15); the Jewish leaders were the experts on the Law, and the ambivalence the gospel displays toward them in this capacity could easily be turned into hate; and, by no means least, the synagogue had persecuted the church.

Literary criticism provides responses to these various observations. The Great Commission is a rewriting of the first

---

[6]On Matthew and this prophetic tradition, cf. Hare, *Jewish Persecution*, p. 152; Gaston, "Messiah of Israel," p. 32; Blair, *Jesus in the Gospel of Matthew*, pp. 42-43; Green, *The Gospel*, pp. 35, 147 (following Hare); and Hummel, *Auseinandersetzung*, p. 142.

mission discourse: the same people, the same location, the same subjects reappear. Matthew 28:16-20 also extends the commands of chapter 10. The disciples, first enjoined only to heal and preach, are sanctioned to baptize and teach. Jesus' authority is now complete, encompassing heaven and earth. And while he had emphasized twice that the mission is only (εἰ μή 15:24; cf. 10:5b) to the house of Israel, there is no "only", no εἰ μή, in the Great Commission. Thus the Jews have lost; or rather, the gentiles have won.

Combined with grammatical considerations, these connections respond to Hare and Harrington's final point: that Matthew would have used πάντας alone -- as Paul does in Rom 11:32 -- if the commission included Israel.[7] The inclusion of ἔθνη, "gentiles," is seen to undercut the universalism of the command. However, a positive reference to one element need not imply a negation of the opposite. Matthew's emphasis is on the extension of the mission to the gentiles, not on the inclusion of the Jews. The evangelist's stylistic interest in recapitulation also commends the specificity of the object of the command: it increases the parallelism between the Great Commission and chapter 10. The inclusion of "gentiles" is, moreover, mandated by the more immediate structure of the pericope. The evangelist has patterned 28:16-20 according to a series of four forms of πᾶς plus a noun. Jesus receives all authority, πᾶσα ἐχουσία; the mission is extended to all the gentiles, πάντα τὰ ἔθνη; all that he has commanded the disciples is reinforced, πάντα ὅσα ἐνετειλάμην ὑμῖν; and he will be with the church all the days, πάσας τὰς ἡμέρας, until the end of the age.[8]

---

[7]"Make Disciples," p. 368; Hare, *Jewish Persecution*, p. 148 n. 3.

[8]De Ridder, *Dispersion*, pp. 183-84; Malina, "Literary Structure," p. 97 (following Bornkamm) and n. 1; Blauw, *Missionary Nature*, p. 85 (following Lohmeyer). On redactional composition, cf. Kingsbury, "Composition and Christology," pp.

In no instance is a previous power or position lessened. The new era witnesses that Jesus has more authority, more potential followers, more commandments, and more time with his disciples. Here all restrictions are ended. In accord with the completion of Jesus' authority -- the emphatic "therefore" of 28:19 -- the mission also reaches its anticipated end. Its extension, specifically to non-Jews, is expressed in Hare and Harrington's translation "all the gentiles." But this extension by no means entails a rejection or an abandonment. Just as the duties of the disciples continue to include healing[9] and preaching, so the mission continues to the Jews.

Source criticism, while by no means definitive, supports this conclusion. Matthew 28:16-20 shares with Dan 7:13-14 (LXX; Theodotian follows the MT) three expressions: ἐδόθη, ἐχουσία, and πάντα τὰ ἔθνη.[10] In Daniel 7, Israel is included in the realm of -- as well as represented by -- the Son of Man.

596-97; Lohmeyer, "Mir ist gegeben," pp. 29-30; Michel, "Der Abschluss," p. 25; Held, "Matthew as Interpreter," p. 171 n. 2; Senior, *Passion Narrative*, p. 159 n. 5.

[9]K. Barth, "Exegetical Study," p. 69, emphasizes christology at the expense of ecclesiology and evangelization by claiming that healings and exorcisms do not appear in 28:16-20 because "the part of Jesus' commandment dealing with doing signs has been fulfilled and become superfluous with the Resurrection of Jesus, the sign of signs."

[10]Blair, *Jesus in the Gospel of Matthew*, p. 47; G. Barth, "Matthew's Understanding," p. 133; Lohmeyer, "Mir ist gegeben," p. 34; K. Barth, "Exegetical Study," p. 61; and, especially, Schaberg, *The Father*, pp. 113, 131, 237, 326. Against the association, see Malina, "Literary Structure," p. 89; Meier, "Two Disputed Questions," p. 410, calls the entire phrase from πορευθέντες redactional. Hubbard, *Matthean Redaction*, p. 128, concludes the phrase was added by someone interested in the gentile mission (cf. Luke 24:47; Mk 16:15; Shaberg, *The Father*, pp. 44, 79 n. 213).

Thus, if Hare and Harrington's restrictive interpretation is correct, "the use of Daniel 7 in the Matthean text would present a startling and direct contradiction to the apparent import of the Danielic passage."[11] This argument holds even if Matthew has not copied the form of the earlier passage; the words of the Great Commission themselves may be sufficiently evocative of the chapter from Daniel. Similarly, that Luke interpreted the phrase as including Israel is indicated in the expression that follows its mention in 24:47 -- "beginning from Jerusalem."[12]

Offering more evidence for the gospel's complete universalism are internal parallels between 28:16-20, the Great Commission, and 4:1-16, the temptation of Jesus and its immediate aftermath. The two scenes share more than an unidentified mountain setting and more than the commonplace of depicting mountains as vantage points from which to survey the world.[13] The setting combines with the dialogue to highlight Matthean universalism: the Devil shows Jesus "*all* the kingdoms of the world" (πάσας τὰς βασιλείας τοῦ κόσμου, 4:8), foremost among which -- given the position of the speaker -- is Palestine. Moreover, just as the Great Commission is the pinnacle of the gospel and so appropriately both a geographical and theological high point, so the first evangelist has made the

---

[11]Schaberg, *The Father*, p. 118.

[12]But see the qualifications in Hare and Harrington, "Make Disciples," p. 366 n. 14.

[13]In addition to Donaldson, *Mountains*; see G. Barth, "Matthew's Understanding," p. 132 and n. 1 (following Lohmeyer, "Mir ist gegeben," p. 24); and, for external parallels, Green, *The Gospel*, p. 69 (II Bar 76:3; I En 24-25); Brandon, *Jesus and the Zealots*, p. 312 (Josephus *War* 6.312-13; Tacitus *Hist*. 5.13; Suetonius *Vesp*. 4); J. Dupont, "L'Arrière-fond biblique du récit des tentations de Jésus," *NTS* 3 (1956/57): 287-304 (Dt 34:1-4).

temptation of world dominion the apex of the Devil's offer.[14]

Connections between the temptation and the Book of Deuteronomy, on the other hand, have on occasion been employed to undercut such universalistic import. For example, the three citations made by Jesus to Deuteronomy have been viewed as indicating "the sad history of Israel's repeated failures in the desert."[15] Yet the temptation is not associated either directly by the verses quoted or indirectly by the context in which it is placed with Jewish infidelity. Indeed, even if Deuteronomy were to be associated with the perfidy of the Jews, the deity nevertheless still brought the people into the promised land. In the context of the first gospel, the references confirm the connection between the time of Jesus and the time of Israel. Contextually, the appeal to Jewish infidelity is also weak. Immediately preceding the temptation Jesus encounters the faithful Jew John the Baptist; no Jews aside from Jesus appear in the temptation; and following his return from the wilderness is the beginning of the public mission and the call of the Jewish and (ultimately) faithful first four disciples. The people in this narrative section between the infancy material and the Sermon on the Mount are quite receptive to Jesus' message: he teaches, apparently unhindered, in the synagogues (4:23); the fishermen leave their nets to follow him (4:18-22); and the crowds spread his fame (4:23-25).

---

[14]P. Pokorny, "The Temptation Stories and Their Intention," *NTS* 20 (1974): 115-16; cf. Allen, *Critical and Exegetical Commentary*, p. 33.

[15]Meier, *Vision of Matthew*, p. 61; cf. B. Gerhardsson, "The Parable of the Sower and Its Interpretation," *NTS* 14 (1968): 171 (following his earlier work, *The Testing of God's Son [Matt 4:1-11 and par]: An Analysis of an Early Christian Midrash* [Lund, Swed.: CWK Gleerup, 1966]).

The thrust of the temptation is not the contrast between Jesus and unfaithful Israel, but the claims to authority made by Satan and, on behalf of God, by Jesus and the storyline. This debate moves beyond the ethnic categories into the realm of the Matthean social axis. Jesus is unable to accept the Devil's offers of power because these offers are illegitimate; only God can bestow upon Jesus "all authority in heaven and earth," as the divine passive in 28:16 implies. Further, since the only christological title associated with mountains in the first gospel is "Son of God" (4:3, 6; 14:23-33; 17:1-5; 28:16-19), Matthew may be read as stressing the familial and non-hierarchical structure of Jesus' mission in opposition to the stress the Devil places on independence and political power. By connecting "a very high mountain" (εἰς ὄρος ὑψηλὸν λίαν) with the granting of royal power (4:8), Satan symbolically attempts to replace the traditional religious and political center, the Temple, with a new center under his own authority. Jesus must reject the offer not only because the Devil lacks the authority to grant universal power but also because acceptance entails the establishment of a new center with its corresponding peripheries. The current center of Judaism, the Temple, will ultimately be replaced with Jesus' continuing -- and decentralized -- presence within the Christian community, but that must wait for the resurrection. The Devil's offer is premature. Finally, Satan's failure to coopt divine power is demonstrated not only by the outcome of the temptation itself, but also by the manner in which it is presented. Both Jesus and the Devil had been moving higher and higher: from the wilderness, to "the highest point (τὸ πτερύγιον) of the Temple" (4:5), to the "very high mountain," but only Jesus remains in the elevated location. The Devil is unable to maintain this situation of priority; those who use power illegitimately are doomed to fall. Satan's emphasis on giving nations to Jesus and so his role as exploiter and slave dealer is replaced by the angels' manifestation of the paradigm of service. The final word in the pericope concerns these other supernatural beings, who "served him" (διηκόνουν αὐτῷ, 4:11).

Returning Jesus to the earthly realm, Matthew also returns to the theme of the temporal division in salvation history. At the close of the temptation narrative, Jesus settles in the Jewish city of Capernaum (4:13) and establishes a program of preaching in Galilean synagogues (4:23). The redactional summary of his activities in 4:23-25 combined with the geographical note in 4:13 provide the contextual frame by which to interpret the ethnic categories in the fulfillment quotation of 4:15-16 (Isa 9:1-2). The people mentioned in 4:16 may inhabit "Galilee of the gentiles" (4:15),[16] but they are Jews. This ethnic distinction is confirmed not only by the mention of synagogues in 4:23 but also by the quotation's own qualification of "Galilee of the gentiles": the setting is the "land of Zebulun and the land of Naphtali" -- regions that passed over from Canaanite to Hebrew control (cf. 15:21-28). Too, the appearance of "people" (λαός) in 4:16 may be connected with the Jewish people of 10:6 as well as 4:23, but, given the evangelist's synonymous use of "people" (λαός) in 4:23 and "crowds" (ὄχλοι) in 4:25; 5:1, this point cannot be forced. Nevertheless, "although the Gospel will eventually surge beyond the borders of Israel and be accepted by Gentiles (cf. 28:19), it is first offered to Jews. They are

---

[16]The JB reads "nations"; reading "gentiles" are the RSV; Tagawa, "People and Community," p. 154; Meier, "Nations or Gentiles," p. 95 ("obviously refers to the large number of Gentile inhabitants in Galilee"); Argyle, *The Gospel*, pp. 41-42 ("heathen Galilee"). R. Brown, *Birth*, equates the verses with Matt 1:1 -- Jesus is the "son of Abraham" by whom "all the nations of the earth shall bless themselves" (Gen 22:18).

the chosen people and Matthew has not lost his sense of continuity."[17]

Davies proposes that Matthew's championship of Galilee (cf. 26:32; 28:7, 10, 16) "inevitably involves in it a rivalry older than Christianity, that between Galilee of the Gentiles and the 'establishment,' if we may so express it, both Pharisaic and Sadducaic, at the Holy City."[18] Additional factors can also be adduced to support such a distinction between the establishment and the marginal. The prophet Isaiah spoke of a light that "shone," but Matthew, reproducing exactly neither the MT nor the LXX, mentions a light that dawns (φῶς ἀνέτειλεν, 4:16).[19] The shift in terminology emphasizes new beginnings: Jesus' mission begins in Galilee, just as does the mission of the disciples in 28:16-20 following the "dawn of the first day of the week" (28:1, ἐπιφώσκω).

Nor does the extension of Jesus' reputation to "all Syria...the Decapolis and Jerusalem and Judea and the Transjordan" (4:25) signal a present gentile mission. The locations represent the borders of Palestine: Galilee in the northwest, the Decapolis in the northeast, Jerusalem and Judea in the southwest, and Perea ("beyond the Jordan"; πέραν τοῦ Ἰορδάνου) in the southeast.[20] The "great crowds" who follow

---

[17]Senior, *Invitation to Matthew*, p. 37; cf. Albright and Mann, *Matthew*, p. 43; Hill, *The Gospel*, pp. 107-8; Green, *The Gospel*, p. 69. J. D. Kingsbury, *Matthew* (Philadelphia: Fortress, 1977); p. 20; cf. *Structure*, p. 465, which suggests that only in 4:18-11:1 is there "'proclamation' in any positive sense to the Jews....following 11:1, Jesus is still pictured as 'teaching' the Jews, but now this activity is colored by the motif of rejection."

[18]*Setting*, pp. 299-300.

[19]Discussed in Stendahl, *School of Saint Matthew*, pp. vii, 105.

[20]Thompson, *Matthew's Advice*, pp. 19-20 and n. 62; following Trilling, *Das Wahre Israel*, pp. 135-36.

him from these areas are Jews. It is to them that the Sermon on the Mount is addressed, and it is for them that the healing miracles in 4:24 are performed. In turn, they correspond to Matthew's social model: they leave their static, secure positions (4:18-22) and their families (4:21-22) in order to follow Jesus (4:25). Unlike their neighbors described in 13:53-58, these crowds are mobile.

Although analysis of grammatical, stylistic, typological, and source-critical considerations of the temptation and the summary section following that pericope have not supported the claim that Jews are omitted from the Great Commission, Hare and Harrington's well-stocked arsenal is not yet exhausted. To support the theory that the deity has rejected the Jews, Hare also appeals to political matters: the Jews' religious leadership does "not constitute a separate group whose destiny is distinguishable from that of Israel." The Pharisees "simply incarnate the spirit of apostasy which has characterized Israel throughout her history."[21] This interpretation is not uncommon in Matthean studies. Those critics of the first gospel who conclude that Matthew depicts the divine rejection of the Jews support their claim through an exegesis of an "impressive succession of stories peculiar to Matthew":[22] 21:28-32; 21:33-43; 22:1-14; 23:37-39; 25:1-13; 25:14-30; and 25:31-46. But examination of these passages does not support their conclusion. Just as the Great Commission equalizes the positions of the Jews and gentiles[23]

---

[21] *Jewish Persecution*, p. 151, cf. p. 153.

[22] Clark, "Gentile Bias," p. 166; cf. Hare and Harrington, "Make Disciples," p. 367; Hare, "Rejection of the Jews," p. 38, citing in particular 21:43; 22:1ff.; 23:37-39.

[23] Tagawa, "People and Community," p. 162; Strecker, "Concept of History," p. 73; Hill, *The Gospel*, p. 43; Senior, *Passion Narrative*, p. 260; Meier, *Vision of Matthew*, pp. 17, 55 n. 19;

and so completes the temporal axis, the cross-ethnic emphasis of the social axis provides the criteria by which those destined for salvation are separated from those to be damned. The followers of Jesus are characterized by mobility, by positions of oppression, subservience, and disenfranchisement, and by faith manifested in action. Those who reject Jesus are distinguished by stasis, by their positions of leadership, and by reliance upon their own authority. These characteristics function to indicate that the Pharisees and priests should not and cannot be lumped together with the entire Jewish community. While the leaders may not be included in the messianic banquet, many among the Jewish people retain their appetite and their invitation.

Matthew 21:28-32

The opposition between the two sons in the parable that bears their name is often interpreted according to ethnic categories. The son who answers "I will not" to his father's request that he work in the vineyard but then repents is seen to represent the gentile, Christian church, while his brother, who first assents but then fails to fulfill his word, represents the Jewish people. Carlston even asserts that the parable is "originally and primarily no doubt an explanation of God's rejection of the Jews."[24] This theory is supported not only by appeals to the gospel's presumed separation throughout all of salvation history of Jews and gentiles, it is also indicated in manuscript tradition by a textual variant. Although most manuscripts mention first the son who originally said "no" and

---

and cf. Garland, *Intention*, p. 214 n. 14.

[24]"Interpreting the Gospel," p. 7; cf. Abel, "Who Wrote Matthew?" p. 149.

regard him as the obedient one, D and several minor texts suggest that the son who answered affirmatively but did not go performed the will of his father. The modification likely was made by copyists who saw in the two sons the contrast between Jews, who said "yes" at Sinai, and gentiles.[25]

Yet the first gospel does not assign ethnic categories to the characters in the parable. Matthew 21:28-32 is the first of three parables depicting the familiar social motif: the religious elite prove inadequate leaders and are consequently condemned; the socially despised and disenfranchised, the tax collectors and prostitutes "who believed" (ἐπίστευσαν, 21:32), are welcomed. Several narrative ploys accentuate the social interests of the pericope. First, the audience and setting are emphasized: Matthew explicitly notes that Jesus is engaged with the "chief priests and elders of the people" (οἱ ἀρχιερεῖς καὶ οἱ πρεσβύτεροι τοῦ λαοῦ, 21:23). Emphasis falls on titles of leadership: not merely priests but chief priests; not merely the people but the elders. The first and only division in the pericope is not between Jews and gentiles but between the Jewish leadership and the people, including Jesus. The leaders do not represent the people; instead they are separated from their nominal constituency by both religious orientation and fear: "But if we say [the baptism of John was] 'from men,' we are afraid of the crowd (ὄχλος); for all (πάντες) hold that John was a prophet" (21:26). Thus the pericope cannot depict the rejection of the Jewish people.

While the discussion is taking place in the religious authorities' home court, the Temple, the advantage belongs to Jesus. He has already bested his opponents once in this location (21:23-27) through a comparison of his authority (cf. 28:18) with theirs. The debate over proper leadership and

---

[25]Hill, *The Gospel*, pp. 297-98; cf. Allen, *Critical and Exegetical Commentary*, pp. 228-29.

social standing continues at the conclusion of the parable of the two sons; here Jesus compares the unrepentant (21:32) elders and priests with members of two groups on the opposite end of the social spectrum: tax collectors and prostitutes. To emphasize the social thrust of the parable, the evangelist repeats the mention of these disenfranchised individuals. They are first to their advantage contrasted with the chief priests and elders (one pair replaces the other), and they are then positively associated with John the Baptist. These marginal members of society repented at John's message, as did the son who originally answered "no"; therefore, they shall enter the *Basileia*. But their entering will not form a new hierarchy. Although the parable suggests that the prevailing social order will be reversed -- "the tax collectors and prostitutes go into the *Basileia* of God before you" -- ultimately the Jewish leaders will not enter at all. The "before" does not imply an "after," and 21:31b indicates exclusion rather than precedence.[26] The Jewish leaders received a second chance to repent, but they did not avail themselves of the opportunity (21:32). Like the second son, they failed to move. To reinforce these social distinctions, Matthew follows the parable of the two sons with a second account that also condemns unfaithful caretakers -- the symbolic equivalent of the priests and elders in control of the Temple (21:33-46).

Matthew 21:33-43

Vineyard parables are fertile fields for those who claim

---

[26]Meier, *Vision of Matthew*, p. 149 n. 162; following J. Jeremias, *The Parables of Jesus*, rev. ed. (New York: Scribner's, 1963), p. 125 n. 48; and against Kümmel, *Promise and Fulfillment*, p. 78 n. 198.

the first gospel depicts the rejection of the Jews. Once one of the parables is interpreted as supporting this theory, the others are seen to follow suit.[27] Such argument from analogy is helpful, but only after the internal contents of the passage in question are analyzed. Further, the argument from juxtaposition can be manipulated to support the theory of any commentator. Thus, the parable of the vineyard and the tenants can be easily shown to conform not to an ethnic division and the consequent rejection of the Jews, but to a pattern that depicts the rejection of patriarchal, exploitative systems of authority.

Those who see an ethnic import to Matt 21:33-46 concentrate on the conclusion of the narrative rather than on the events in the parable itself. In 21:43, Jesus tells his audience that "the *Basileia* of God will be taken away from you and given to a nation (ἔθνει) producing the fruits of it," and commentators tell their readers that this nation is the *gentile* church.[28] The various difficulties in translating ἔθνος render suspect any conclusion that the term refers only or even to gentiles. But even when the term is translated "nation," the argument that the pericope indicates the rejection of the Jews is still made. Hare, for example, concludes that the unfaithful tenants "represent Israel as a whole, not its religious leaders only as in Mark. What is taken away, therefore, is not the privilege of leadership but the status of being God's special people." The parable therefore depicts a rejection of the Jews

---

[27]E.g., Carlston, "Interpreting the Gospel," p. 7.

[28]Fenton, *Saint Matthew*, p. 345 (on 21:43, but cf. p. 343 on 21:41); Jeremias, *Rediscovering the Parables*, pp. 51, 57, 63; Abel, "Who Wrote Matthew?" pp. 149, 151; and cf. Bornkamm, "End-Expectation," p. 43. On the complementary view that the mission is now turning to the gentiles, see Strecker, *Der Weg*, pp. 33, 110-13; cf. Senior, *Invitation to Matthew*, p. 211.

as an ethnic group, the rejection of "Israel according to the flesh."[29] On the other hand, Hill equates the tenants with the Jewish leaders,[30] and thus he proposes that Israel retains its earlier soteriological benefits.

The summary statements in 21:43-45[31] combined with details in the parable itself support Hill's conclusion. The reidentification of the audience, now the odd alliance of the "chief priests and Pharisees" (21:45) instead of the "chief priests and elders of the people" (21:23) suggests that the various leadership groups within the Jewish community have

---

[29]"Rejection of the Jews," pp. 38-39, cf. p. 33; and *Jewish Persecution*, p. 151; Trilling, *Das Wahre Israel*, pp. 45, 95-97, 162, 213, and J. Reumann's review of the first edition of Trilling in *JBL* 79 (1960): 376; Green, *The Gospel*, p. 180; Brandon, *Jesus and the Zealots*, p. 305; Hummel, *Auseinandersetzung*, pp. 148-50; Meier, "Nations or Gentiles," p. 98; *Vision of Matthew*, pp. 17, 55 n. 19; *Antioch and Rome*, p. 61. See also M. Kiddle, "The Death of Jesus and the Admission of the Gentiles in St. Mark," *JTS* 35 (1934): 45-50; and following Kiddle, Dahl, "Passion Narrative," p. 50. Dahl connects 21:43 with the theme of Jewish guilt, as does Tilborg, *Jewish Leaders*, pp. 70-71.

[30]*The Gospel*, p. 298; cf. the section title in Gundry, *Matthew*, p. 424: "The Transferral of God's Kingdom from the Jewish Leaders to the Church..."; Martin, "Recent Study," p. 136 (against Hare).

[31]Allen, *Critical and Exegetical Commentary*, p. 231; Manson, *Sayings of Jesus*, p. 224; Kilpatrick, *Origins of the Gospel*, p. 30; Hare, *Jewish Persecution*, p. 153. Strecker, *Der Weg*, p. 169; and Hill, *The Gospel*, p. 301, argue for a pre-Matthean origin, but all suggest the evangelist placed it at the end of the parable; cf. Held, "Matthew as Interpreter," p. 239; Kümmel, *Promise and Fulfillment*, p. 53 n. 111 (following Klostermann and Dahl); Hare, *Jewish Persecution*, p. 153 n. 3, correctly rejects Lohmeyer's claim that the verse derives from a Jewish-Christian community.

banded together against Jesus and the people. The editorial note that these authorities perceived that Jesus was speaking about them (ἔγνωσαν ὅτι περὶ αὐτῶν λέγει, 21:45) further serves to distinguish between the leaders and the lost sheep, the house of Israel.

That the repetition of the audience is a deliberate redactional insertion is also indicated by the similarly repeated reason for the separation between the leaders and the people: the chief priests and Pharisees are unable to arrest Jesus because "they feared the crowds (τοὺς ὄχλους) who believed him to be a prophet" (21:46). These parallels between the crowds' acclamation of Jesus in 21:46 with the references to John the Baptist in both 14:5 and 21:26 are striking. Three times people in authority (Herod Antipas, the chief priests, the elders, the Pharisees) condemn individuals acclaimed by the crowds as prophets; three times the leaders fear reprisals from the people; three times the leaders are therefore separated from the people.

The characters in the parable of the vineyard and the tenants confirm the distinction between faithless Jewish leaders and faithful Jewish crowds. The servants (δοῦλοι) mentioned throughout 21:33-43 are the symbolic equivalents of the Hebrew prophets; the son who fulfills the same role and suffers the same fate (cf. 23:34) as these earlier messengers is the last and greatest in this line. Therefore the parable confirms the perceptions of the crowds. The connection of the parable to the prophetic tradition itself underlines the distinction between leaders and the people as well as the Jewish agenda of the narrative. The metaphor of the vineyard is most clearly articulated in Isaiah 5, where it represents Jerusalem/Judea (Isa 5:3, 7) and where too the nobility of Jerusalem and those lacking humility are specifically mentioned (5:13b, 14c). Such allusions as well as the citation of Ps 118:22-23 in 21:42 reinforce the address of the pericope to the Pharisees and priests; biblical interpretation was their sphere. Similarly, the wicked tenants hold the power of capital punishment, a prerogative of the Sanhedrin and not of the general population. And these tenants are interested in maintaining their elite and static position: they kill the heir in order to obtain his inheritance (21:38; cf. Mk 12:7; Lk 20:14). The parable thus plays upon the discrepancy between those who appear to hold authority over the land and the legitimate owner. Producing ironic effect, Matthew rewrites Mark's version to indicate that the son is killed outside the vineyard. While this shift may increase the christological assocations of the death of the son (cf. Acts 7:58), it also confirms the gospel's distrust of centers. The salvific acts of both crucifixion and resurrection appearances must be away from the locus of earthly power. The move outside of symbolic Israel also foreshadows the continuity of Israel in the new era. While the son is brought outside the vineyard, ultimately the vineyard itself will be repopulated with faithful tenants. The focus on Israel itself remains constant; the only element that changes is the leadership. Finally, the Matthean criterion of legitimacy reappears in the description of these characters. The faithless tenants attempt to reinforce their false claim through stasis: they remain on the land. The mobility of the servants and the son -- their entry into the vineyard -- threatens the tenants and calls into question their claims of power.

The tenants in the vineyard are comprised of two groups: those who will pay the master what is required and those who attempt to usurp everything for themselves. So too the Jewish community may be divided into two groups: on the one hand are the crowds, the prostitutes, and the tax collectors who listen to John the Baptist and Jesus; on the other are the political and religious authorities who reject both prophets. But in neither Matt 21:33-46 nor 21:28-32 do gentiles enter the picture directly. A division is made between faithful and faithless tenants; the subject -- the Jewish community -- remains the same. And because the ambiguous ἔθνος of 21:43 is associated with these good tenants, so the referent of the term here cannot be only, or even primarily, to the gentiles. The best explanation of this "nation" is that it symbolizes the church constructed on an egalitarian framework and along both temporal and social axes. The temporal emphasis appears in the future tenses of the verbs; only after the resurrection will this new nation receive the *Basileia*, and the social axis supplies the division between repentent marginals and unfaithful leaders.

Matthew 22:1-14

A majority of scholars commenting on the parable of the wedding feast agree that the second invitation is directed to or at least includes gentiles.[32] In turn this acceptance of gentiles has been understood to imply the elimination of the

---

[32]E.g., Jeremias, *Jesus' Promise*, p. 24, and *Rediscovering the Parables*, pp. 51, 56-57; Manson, *Sayings of Jesus*, p. 130; Hahn, *Mission*, p. 130; Meier, *Vision of Matthew*, p. 153; Fenton, *Saint Matthew*, p. 349; Davies, *Setting*, p. 329 (on Matthean universalism); and cf. Argyle, *The Gospel*, p. 165 (on the invitation to "tax-gatherers, sinners, gentiles"); Schweizer, *Good News*, p. 419; Plummer, *Exegetical Commentary*, pp. 301-2; Wilson, *Gentiles*, pp. 6-7, 34; V. Hasler, "Die königliche Hochzeit: Matt. 22.1-14," *TZ* 18 (1962): 25-35 (cited in Rohde, *Rediscovering*, p. 50 n. 4); C. H. Dodd, *The Parables of the Kingdom* (New York: Scribner's, 1961), p. 94; S. Brown, "Matthean Community," p. 195 n. 10.

Jews from the *Basileia*. Hare succinctly states, "The theme of the allegory is clearly the rejection of God's messengers by Israel and the consequent rejection of Israel by God."[33] While according to Matthew gentiles will certainly be welcome in the new era, application of ethnic categories to the parable is not warranted. Like the preceding material, Matt 22:1-14 depicts the rejection of members of elite groups and the invitation to all lacking status and authority in the social structure.

The address of the parable to chief priests and Pharisees (22:1, 15), with its consequent emphasis on people in hierarchical and static positions, is reinforced by details within the parable itself. The first guests, those who refuse the invitation, share two characteristics: they are members of the establishment and they are well-grounded. These individuals are the first invited; they are the ones expected to associate with royalty; they are the initially privileged. While these motifs are apparent in the Matthean version, a comparsion of Matt 22:1-14 with Lk 14:15-24 highlights the first gospel's social concern. Unlike Luke's version, in which one guest refused the invitation because he had just married (14:20), Matthew places complete emphasis on business concerns (22:5). And unlike Lk 14:15-24, the guests in the first gospel are not characterized by movement. Luke's guests excuse themselves in order to "go" (ἐξελθών, 14:18; πορεύομαι, 14:19; cf. ἐλθεῖν, 14:20), but Matthew's contingent simply "would not come" (οὐκ ἤθελον ἐλθεῖν, 22:3).

The juxtaposition of Matt 22:1-14 with the parable of the vineyard also directs attention to the social axis. The guests invited first to the wedding feast share with the self-serving tenants of 21:33-41 both the same attitude toward

---

[33] *Jewish Persecution*, pp. 121-22, cf. p. 154.

their superior (the householder and the king, respectively) as well as the same activities: both groups are characterized by stasis, and both attempt to secure their positions by precluding the mobility of the servants through seizing and killing them (22:6). Thus the identification of the wicked tenants in 21:33-46 may be applied to the unreceptive and consequently unreceived guests in 22:1-14. The guests are not all the people of Israel, they are only the Jewish leaders.

The converse of this point -- that those called in the second invitation are the marginal members of society and not primarily or even gentiles -- is also confirmed by the parable. The second invitation is addressed to those characterized by movement; they are in the thoroughfares (διεξόδους τῶν ὁδῶν, 22:9, cf. Lk 14:21) rather than on farms or in businesses. Like the faithful and faithless tenants in the parable of the vineyard, both the first and the second group are identified by the same term: they are "invited" or, more literally, "called" (καλέω). While the description of the second group of guests does not exclude the possibility that gentiles are implied, nothing in the parable suggests any ethnic distinctions. Matthew has separated the guests in terms of social position: the church is to welcome those in the streets, the "street people": prostitutes, sinners, and tax collectors. Further, the eschatological judgment has a cross-ethnic or non-ethnic orientation: salvation is granted to those, regardless of ethnic origin, who respond fully to the invitation, to those who "do the will of the Father."

These observations render unlikely Strecker's claim that the burning of the city described in 22:7 indicates the end of the Jews' ability to act on their own behalf for salvation.[34] While the statement that the king "sent his troops and

---

[34] *Der Weg*, p. 117.

destroyed those murderers [cf. 21:41] and burned their city" may suggest the destruction of Jerusalem in 70 C.E., and while Manson may even be correct in his claim that the second invitation means that the servants are to approach [Jewish?] refugees from the city,[35] the emphasis of the parable remains on the fate of the leaders and outside of historical referents. For example, although 22:7 causes a break in the parable's narrative -- the supper must be delayed while the city is destroyed -- the delay follows the apocalyptic pattern: destruction of the wicked usually precedes eschatological reward of the faithful. And, it is the leaders' city, "their" (αὐτῶν) city and hence their center which is burned; the people -- enough to fill the wedding hall (22:10) -- survive.

Social rather than ethnic categories also explain the brief account of the unprepared guest appended to the parable. Brandon suggests that the missing wedding garment is a "qualification an alien guest, i.e., a Gentile convert, might not have."[36] But the garment does not represent the cultic or ethnic qualification: as in Rev 3:4, 5, 18; 19:8; 22:14; and I En 62:15-16, it indicates faith in and obedience to God. The concluding statement that "many are called but few are chosen" (22:14) also suggests that the Jews neither are nor will be rejected. Because they are included in the second invitation, they have the same opportunity for salvation as their non-Jewish counterparts. The distinction between the many and the few functions as a warning against complacency, a characteristic already manifested not only by the Jewish

---

[35]*Sayings of Jesus*, pp. 225-56. Meier, *Law and History*, p. 7 n. 30, cites K. Rengstorf ("Die Stadt der Morder [Mt 22,7]," in W. Eltester (ed.), *Judentum, Urchristentum, Kirche* [Berlin: Topelmann, 1960], pp. 106-29), who claims 22:7 is a "fixed *topos* used to portray punitive expeditions."

[36]*Jesus and the Zealots*, p. 174, cf. pp. 173, 305.

religious authorities but also by the disciples. Finally, the parallels between 22:9-10 and 8:11 on the one hand, and 22:13-14 and 8:12 on the other, confirm the parable's emphasis on social rather than ethnic categories. The eschatological logion in chapter 8 has a cross-ethnic focus as well as an implicit concern for social distinctions. The same two motifs plus, in the case of 22:13, the same wording reappear in the parable of the marriage feast. The parable ends with the warning to those who abuse their authority and who fail to act: they will be cast into the outer darkness where all activity consists of weeping and gnashing teeth (8:12; 22:13).

Matthew 23:37-39

The lament over Jerusalem provides the strongest case for those who claim Matthew depicts God's rejection of Israel. The Jewish leaders are viewed not merely as having failed their people; rather, "the failure of Israel" is seen to be the logical consequence of the "failure of her self-appointed leaders."[37] Yet a close reading of Matthew 23 reveals only a condemnation of the Jewish leadership. The people of Israel, as distinguished from their faithless elite, is provided the same opportunity obtained by the gentiles at the Great Commission: salvation for the Jews is contingent upon their response to the

---

[37]Garland, *Intention*, p. 116 cf. pp. 39, 203, 211-12; Strecker, *Der Weg*, p. 35; Hare, *Jewish Persecution*, p. 155; and "Rejection of the Jews," p. 39; Walker, *Heilsgeschichte*, pp. 56-57; Trilling, *Das Wahre Israel*, pp. 85-86; Frankemölle, *Jahwebund*, pp. 250-59; Hummel, *Auseinandersetzung*, pp. 87-88; and additional citations in Dale C. Allison, Jr., "Matt. 23:39 = Luke 13:35b as a Conditional Prophecy," *JSNT* 18 (1983): 75-84.

gospel.[38]

Although Matthew 23 repeatedly addresses the scribes and Pharisees with the emphatic second person construction (cf. Lk 11:49ff.), the chapter is not directed only to them. In 23:1 the crowds (ὄχλοι) and the disciples are for the first time "unequivocally addressed together and on the same level in a discourse."[39] This address separates the crowds and the disciples from the already-condemned Jewish leaders. Through its inclusive audience, Matthew 23 becomes a practical warning to leaders of the church not to engage in the exploitative practices that characterize the Pharisees and scribes.

The distinction in audience is reinforced by the particular descriptions of the Pharisees in the chapter: they require the people to practice what they themselves do not; they seek to distinguish themselves in dress, activities, and seating in the synagogues. They thereby separate themselves both by lack of action and by interest in social trappings from the corporate community, who, by implication, are mobile and less concerned with status. Thus this chapter does not depict "an explicit explanation for the failure of Israel," or a "solution for the Christian problem of Israel's rejection of

---

[38]Allison, "Matt. 23:39," p. 80. Garland, *Intention*, p. 204 and n. 128 (following Stagg), lists several passages suggesting the fate of the Jews is "chosen not imposed."

[39]Garland, *Intention*, p. 37, cf. pp. 34-39 and contrast his conclusion, p. 39, that from Matt 21:1 on "the crowds" are in league with the authorities against Jesus. Gaston, "Messiah of Israel," p. 37, elides the social and ethnic divisions in asserting the polemic is only against "lawless, legalistic, Christian enthusiasts." However, Tilborg, *Jewish Leaders*, p. 17, notes similar charges against "official Judaism" in AssMos 7:3-10 and TAsh 2:5-8.

Jesus."[40] No "explanation" per se is offered. And because Matthew's church has members of Jewish background and members who subscribe to Jewish customs, no "solution" is needed. "Israel" does not reject Jesus; individual Jews as well as individual gentiles -- primarily those content with their place in the status quo -- do.

Distinctions between the leadership and the community are maintained in 23:29-33, the seventh woe. The evangelist has added the direct address to the scribes and Pharisees (cf. Lk 11:47-48) as well as their direct condemnation as a "brood of vipers" (γεννήματα ἐχιδνῶν) in v. 33. This expression had earlier been applied to "many of the scribes and Pharisees" (Matt 3:7; the Lucan parallel, also 3:7, is to the crowds) and in 12:34 to the Pharisees alone. The focus consequently remains on the leadership. The members of the Jewish elite in 23:32-33, unlike the crowds and the disciples of 23:1-12, are not exhorted to repent. Because they remain insistent on placing their own power and status above that of Jesus and the rest of the people -- because they have established and maintained hierarchical divisions on the patriarchal model -- their damnation and consequent loss of power are inevitable.

Attempting to expand the referent of 23:29-33, Garland proposes that the woe indicates a subtle incrimination of the present generation of Israel in past guilt, and Hare adds that the condemnation of the Pharisees in 23:29 "shades almost imperceptibly into a condemnation of the people as a whole, symbolized by 'this generation' (23:36) and Jerusalem (23:37)."[41] Yet what is "imperceptible" may not be there at all. Both the notice of "this generation" and the address to

---

[40]Garland, *Intention*, pp. 211-12.

[41]Ibid., pp. 166, 186 and n. 78; Hare, *Jewish Persecution*, pp. 151-52, cf. p. 94 which describes 23:35 seeing "apostate Israel" as a "corporate whole."

Jerusalem continue the same subject matter: the Jewish leaders. The Greek reinforces the connection through the similarities in sound among the terms for "generation" (γενεὰ, 23:36); viper's "brood" (γεννήματα, lit.: offspring, 23:33); and "hell" (γέεννα, 23:33). Thus the generation condemned cannot refer to all of Israel. Rather, the various charges in 23:34-36 of persecuting the wise, killing the prophets, and being children of serpents are all laid against the Jewish leaders. They are responsible for the failings of Israel's past, and they will be denied salvation in the future. The referent to "this generation" is confined to the leaders of the Jewish people."[42] Matthew does not note a change in audience or subject that would suggest the term applies to all Israel, and the focus on leadership is reinforced by the appearance of the term "generation" in 17:17, where it may apply to Jesus' own disciples (17:16). But the people themselves, together with the disciples if they heed the warnings about abuse of power, have a chance at salvation.

Several elements in 23:34-36 reinforce the thematic focus on those in positions of authority. The complaint that the Pharisees and scribes make a habit of killing messengers from God (23:34; cf. Lk 11:50) recalls the parables of the vineyard (21:33-43) and the wedding feast (22:1-14); in each the murderers are the allegorical equivalents of the Jewish leadership and not of the corporate community. Second, Matt 23:34 suggests that missionary activity among the Jewish people will continue during the age of the church;[43] the

---

[42]Tilborg, *Jewish Leaders*, p. 67, but p. 46 suggests the judgment about killing the prophets expresses Israel's permanent disobedience.

[43]Kingsbury, *Matthew*, p. 99; Garland, *Intention*, p. 176 (comparing verb forms in Matt 23:34 and Lk 11:50). On the persecution of missionaries see Suggs, *Wisdom*, p. 15; Garland,

mention of those messengers to be "scourged in your synagogues" follows the reference to crucifixion. But the previous parables have alerted the reader that those who persecute such messengers are the leaders, the elite, the nonmobile. Thus the Jewish people, as distinguished from their leaders, not only retain the opportunity to repent, they are assured through the parables that they will be given the benefits revoked from those first invited to the banquet.

The charge in 23:34 of killing the prophets is repeated in verse 37, where it is directly associated with Jerusalem. Two Matthean themes, combined as early as the infancy accounts in chapter 2, here reappear. The cultic center which established peripheries and so created locative as well as social inequalities is combined with the condemnation of the leaders of the people. The patriarchal associations of the city are ironically contrasted to Jesus' feminine language: rather than divide individuals into elites and marginals, he would have gathered the children of Jerusalem together "as a hen gathers her brood under her wings" (23:37).

In continuity with his theory that Jesus' lament indicates God's abandonment of Israel, Hare proposes that the house (οἶκος) declared "forsaken and desolate" (23:38) refers to the nation of Israel.[44] Such a broad definition is not, however, adopted by others in the scholarly community. Some associate the house with the Temple, others stress the connection with the city; and still others argue that because the city cannot be

---

Intention, pp. 176-77; Haenchen, "Matthäus 23," p. 53; and Hare, *Jewish Persecution*.

[44]*Jewish Persecution*, p. 154 (specifically against Davies); Green, *The Gospel*, p. 195. Hill, *The Gospel*, p. 316, offers "the people in its entirety symbolized by the Temple"; cf. Trilling, *Das Wahre Israel*, p. 67; Garland, *Intention*, p. 199.

distinguished from the Temple the reference is to both.[45] Of these various possibilities, Hare's suggestion receives the least support from the gospel. Matthew has indicated that centers are dangerous because they necessarily create distinctions between elite and marginal. Further, the Great Commission replaces both centers of Israel -- the city and the Temple -- with new but diffused focal points -- the proclamation on an unidentified mountain of the continuing presence of Jesus within the community. The combination of these motifs with the frequent complaints in the gospel against both city and Temple confirm that the desolate house refers not to an abandoned people but to a rejected religious and political establishment.

The final element in the lament over Jerusalem which may suggest Israel's rejection is Matthew's insertion of the phrase usually translated as "until", ἀπ' ἄρτι, in 23:39 (cf. 26:29, 64). According to Garland, the phrase "makes it less likely that the acclamation looks forward to a redemptive encounter between Christ and Israel, or any implication that Israel will be converted before the parousia...the context implies no positive expectations for Israel (8:12; 21:43; 22:7); 24:30-31 gives no hint of a time for repentence."[46] Yet all four passages to which Garland appeals -- 8:12; 21:43; 22:7; 24:30-31 -- directly concern only the Jewish leadership, not the

[45]On the Temple, cf. Kingsbury, *Matthew*, p. 52; and the list in Garland, *Intention*, pp. 198-99. Meier, *Vision of Matthew*, p. 146 n. 158, notes the contrast of "my house" (21:13), where the reference is clearly to the Temple, and "your house," in 23:38. On the city, Garland cites Klostermann, McNeile, Plummer, Steck, and Hoffmann; on both city and Temple, cf. Davies, *Setting*, pp. 144, 152; and following him Allison, "Matt. 23:39," p. 82 n. 12.

[46]*Intention*, pp. 206-7, cf. p. 208; Green, *The Gospel*, p. 195.

corporate community. And, the temporal connotation of the phrase anticipates both the eschatological discourse which follows in chapter 24 and the turn of the era at the resurrection.[47] According to the Great Commission as well as such passages as 24:14, there will be a delay between the resurrection and the parousia; the same point is made by the inclusion of ἀπ' ἄρτι in 23:39.[48] During this time -- the era of the church -- Jews and gentiles both have the opportunity to obey the message of the eleven sent out by Jesus. Nor does the lament indicate that when the last days arrive "it will be too late" for the Jews to respond properly. As Allison notes, the acclamation of the term "blessed" (εὐλογημένος) is not usually associated with fear, despondency, or mourning. In the Hebrew of Ps 118:26, the term is ברך, which also has extremely positive connotations. "It is not easy to envision the words of Ps. 118[117]:26 as coming, begrudgingly or otherwise, from the lips of those for whom the messianic advent must mean only destruction."[49]

These several observations reveal that even if the pericope concerns all of Israel rather than just the leadership or the population of Jerusalem, it does not testify to rejection or abandonment. Rather, the lament over Jerusalem contains both the threat of judgment and the opportunity of salvation,

---

47 Garland, *Intention*, p. 206 and n. 134; Hummel, *Auseinandersetzung*, p. 141; Trilling, *Das Wahre Israel*, pp. 68, 86-87; Senior, *Passion Narrative*, pp. 179-83; Hare, *Jewish Persecution*, p. 154; and Rohde's comments on Hummel in *Rediscovering*, p. 105.

48 C. K. Barrett, *Jesus and the Gospel Tradition* (London: S.P.C.K., 1967), p. 76; cf. Hare, *Jewish Persecution*, p. 95; Hill, *The Gospel*, p. 316.

49 Allison, "Matt. 23:39," p. 75.

the two possibilities shared by Jew and gentile alike at the Great Commission.

The Eschatological Discourse

The first four pericopes invoked by those claiming that Matthew depicts the rejection of the Jews are most frequently approached in ethnic terms; rather than see the various characters as separated into faithful and faithless members of one group -- be that the Jewish community or the church -- the view persists that the faithful must be gentiles and the recalcitrant, Jews. This classification in turn becomes theologically coded: the faithful gentiles symbolize the Christian, gentile church; the disciples and the other non-gentiles who follow Jesus are implicitly stripped of their Judaism by the commentators, and so Jews as a whole remain Jews, separated from and rejected by both church and deity. These same reductive conclusions are also applied to the final three pericopes that purportedly indicate the rejection of the Jews: the parables that constitute chapter 25.

And again, the context of the narratives and the images they depict fail to support such divisions. The eschatological discourse of Matthew 24-25 reveals the cross-ethnic focus of the gospel's salvation history. In the era of the church, Jews and gentiles have an equal opportunity to hear the gospel. Further, since the mission to the Jews continues and since the church is founded both by and upon members of the Jewish community, it is more appropriate to speak of the gentiles gaining a greater place after the resurrection rather than of the Jews having lost the promise of the *Basileia*. The ultimate distinction in the gospel remains along the lines of the social axis: judgment is based on faith manifest in action and not on ethnic origin or elite-group affiliation.

Both sections of the eschatological discourse stress the equal status of Jews and gentiles in the new era. The first part, the description of the end in 24:1-51, predicts not only the extension of the mission to the gentiles (24:14; cf. 28:19) but also the equal participation of Jews and gentiles in the apocalyptic tribulations. The universality of the Great Commission is anticipated in the second section of the discourse as well: the three parables of 25:1-46 illustrate that all individuals will be judged by the same criteria. As Günther Bornkamm states: "It would be difficult to maintain that the description of the judgment of the world, with which -- no longer in parabolic form -- the whole construction of the discourse concludes, refers only to the judgment that is come upon the Gentiles in distinction from the members of the community of Jesus. Rather it is typical for the end-expectation of Matthew that by means of a great picture already current among the Jews the judgment of the world is announced as applying to all nations, but now in such a way that no distinction is made between Jews and Gentiles, nor even between believers and unbelievers."[50] The universalistic picture of Matthew 24 is painted in bold colors by verses 7, 9, 14, and it is accentuated in more subtle shades by 20, 27, 30, and 45-51. This universalism in turn provides the context by which to interpret the three parables of chapter 25.

Among the signs of the eschaton, Matthew follows Mark in announcing that "nation will rise against nation (ἔθνος ἐπὶ ἔθνος) and kingdom against kingdom" (24:7; cf. Mk 13:8; Lk 21:10).[51] This possible *vaticinium ex eventu* is the gospel's

---

[50]"End-Expectation," p. 23.

[51]Hare and Harrington, "Make Disciples," p. 362, agree with Meier, "Nations or Gentiles," p. 98, that ἔθνος may "retain the original meaning as a national group or collective."

first indication that the Jews -- here fitting under the categories of nation as well as kingdom as they do in 24:14 -- will participate in the same apocalyptic signs as the gentiles. The prediction corresponds to Isa 19:2 in the phrase "kingdom against kingdom" (βασιλεία ἐπὶ βασιλείαν) only; no Hebrew version speaks of nations rising against nations. While this modification indicates the typical reluctance of apocalypticists to quote sources directly, it also reinforces the complete ethnic inclusivity of the prediction. Just as Jews will share with gentiles the benefits of salvation history, so they must share in the eschatological woes.

Nor will the Jews be distinguished from the gentiles in the new era on the basis of their treatment of the disciples: Jesus' followers will be hated by "all the nations" (πάντων τῶν ἔθνων, 24:9), Jew and gentile alike. Taking their cue from a comparison of Matt 24:9 with Mk 13:9b-13a, several commentators have suggested that the first evangelist includes the words τῶν ἔθνων and eliminates Mark's reference to the synagogue (13:9) in order to narrow the category of persecutors to gentiles.[52] Yet persecutions in synagogues are explicitly mentioned in Matt 10:17, a verse which both depends on Mark's little apocalypse and refers to the era of the church. That Jews will play a role in persecuting the church is indicated in 10:22 and 23:34 as well. However, they will not be alone. The absence of the reference to synagogues in Matt 24:9-13 is due to the universal nature of the passage: the evangelist emphasizes worldwide tribulation, not just

---

[52]Hare and Harrington, "Make Disciples," p. 366, but cf. p. 362. Thompson, "Historical Perspective," pp. 254-55; cf. Plummer, *Exegetical Commentary*, p. 331; Walker, *Heilsgeschichte*, pp. 83-86. Supporting the inclusive reading "nations" are Trilling, *Das Wahre Israel*, p. 28; and Meier, "Nations or Gentiles," pp. 96-97 n. 9, 99.

problems in Palestine or in Jewish institutions.

The addition of "the nations" (τῶν ἔθνων) to Mark's simple "all" (πάντων) also anticipates both the next appearance of the phrase in 24:14 and its final mention in the Great Commission. Just as all nations will display antipathy toward the representatives of the gospel, so all will have the opportunity to hear it. However, while Matt 28:19 is best translated "all the gentiles," the context of 24:9 suggests the more inclusive reading of "all the nations." While a consistent translation of a term or phrase throughout a document has much to commend it, critics must seek the appropriate connotations of each expression within its particular context. Thus, the reference to "nation against nation" in 24:7 has a greater influence on 24:9 than does the Great Commission's application of the term in 28:19. Although connections between the eschatological discourse and the Commission are emphasized by the evangelist, the internal content of the discourse itself is the deciding factor in determining the translation of its vocabulary. The eschatological discourse stresses equality of Jews and gentiles in the new era; therefore the inclusive reading "nations" is more appropriate.[53]

The repetition of the inclusive phrase πάντα τὰ ἔθνη is not the only connection between 24:14 and 28:16-20. Matthew's prediction that the "gospel of the kingdom will be preached throughout the whole world" (ἐν ὅλῃ τῇ οἰκουμένῃ) indicates both

---

[53]On the future thrust of Matt 24:9-14, see Hare, *Jewish Persecution*, pp. 124, 177-79; Thompson, "Historical Perspective," pp. 249, 254-55 (against Walker, *Heilsgeschichte*, p. 84 n. 34). Thompson (pp. 255-57) and Hare, (p. 144 n. 4) propose that the gentile mission is the precondition of the eschaton. This conclusion is better associated with Mk 13:10, where the temporal indicator πρῶτον appears; see Kümmel, *Promise and Fulfillment*, p. 84 and n. 220.

that the command to preach given in 10:7 continues in the new era and that the preaching will be addressed to Jews and gentiles alike. Hare and Harrington, employing 24:14 as evidence that the mission will not continue to the Jews, counter this claim with two suggestions: first, that although "the phrase *pasin tois ethnesin* could conceivably include Israel...some contrast between Israel and the whole world is implied"; and second, that "the assumption underlying 24:14 (and Mk 13:10) is that the Jewish nation in Palestine has *already* heard the gospel."[54]

Neither of these suggestions is fully supported by the text. Unlike the rest of the gospel, which refers to the era of Israel and so preserves the privilege of the Jews in salvation history, the eschatological discourse is concerned entirely with the new era and so appropriately eliminates any distinction between Israel and the rest of humanity. Hare and Harrington's second claim makes a subtle shift from Israel as a nation or people to Israel as a geographically bound community: neither gentiles nor the Jews of the diaspora had heard the gospel message during the time of Jesus. If Matthew is in fact a product of the diaspora community in Antioch, Hare and Harrington's geographical focus becomes even more difficult to support. Nor can their theory account for the very problematic comment in 10:23b that the disciples "will not have gone through all the cities (οὐ μὴ τελέσητε τὰς πόλεις) in Israel before the Son of Man comes." If this verse is consistent with the rest of the gospel, all the Jews in Palestine will not have "already" heard the message; their time for evangelization will follow the resurrection. Finally, Meier observes that Matthew 24 concerns the mission of the disciples, and "in the immediate context of 24:14, there is no

---

[54]"Make Disciples," pp. 363, 366; cf. Green, *The Gospel*, p. 199.

explicit mention of an earlier, separate mission to the Jews."[55] There is, in fact, no mention of an earlier mission of the disciples anywhere in the first gospel (cf. 11:1).

The inclusion of the Jews in all facets of the eschatological era receives indirect support from the description of the apocalyptic signs in 24:15-26. Most significant is the warning in verse 20: "Pray that your flight may not be in winter or on a sabbath." The verse does not, as Giblin claims, juxtapose a "world perspective" to a "specifically Judean perspective,"[56] particularly since diaspora Jews and Judaizing gentiles also kept the Sabbath, nor does it indicate that the congreagation is a "strict Jewish-Christian community" with all the baggage of antipathy toward gentiles attached to that term. Rather, Matt 24:20 complements such passages as 5:17-20: the church comprised of both Jews and gentiles preserves, interprets, and obeys the biblical Law.[57]

The heavenly portents which accompany this earthly struggle to keep the Sabbath continue the universalistic theme of the passage. W. D. Davies notes that the lightning which comes from the east (ἀπὸ ἀνατολῶν) and shines as far as the west (ἕως δυσμῶν, 24:27) indicates the nonlocalized appearance of the Son of Man.[58] The verse also subtly recalls the inclusion of both gentiles and the marginal members of the Jewish community in the church of the new era: from the Magi who come "from the east" (ἀπὸ ἀνατολῶν) in 2:1 to the Romans in the west to that undefined, mobile "many" who join the

---

[55]"Nations or Gentiles," p. 99 n. 16.

[56]"Theological Perspective," p. 657 n. 44.

[57]Bornkamm, "End-Expectation," p. 22; Green, *The Gospel*, p. 200; and Schweizer, "Observance of the Law," p. 214.

[58]*Setting*, p. 152.

patriarchs at the eschatological banquet (8:11). And just as the entire world will view this apocalyptic portent, so 24:30-31 indicates that everyone will be affected by it. The category of those who mourn (24:30) is not, as Hill proposes, restricted to unbelieving Jews as it is in Zech 12:10-12. "Tribes" (αἱ φυλαὶ) is not a technical term for the Jewish community in the first gospel (cf. 19:28), and the universalistic context eliminates the possibility that the text is concerned only with diaspora Jews.[59] The elect who, according to the following verse (24:31), are gathered from the four winds include both Jews and gentiles; the wind continues to blow both on Palestine and on the diaspora communities as well as on the gentiles. The tribes who mourn, consequently, are those members of both Jewish and gentile groups who have not acted upon the message of the gospel.

Following the list of apocalyptic signs, Matthew offers several examples of the process by which the final judgment will occur (24:40-51). In no instance is the ethnic background or even the confessional orientation of the person saved or damned admissable evidence; the complete universalism of the discourse is maintained. Clark's suggestion that the faithful slave of 24:45 represents the "Gentile Christian who stands ready for the imminent coming of his Lord, while the wicked slave...represents recalcitrant Judaism condemned in wailing and gnashing of teeth to the lot of the 'hypocrites' (24:51)"[60] should therefore be rephrased. Although the reference to the hypocrites in 24:51 is not directly applied to scribes and Pharisees, the association of the verse with Matthew 23 is unavoidable. The underlying theme in the

---

[59]Hill, *The Gospel*, p. 322; against his interpretation see Manson, *Sayings of Jesus*, p. 242. Argyle, *The Gospel*, p. 185, connects the verse with the universalistic Isa 11:12.

[60]"Gentle Bias," p. 167.

eschatological discourse is that the social category of leaders is the group destined for damnation. The wicked servant who exploits the absence of the master by lording it over the others in the household is a cipher for any patriarchal system and not for the Jewish community. Finally, according to 24:3 the discourse is given to the disciples privately (κατ' ἰδίαν) and, by extension, to the church. The disciples were warned in 23:1 to avoid exploiting their leadership roles, and in the following chapter the evangelist repeats the message.

These several observations have a direct bearing on the interpretation of the three parables in Matthew 25. Like the men in the field (24:40), the women at the mill (24:41), and the servants waiting for their master (24:45-51), the characters who populate the pericopes of 25:1-46 are separated in the new era·according to faith manifest in action and not according to ethnic group, church affiliation, or religious confession.

Matthew 25:1-13

According to Jeremias, the foolish women in the allegory of the ten virgins early on came to represent Israel, and the wise women symbolized the gentiles; Manson, noting the variant in 25:1 which states the women went to greet not only the groom but also the bride, conjectures that the bride represents true Israel, the ten women gentile converts, and the five among them who are wise those who accept "Jewish-Christian conformity to the law."[61] However, neither the context, nor the images -- oil, lamps, the bridegroom, the women -- in the parable, nor its vocabulary connote ethnic

---

[61]Jeremias, *Rediscovering the Parables*, p. 39; Manson, *Sayings of Jesus*, p. 244.

categories. Matthew 25:1-13 repeats a central theme of the first gospel: doing the will of God by actively manifesting faith.

The ten virgins are not only connected to the two women grinding at the mill in the previous chapter (24:41), they are also framed by accounts of faithful and faithless servants (24:45-51; 25:14-30). These juxtapositions first confirm the unlikelihood that the virgins can be ethnically categorized: the women at the mill, for example, have no Jewish or gentile markers. Analyzing the symbolic vocabulary of the pericope and concentrating on the interpretation of the oil, which the foolish virgins lack and which the wise virgins will not share, for understanding the allegory, K. Paul Donfried confirms this observation.[62] Although "oil" does not appear elsewhere in the New Testament's symbolic repertoire, "light" and "lamps" -- its two corollaries in 25:1-3 -- are specifically mentioned in 5:14-16. These earlier verses establish the themes reiterated in the fifth discourse: that the church has a worldwide focus and that all the earth's inhabitants will be judged according to the same standard of good works. Jeremias proposes that 5:14-15 refers to the eschatological ingathering of the nations,[63] but the two verses do not address the ethnic makeup of the recipients of the light; indeed, the concern is not with the recipients at all. Emphasis falls on the senders: the Jews addressed in the crowd and, by extension, the members of the church. This focus on the Jewish people is also supported by a comparison of Matt 5:15 with Mk 4:21 and Lk 11:33. While Mark indicates simply that the lamp is "brought in" (ἔρχεται), the third gospel suggests that the lamp provides light for those

---

[62]"The Allegory of the Ten Virgins (Matt 25:1-13) as a Summary of Matthean Theology," *JBL* 93 (1974): 424-27.

[63]*Jesus' Promise*, p. 66.

outside the house, so "that those who enter may see the light." This reading appears to anticipate conversions from among the gentiles. Matthew however, stresses the lamp which "gives light to all in the house" and so retains an emphasis on the house of Israel.[64]

Connections between Matt 25:1-13 and 7:13-27 are also numerous, and the shared imagery mitigates against interpreting the parable in ethnic terms. The distinction between wise and foolish individuals (7:24-27), the rejection of those not adequately equipped with good deeds (7:17, 21-23), the closed door (cf. 7:13-14), and even the confessional cry "Lord Lord" (7:22) by no means indicate that the Jews in particular have been or will be rejected. Schweizer proposes that the wolves mentioned in 7:15 symbolize gentiles (cf. Jer 5:6) as well as faithless leaders in general (Ezek 22:27-28; Zeph 3:3-4; Jn 10:12; Acts 20:29).[65] While the latter interpretation is in harmony with the gospel's condemnation of those in elite positions, a particular reference to gentiles -- as distinguished from gentile leaders -- is not. The social axis indicates that salvation and condemnation transcend both religious affiliation and ethnic category; gentile leaders who abuse their position are condemned along with Jewish leaders who also fail to bear good fruit.

That the characters who populate this parable are women does not undermine Matthew's distinction between elite and marginal. In the first gospel, faithfulness is not directly associated with sex or economic position any more than it is with ethnic origin. Just as Jews can be either for Jesus or against him, so too can gentiles, men and women, servants and

---

[64]See Manson, *Sayings of Jesus*, p. 93, followed by Hill, *The Gospel*, p. 116.

[65]*Good News*, p. 186.

masters. While Peter's mother-in-law and the centurion of chapter 8 signify the marginalized position of women and gentiles within the official socio-religious system of Palestinian Judaism, they do not indicate that all women and all gentiles are or will be among the saved. Similarly, the equal status of the ten virgins, like that of the servants with the talents and the women at the mill, indicates that group membership does not guarantee salvation. Once people are within the system, be they virgins responsible for keeping their lamps full or servants entrusted with the master's talents, they must remain both watchful and active. For those within the church, the faith must have an active corollary; protestations of "Lord Lord" are insufficient.

Matthew 25:14-30

The parable of the talents appears within the same universalistic, eschatological context as the pericope it follows, and it makes the same point as that earlier narrative. Matthew 25:14-30 is not "part of Jesus' denunciations of the scribes, who had 'buried' the Law under the mass of their traditions and regulations."[66] It denounces in vivid terms church members who -- to extend the metaphor of chapter 5 -- put their lamp under a bushel rather than allow it to shine before all. A distinction is made among the servants based on their activities, not on their ethnic background or religious orientation. Nor are these activities symbolically connected, as Fenton suggests, to the Oral versus the Written Law. Indeed, using his same criteria of analysis, one might conclude that the first two servants are to be commended for proliferating

[66]So Fenton, *Saint Matthew*, p. 398.

legal requirements within the church. Further, Matt 23:2-3 indicates that the evangelist thinks quite highly of this "mass of traditions and regulations." The last verse of the pericope confirms the observation that the thrust of 25:14-30 crosses ethnic lines: the slothful servant will take up residence in the same area where others, Jews and gentiles alike, who displayed only their talents for stasis and self-protection have been sent: the outer darkness where no light can be seen (25:30; cf. 8:12; 22:13).

Matthew 25:31-46

The third of the three eschatological parables repeats several of the gospel's principal themes: an association of the phrase πάντα τὰ ἔθνη with the new era, an eschatological judgment that distinguishes saved from damned on the basis of faith manifested in action, and a body of instruction for a *corpus mixtum*, a church comprised of Jews and gentiles, good and bad. Debates on the specific interpretation of these themes continue, however. While some suggest that the final judgment between the sheep and the goats is universal, others maintain that even in this eschatological context the Jews form a separate category. Rather than judged on the same basis as the gentiles and/or the church, the Jews are already judged, and damned.

According to Matt 25:32, πάντα τὰ ἔθνη will be gathered at the coming of the Son of Man. He, in turn, will separate this group into the sheep, bound for salvation, and the goats, bound for hell. Jeremias, who connects the parable with the eschatological pilgrimage of the gentiles to Zion, renders along with a host of others the problematic phrase "all the gentiles"; the final judgment upon the Jews has already been pronounced.[67] This interpretation is based on three claims: that ἔθνη in Matthew's gospel necessarily means gentiles; that "just as there are three kinds of humanity -- Jews, Christians, and pagans -- so there will be three separate judgments," with 25:31-46 addressing the criteria by which those [pagans] unacquainted with the gospel will be judged;[68] and that those being judged in 25:31-46 have had no direct contact with either Jesus or his gospel.[69]

The appeal to the translation of the term ἔθνη is the weakest of the three points.[70] The word must be analyzed each time it appears, and the universalistic/eschatological thrust of this section of the gospel commends the reading "nations" rather than "gentiles." Because the connection drawn within the eschatological discourse (24:7) between kingdoms and "nations" includes Palestine -- this country is not merely a

---

67Jeremias, *The Parables of Jesus* (New York: Scribner's, 1966), pp. 206, 209; cf. *Jesus' Promise*, pp. 64-68; and see Blauw, *Missionary Nature*, p. 70; Gaston, "Messiah of Israel," p. 32; Green, *The Gospel*, p. 206; Brandon, *Jesus and the Zealots*, pp. 182, 200; Hare and Harrington, "Make Disciples," p. 363; Hooker, "Uncomfortable Words," p. 363 n. 2 ("should probably be understood as meaning the Gentiles; certainly it includes them"). Manson, *Sayings of Jesus*, pp. 249-50, reads "all the gentiles" but proposes that "true Israel is covered by the concept 'Son of Man' interpreted as 'the people of the saints of the Most High' while the Jews who have rejected the Kingdom as preached to them by Jesus and His disciples are reckoned among the Gentiles."

68Hare, "Rejection of the Jews," p. 44; cf. Hare and Harrington, "Make Disciples," p. 363.

69Hare and Harrington, "Make Disciples," pp. 364-65; Wilson, *Gentiles*, p. 5; Jeremias, *Rediscovering the Parables*, pp. 162-63.

70See O. L. Cope, "Matthew xxv:31-46, 'The Sheep and the Goats' Reinterpreted," *NovTest* 11 (1969): 37.

kingdom, it is one that had recently "risen up against [another] kingdom" -- it is more likely that a consistent translation of the term ἔθνη as "nation" rather than "gentile" is here warranted.

The second claim is supported by appeals to three bodies of literature. From the Hebrew Bible Hare and Harrington cite Joel 4 (MT) and Ezekiel 39, passages suggesting that the (gentile) nations (גוים) will be judged in regard to their treatment of Israel. From the Pseudepigrapha, they cite the two judgments mentioned in II Baruch 72 (Israel and the nations), and compare them with similar motifs in IV Ezra 13:33-49; PsSol 17:27-28; and TBenj (Armenian) 10:8-9; as well as with Enoch 90:20-27; and 91:12-15. And from the Christian scriptures they cite I Pet 4:17; I Cor 6:2-3 (cf. II Cor 5:10); Rom 2:9-10; and Matt 19:28.[71] Hare and Harrington are both thorough and correct in noting that several ancient sources depict separate judgments for Israel and the gentiles. However, while the first gospel follows the pattern of these other scenes, Matthew's version has a cross-ethnic cast. The people who represent Jesus in 25:40, 45 take the place of the prophets' "persecuted Israel," and their description further serves as a connection to all other marginal, Jewish as well as gentile, characters in the gospel. Hunger, thirst, outsider status ("stranger," ξένος), nakedness, sickness, and imprisonment indicate that these least among the brothers and sisters have followed the models established by the Baptist

---

[71] Hare and Harrington, "Make Disciples," pp. 364-65. On the Christian interpolations in TBenj 10:9-10 and their connections with both the translation of πάντα τὰ ἔθνη and the *Sitz im Leben* of the Matthean community, see J. H. Charlesworth, "Christian and Jewish Self-Definition in Light of the Christian Additions to the Apocryphal Writings," in Sanders et al. (eds)., *Jewish and Christian Self-Definition*, vol. 2, p. 40.

and Jesus. Their description recalls those very people whose faith in Jesus has been commended in Matthew 8-9.[72]

This social rather than ethnic emphasis calls into question the claim that Matt 25:40 refers to the disciples who were preaching to the gentiles. While the disciples are included among the "least" (ἐλαχίστοι), the group need not be limited to missionaries and cannot be limited only to those who preach to the gentiles; Matt 10:40-42 applies the comparative version of the term, "little ones" (μικρός) to the twelve commissioned to evangelize the Jews. Because these "least ones" are economically, socially, and politically marginal to and excluded from positions of patriarchal leadership, the parable's emphasis falls not on Jews and gentiles but on the divisions established by the social axis.[73] It is the responsibility of everyone, member of the church or not, to care for those somehow outside of the prevailing system. Again, confessionalism is subordinated to action.

This social rather than ethnic or group focus is not contradicted by Hare and Harrington's appeal to Matt 19:28.

---

[72]Those interpreting the "least" as referring to anyone in need include Meier, *Vision of Matthew*, p. 178 n. 206, "Nations or Gentiles," p. 99 and n. 18 (citing Grundmann, Bonnard, Schweizer, and Jeremias, *Parables*, p. 207); and Wilson, *Gentiles*, p. 5. On connecting the "least" with the disciples see Cope, "Matthew xxv," p. 39; Jeremias, *Jesus' Promise*, p. 24 (disciples preaching to gentiles); Thompson, "Historical Perspective," p. 258; Hare and Harrington, "Make Disciples," p. 365 n. 13; W. D. Davies, *Setting*, p. 98 (on Christians in a pagan environment); and the extensive discussion in Michaels, "Apostolic Hardships," pp. 27-37.

[73]Cope, "Sheep and the Goats," p. 37, states that πάντα τὰ ἔθνη "are those *other than the brothers of the Son of Man*....When this is seen, the question of whether or not Israel is included becomes academic."

Although the church is not elsewhere in the gospel explicitly referred to as Israel, Jesus' comment to his disciples that "in the new world (παλιγγενεσία), when the Son of Man will sit on his throne of glory, you who have followed me will also sit on twelve thrones, judging the twelve tribes of Israel" maintains a cross-ethnic ecclesiology. The verse most probably concerns the fate of the church (cf. Rev 7:4-8; Rom 2:29; Gal 3:29; 6:16; Phil 3:3; I Pet 1:1; James 1:1) and not a separate judgment of the Jews.[74] Had Matthew meant the "twelve tribes" to indicate Jews as a corporate community distinct from the church, then the mention of Ἰουδαίοι (cf. 28:15) would have been more appropriate. The conclusion that the judgment in 19:28 is applicable only to the Jews also contradicts the theory that the Jews have rejected the deity and in turn have been rejected. Judgment in the first gospel means that some will be saved, some will not. Even the following verse, 19:30, indicates that many -- among the "twelve tribes of Israel" -- who are now last will be among the first. If the reference is therefore only to the Jews, then the conclusion that the Jews as a corporate community have lost the chance at salvation is inconsistent with the interpretation of this passage. Meier points to yet another problem with inconsistency: completing this particular argument against Hare and Harrington's second point is his appeal to other statements in the first gospel that

---

[74]Manson, *Sayings of Jesus*, p. 217, cf. Hill, *The Gospel*, p. 284; Fenton, *Saint Matthew*, p. 317; Jeremias, *Jesus' Promise*, p. 21; Meier, *Vision of Matthew*, p. 141 and n. 151; and Green, *The Gospel*, p. 173, who takes a reverse approach: "This for Matthew must mean the new Israel, since he regards the judgment of the old as already executed." On the pre-Matthean version (and Lk 22:28, 30) as perhaps referring to the Jews, see Kümmel, *Promise and Fulfillment*, p. 47; Manson, *Sayings of Jesus*, p. 216.

concern a single, universal judgment: 8:11-12; 11:20-24; 12:41-42; and 13:36-43.[75]

The juxtaposition of 19:28-30 with the parable of the laborers in the vineyard (20:1-16) supports the identification of the twelve tribes of Israel with the church. Again, the parable is often interpreted in terms of ethnic categories: the laborers who work the entire day are those Jews who have remained faithful to God, and the latecomers are the gentiles who join with these earlier disciples in the new era.[76] However, given the first evangelist's social thrust, the richness of the message appears only when ethnic categories are downplayed. Not only does the parable break down economic hierarchies by depicting the equal payment of all, it elevates those on the outside of the system to a place equal to those within. The original workers have not lost anything; it is the new workers who have gained. Moreover, those laborers called in the third, sixth, ninth, and eleventh hours are those who heeded the call of the householder and replaced their "standing idle" (ἑστῶτας...ἀργούς, 20:3) for working in the vinyard. The emphasis consequently falls both on their shift from stasis to mobility and on the equality within the vineyard system of all those who enter regardless of the time they do so.

The third argument, that Matt 25:31-46 concerns the judgment of the gentiles only and so indicates that the Jews have already been damned, claims that those who comprise πάντα τὰ ἔθνη have not heard the message of the gospel. Yet in the eschatological context of the parable the missionary endeavors of the new era are complete: the disciples will have followed Jesus' command to evangelize not only the Jews but

---

[75]"Nations or Gentiles," p. 100.

[76]See Green, *The Gospel*, p. 173; Carlston, "Interpreting the Gospel," p. 7; Argyle, *The Gospel*, p. 151.

also the gentiles (28:19), and the gospel will have been preached to the whole world (24:14). Consequently, while the message has gone out, those from all nations being judged have failed to fulfill all its requirements. Those judged to be among the goats may well have said "Lord, Lord," but they did not care for the Lord's "least ones." The comments made by both righteous and sinners in 25:37-39, 44 -- "Lord, when did we see you hungry or thirsty...?" -- do not indicate that the sheep and the goats did not hear the message of the gospel. They rather indicate the pragmatism of the first evangelist. Matthew is aware both that membership in the church does not guarantee salvation (cf. 7:21-23; 18:17; 25:11-12; etc.) and that a major danger facing the survival of the new community is stasis with its attendant problems of complacency and exploitative hierarchies.

Thus the eschatological predictions and the parables of judgment reinforce the gospel's theme: salvation is obtained by those of all the nations -- Jews, pagans, and Christians -- who demonstrate their faith by doing good works.[77] Group membership, be it through the synagogue, the church, or gentile descent, is no guarantee of salvation. And again, the argument that the first gospel both depicts the rejection of the Jews and proclaims a Great Commission limited to the gentiles is refuted.

---

[77]Hill, *The Gospel*, p. 331; Meier, "Nations or Gentiles," pp. 99-101; Thompson, "Historical Perspective," p. 258 n. 31; Wilson, *Gentiles*, p. 5; Trilling, *Das Wahre Israel*, p. 14; and Rohde's summary, *Rediscovering*, p. 50, of Bornkamm, "End-Expectation," pp. 23f. See also Manson, *Sayings of Jesus*, p. 249; J. A. T. Robinson, "The 'Parable' of the Sheep and the Goats," *NTS* 2 (1955/56): 225; Cope, "Matthew xxv," pp. 32-34.

VIII

Jewish Guilt, Jewish Innocence, and the True Israel

The seven pericopes most often cited as examples of ethnic divisions within the gospel's program of salvation history do not support the theory that Matthew's deity has rejected the Jews. The mission of the church continues to include the Jews and has been extended to "all the gentiles," such that by the end of time "all the nations" will have heard the message of the gospel. Consequently, in the eschatological judgment distinctions between Jews and gentiles are eliminated. Salvation for all people will be based on good works and not membership in a particular ethnic group, religious institution, or social class.

These observations do not, however, complete the picture of Matthean soteriology; they instead lead to two further areas of debate. First, although God does not reject the Jewish corporate community, have the Jews as a whole rejected God? And if they have, is this the prerequisite for the gentile mission? In other words, has Jesus' mission been restricted to the Jews *in order that* their guilt be established?[1] Second, since the seven pericopes indicate that the rejection of Jesus'

---

[1]See Trilling, *Das Wahre Israel*, esp. pp. 103-5, 138-40, followed by Hare, *Jewish Persecution*, pp. 146 n. 1, 151. See also the discussions in Wilson, *Gentiles*, p. 8; Gaston, "Messiah of Israel," p. 32 n. 20 (following H. Schlier, "Die Entscheidung für die Heidenmission in der Urchristenheit," in *Die Zeit der Kirche* [Freiburg: Herder, 1942], pp. 90-107); Green, *The Gospel*, p. 147; Hooker, "Uncomfortable Words," p. 364.

message crosses ethnic categories, what is the relationship between the church and those who refuse the gospel message? Is the church the true Israel, or is it a new community distinct from Israel and "all the nations" of the world?

As the argument that the Jews are rejected rests on particular narratives within the first gospel, so too the complementary theory that the Jews have rejected God is principally based on three passages: 11:1-12:50; 13:1-51; and, especially, 27:25. Analysis of this material has led to the conclusion that Matthew indicts Judaism based on religious rather than national criteria: "The Jew is indicted because of what he has done with God's gifts to him, not because he is a Jew."[2] However, the distinction is both too facile and not supported by a close reading of the various pericopes involved. The Jews claim descent from Abraham (3:9) and so do not separate the nation from the religion; the Romans make the same connection but emphasize ethnic rather than religious matters (27:11, 37); and Matthew's temporal axis concerns the Jews' national identity rather than their religious practices. Finally, 11:1-12:50; 13:1-51; and 27:25 do not indicate that the Jews have rejected "God's gifts." Only some among this group have chosen to reject the gospel, and these are the leaders, the static, and the complacent.

The mission to the gentiles requires only the positive change in Jesus' position and the fulfillment of the promises on which the temporal axis is based; it needs no justification such as the completion of the guilt of Israel. In turn, because Jews and gentiles are equals in the new era, the time of Israel -- as well as the existence of a body called "Israel" -- ceases to exist in the gospel's purview. The Great Commission inaugurates not only a new era but a new body: not Israel, not a

---

[2]Franzmann, *Discipleship*, p. 172.

Jewish or a gentile group, but the ἐκκλησία, the church.

Matthew 11:1-12:50

In the critical literature, the narrative section following the second discourse is often interpreted as depicting the Jews' failure to accept the good news of the *Basileia*. Although Jesus has clearly presented his message in the synagogues of Galilee, has explained his gospel in the Sermon on the Mount, and has demonstrated his authority to heal and to control nature, all segments of Israel -- from the general "this generation" (11:16) to Jesus' own family (12:46-50) -- are seen to reject both messenger and message.[3] This theory downplays the distinction among characters drawn in Matthew 11-12: the crowds continue to follow Jesus and he continues to heal them and preach to them; only the Jewish leaders and groups associated with them remain hostile or unconvinced. Thus the discourse in chapter 10 leads into the practical implications of separating elites from marginals, static from mobile, and so prepares the way for the parables of the *Basileia* in chapter 13.

According to the first verse of Matthw 11, "When Jesus had finished instructing his twelve disciples, he went on from there to teach and preach in their cities." Noting that, unlike in

---

[3]Kingsbury, *Matthew*, pp. 48, 50-51; and "Structure of Matthew's Gospel," pp. 462-63; cf. Fenton, *Saint Matthew*, p. 173; Hill, *The Gospel*, p. 197; Clark, "Gentile Bias," pp. 167-68; Meier, *Vision of Matthew*, pp. 165-66; Albright and Mann, *Matthew*, p. 160. See also Hummel, *Auseinandersetzung*, pp. 122-23; Walker, *Heilsgeschichte*, pp. 52-53 (on 12:22-24); and, on the failure of the mission to the Jews, Hare, *Jewish Persecution*, pp. 128-29; Garland, *Intention*, p. 89 (citing E. Kinniburgh, "Hard Sayings III," *Theology* 66 [1983]: 416).

4:23 and 9:35, "to heal" is not mentioned among the list of Jesus' activities, Fenton proposes the evangelist deliberately omitted the third verb to demonstrate that "Jesus is beginning to withdraw his miraculous power from Israel" because of their unbelief.[4] Yet the mention of healing is unnecessary since Jesus continues to heal Jews (12:9-14, 22-23; 15:30-31; 17:14-18; 20:29-34; 21:14) as Fenton himself notes. Further, because the conventional missionary descriptions are presented in chapters 4 and 9 as well as confirmed in the commands to the disciples in 10:1, the reader is prepared to fill in the mention of healings in 11:1. Unlike the addition of the command in 28:20 enjoining the disciples to "teach," the absence of a frequently repeated term does not carry the same weight: in the former case, something new has clearly been added; in the latter nothing has been in fact removed. Indeed, the emphasis on healings plus exorcisms in 10:1 suggests not the separation of Jesus from the Jews but the beginning of the transfer of responsibility from Jesus to his followers. Finally, there is no indication either in this section of the gospel or in the material preceding it that the Jewish people, as opposed to the leaders, have rejected Jesus or he them. Quite the opposite: Jewish crowds have followed Jesus (chapters 5-7); individual Jews have demonstrated their faith in him (chapters 8-9), and Jesus himself has stressed the close connection between his mission and his people (10:6, 23). Thus for Jesus to begin to separate himself from the Jews in 11:1 is premature at best and inconsistent given his own exhortations in 10:5b-6.

Any mention of healing in 11:1 would appear redundant in light of Jesus' response in 11:4 to the Baptist's disciples. Confirming the gospel's separation not of Jesus from the Jews but of elites from marginals, Matt 11:2-6 recapitulates 9:14-

---

[4] *Saint Matthew*, p. 174.

17 by demonstrating the failure of John and his followers to recognize what the tax collectors, prostitutes, and readers already know. The disciples and their master have heard of Jesus' healing the blind, the lame, the deaf, lepers, even the dead, but they remain overly concerned with confessionalism. They want to know to whom they should address their petitionary "Lord, Lord." Jesus, in turn, responds by emphasizing the reversals of fortune: those on the hygienic, political, and economic peripheries continue to be brought into contact with the *Basileia*.

When Jesus explicitly mentions that through his mission the "blind receive their sight...and the deaf hear," he begins his response to the Baptist's disciples with the comment "Go and tell John what you see and hear" (11:4). The implication of the disciples' blindness subtly connects them to the unperceiving Pharisees of 15:14 and 23:16 as well as, potentially, to those among the crowds who "shall indeed hear but never understand" (13:14). Also conveying an implicit connection between the disciples and the Jewish leadership is Jesus' parting comment, "blessed is the one who takes no offense at me" (11:6). The Pharisees take offense at Jesus because he dines with tax collectors and sinners (9:11), the followers of the Baptist question why they and the Pharisees fast while Jesus' disciples do not (9:12), and both queries presuppose a judgment of scandalous action: Jesus is not behaving in a socially acceptable manner for a religious leader. Thus Jesus warns these groups that their own social agenda is misguided; fasting is less important than fulfilling the demand of "mercy, not sacrifice." Similarly, in the eschatological discourse Jesus will speak of righteousness manifested by visiting those in prison (25:36). John's concern and that of his disciples should have been with those imprisoned with him, not on the particulars of Jesus' person.

Matthew's social emphasis is continued, albeit less dramatically, by Jesus' address to the crowds (ὄχλοι) in 11:7-30. Here John the Baptist functions as an explicitly positive example. Just as membership within the Baptist's circle does not guarantee salvation, so too criticism of this same group will not grant entry into the *Basileia*. One negative evaluation based on stereotypes that preserve the oppressive status quo cannot be substituted for another. Jesus' reassessment of John, which highlights his peripheral status -- he is not dressed in the clothes of courtiers and does not sit in "kings' houses" (11:8) -- returns the subject to the social axis. Unlike his disciples, John is not primarily categorized as a group member; he is both a solitary prophet and unique "among those born of women" (11:11). Therefore John, as well as his disciples if they modify their beliefs, have a good chance of perceiving correctly.

This possibility of redemption may even be extended to the residents of Chorazin, Beth-Saida, and Capernaum. Like the disciples of the Baptist, they are compared unfavorably with the marginal and the mobile, have not realized the implications of what they have seen and heard, and are associated with the Jewish leaders. Too, like the Baptist's disciples, these people might still repent. The cities are also connected to Jesus' own followers in 11:1 through the pronoun "their" (αὐτῶν); the antecedent can only be to the twelve. In turn, through a similar grammatical juxtaposition the members of "this generation" in 11:16 are connected not with those who reject the music of the pipes and the wailing but with those who played the music and mourned. Symbolically, "this generation" includes the followers of Jesus. Thus the evangelist in several ways both indicates that even those now separated from the *Basileia* have the potential to join and confirms that the mission to the Jews will continue.

While the potential conversion of the crowds and disciples is expressed, the chapter also indicates the separation the gospel message occasions between elites and marginals: 11:19 describes the dissociation of the static who would neither dance nor mourn (11:17) from tax collectors and the sinners; 11:25 distinguishes those who claim wisdom and understanding (σοφῶν καὶ συνετῶν) and so represent the religious and political elite from the babies (νηπίοις) who either do not know the traditions of intepreting the Law[5] or who refrain from exploiting their knowledge. And Jesus offers his appeal specifically to those who "labor and are heavy laden" (11:28). While the connotations of this last reference immediately concern economic oppression, the final emphasis remains on the distinction between the general population and the leadership. In 11:29, the heavy yoke is connected not with physical labor but with the prevention of "rest for your souls" (ἀνάπαυσις ταῖς ψυχαῖς ὑνῶν); in 23:4 these burdens are explicitly identified as Pharisaic creations. For the first gospel, social distinctions go beyond economic standing; even the rich, such as Joseph of Arimathea, can still be separated from the ruling class.

The burden of the controversy story that follows Jesus' invitation to those who are heavy laden continues the critique of those in positions of patriarchal authority. In chapter 12, the Pharisees appear as the gospel's principal representatives of the elite, and again, as in chapters 2, 8-9, the ever-present religious leaders (12:2, 14, 24, 38) are contrasted to rather than associated with the crowds who follow Jesus. The opening pericope continues the discussion of the Pharisaic yoke. In Matt 12:1-8 the representatives of the religious establishment accuse the disciples of transgressing the

---

[5]Gundry, *Matthew*, p. 216.

Sabbath by "plucking heads of grain," by engaging in the labor of harvesting (Ex 20:8-11). Jesus' response, based on I Sam 21:1-6, concerns not only religious egalitarianism but also the misapplication of Sabbath regulations created when social rank supersedes personal need. Just as David's hunger motivated him to eat the showbread set aside for the priests, so the disciples' need supersedes the Pharisees' complaint. Manifesting his compliance with biblical precedent, Jesus substitutes one passage for another (cf. the divorce regulations in 19:3-9) and announces that not only the priests (12:4, 5) but everyone is entitled to the full benefits of the Sabbath. The leadership has not lost any of its privileges; instead, the people who are not in positions of authority or members of elite groups now share in priestly prerogatives.

The controversy story ends with a comparison of Jesus' authority to that of the religious establishment. After invoking Temple practices (12:5) to justify his disciples' action, Jesus announces that the Temple itself is transcended by his own power (12:6, 8). Since the institution is replaced and the privileges of the priesthood have been extended to all the people, the category of "priest" with its elitist implications is rendered meaningless. Nor does the domain of the Pharisees, the self-given authority to interpret the Law, escape Jesus' notice. First, he specifically mentions that their somewhat selective interpretations can be both inadequate and harmful (12:7), and he then replaces their earthly claims to authority with his heavenly mandate (12:8). These comments do not, however, contradict Jesus' contention that the scribes and Pharisees sit on Moses' seat (23:2). While their general interpretation of orthopraxy is to be followed, Matthew requires that church members judge any such pronouncement according to the criterion of "mercy not sacrifice" (9:13; 12:7). Thus, each time this quotation of Hos 6:6 appears, it comments on a Pharisaically engineered distinction between groups. In chapter 9, the saying is in the context of Jesus' dining with tax collectors and sinners; in chapter 12 it concerns the disciples' plucking grain on the Sabbath.

The next pericope in chapter actualizes Jesus' claims. The healing of the man with the withered hand in the Pharisees' domain (12:9-14) proves the Son of Man to be Lord of the Sabbath but does not, as K. M. Bishop suggests, indicate an increasing separation between Jesus and his people. According to Bishop, since Jewish readers would know that no member of their community would break the Law by permitting Jesus to heal on the Sabbath, the handicapped man must have been a gentile employed by the Pharisees; neither he nor most of those cured later that day (12:15) were Jews.[6] This suggestion not only ignores the distinction between crowds and rulers, the absence in the pericope, and even in the surrounding narratives, of a reference to gentiles, the observation that people in Galilean synagogues are more likely to be Jews rather than gentiles, the injuction in 10:5b-6, and the fact that Jesus too was a Jew who had just in the previous pericope expressed his fidelity to scriptural models, it also presupposes a monolithic characterization of first-century Judaism. Just as the Jews in the gospel accounts disagree over the messianic claims made for Jesus, so they disagree over the proper interpretation of the Law. In 12:9-14, Jesus offers his own interpretation of Sabbath regulations as well as remains consistent with his emphasis on rest (11:28): he heals the man without touching him, and so does not violate the day of rest by "working." Neither the man nor Jesus can be classified as "un-Jewish"; they have merely thwarted the Pharisees' plan.

Following Jesus' successful demonstration that his

---

[6]"St. Matthew and the Gentiles," *ET* 59 (1947-48): 249.

authority surpasses theirs, the Pharisees leave the synagogue to plot his destruction (12:14). Jesus, however, remains inside, surrounded by Jewish people in the Jewish house of worship. When he does withdraw (ἀνεχώρησεν), he is accompanied by many (12:15). Spatially as well as religiously, therefore, Jesus and the people are connected, and both are distinguished from the Pharisees. That Jesus continues to perform healings -- of the "many" (πολλοί) or, according to several texts, "many crowds" (ὄχλοι πολλοί), he "healed them all" -- separates the crowd even more from the interests of the religious elite. Through the hyperbolic suggestion in 12:15 that "all" among these "many" required healing, Matthew creates yet another allusion to the debates with the Pharisees in chapter 9. There Jesus explicitly states that the mandate of "mercy, not sacrifice" involves caring for those whom the religious establishment does not deem "righteous": people identified as the "sick" and who are "in need of a physician" (9:10-13). "All" have been subjected to the indoctrination of the Pharisees and the control of the Roman Empire (symbolized by the several references to tax collectors); all are therefore in need of Jesus' ministrations.

The crowd's approval and the Pharisees' plot provide the context for the fulfillment quotation in 12:18-21. Moreover, by framing the positive *future* references to gentiles[7] in verses 18 and 21 with negative *present* references to Pharisees (12:1-14; 24ff.), Matthew indicates that in the new era the

---

[7]Both Meier, "Nations or Gentiles," p. 95; and Hare and Harrington, "Make Disciples," p. 362, agree that the better translation of ἔθνη here is "gentiles." See the extensive discussion of the citation in J. Grindel, "Matthew 12, 18-21," *CBQ* 29 (1967): 110-15, as well as Cope, *Matthew, A Scribe*, pp. 34-36 (particularly on the difficulties of relating the verses to their narrative context); Stendahl, *School of St. Matthew*, pp. 39-40, 109-11, 114-15.

mission will be extended to the gentiles, and that both now and in the future the power of patriarchal leadership is broken. The gentiles are therefore not contrasted with the "many" Jewish people; they are separated from the Jewish ruling establishment.

Holding to the temporal axis, Matthew also connects the quotation from Isaiah with the motif of the "messianic secret." While Mark does not record the prophecy and so associates "and he strictly ordered them not to make him known" (Mk 3:12) with the preceding material concerning the healing of the crowds, Matthew connects Jesus' command in 12:16 explicitly with the quotation that follows: "This was to fulfill what was spoken by the prophet Isaiah" (12:17). Thus, Jesus both informs the crowds that in the future "he shall proclaim justice to the gentiles" (12:18) and that, for the present, these followers are not to bring the good news to non-Jews. The gentiles will "hope in his name" (12:21), but not yet. The focus of the narrative remains on the mission to the Jews.

The christological titles in the following pericope (Matt 12:22-29) reemphasize the Jewish context of Jesus' activities. At the healing of the blind and mute demoniac, "all the crowds" (πάντες οἱ ὄχλοι) are amazed and wonder if Jesus is the "son of David" (12:23); the title connects the people with the disciples who, like the Jewish king, ate the food reserved for the priests. The Pharisees also recognize royalty in Jesus, but associate him instead with the "ruler (ἄρχον) of demons," Beelzebul (12:24). Even this choice of name, "lord (Ba'al) the prince" or "lord of the divine realm," for the demonic ruler carries connotations of authority. Underlying the debate over the origins of Jesus' power is not merely the contrast between David and Beelzebul, it is also between "son" and "ruler" and so has implications for Matthew's social axis. The people associate Jesus with sonship and with David the ideal king who himself is able to recognize Jesus' authority (cf. 22:41-46). Thus the people see a "son"; their "blind guides" see only a threat to their own power.

Following Jesus' condemnation of these leaders, "some of the scribes and Pharisees" ask to see a sign. The reference to "some" (τινες) suggests that the leadership has become a "house divided against itself" (12:25), and that their "kingdom" will be replaced by the *Basileia* of Heaven. Although the pre-Matthean version of Jesus' response, the discussion of the sign of Jonah (12:38-40), may have highlighted the reaction of "non-Jews to a former Jewish prophet and a former Jewish king,"[8] the evangelist undercuts this ethnic reading by interpreting the sign as the period between Jesus' crucifixion and resurrection; of the synoptic writers, only Matthew states: "For as Jonah was three days and three nights in the belly of the whale, so will the Son of Man be three days and three nights in the heart of the earth" (12:40). Thus the discussion both condemns the Jewish leaders (cf. 16:4) and retains the emphasis on the restricted mission. The men from Nineveh -- presumably those who received Jonah's warning -- will condemn "this generation" of "scribes and Pharisees," but they will not do so until the judgment day (12:41).

That Matthew has eliminated the connection between the sign of Jonah and the gentile mission argues against Fenton's

---

[8]Cope, *Matthew, A Scribe*, p. 43, cf. pp. 33-40 and, on the pre-Matthean logia, pp. 43-44; cf. Cox, *The Gospel*, p. 91; Manson, *Teaching of Jesus*, p. 219; and *Sayings of Jesus*, pp. 89-92; Argyle, *The Gospel*, p. 98; J. Howton, "The Sign of Jonah," *ScottJT* 15 (1962): 288-304; N. Walker, "The Alleged Matthean Errata," *NTS* 9 (1962/63): 393; A. J. B. Higgins, "The Sign of the Son of Man (Mt xxiv, 30)," *NTS* 9 (1962/63): 381; Hill, *The Gospel*, pp. 219-20; Wilson, *Gentiles*, pp. 4-5; Kümmel, *Promise and Fulfillment*, p. 68; Jeremias, *Jesus' Promise*, p. 50 and nn. 3-5; Tilborg, *Jewish Leaders*, pp. 30-31.

interpretation of the next pericope. For Fenton, the possessed man of 12:43-45 is the symbolic equivalent of "this generation" (cf. 12:39, 42) of Jews, the exorcism is Jesus' ministry, the emptiness of the house is "the unbelief and unrepentance of the Jews, and their 'last state' is their condemnation at the eschatological judgment."[9] This interpretation -- although it is prefaced by the comment that 12:43-45 "continues to warn the scribes and Pharisees" -- suggests that not only the leadership but the Jewish people as a whole have rejected their God and that they in turn have been rejected. Fenton's theory is belied by both the form and the context of the parable. Seeking a symbolic correspondence between each element in the story and the external narrative is unnecessary; even Fenton offers no analogies for the unclean spirit, the waterless places, and the seven other spirits. Nor are these equivalents needed to make the passage comprehensible; it is a parable rather than an allegory. Further, some of the connections Fenton draws are not supported by the story itself: since Jesus notes that the house is "swept and put in order" the emptiness cannot symbolize unbelief or unrepentance. It is more likely that the empty house indicates those who accept Jesus' message but fail to take the next step and furnish it, that is, those whose statements of faith yield no active results. Thus the warning is not just to the leaders, it is applicable also to the people, as 12:46 indicates. The people must dissociate themselves from the leadership lest they become increasingly damaged. Finally, Tilborg notes that the difference between Matt 12:43-45 and Lk 11:24-26 is restricted to the apparently redactional assertion of Matt 12:45c, and concludes: "The sentence applies the parable to the leaders of the people, for the γενεᾷ πονηρᾷ

---

[9] *Saint Matthew*, p. 204; cf. Strecker, *Der Weg*, pp. 105-6; Green, *The Gospel*, p. 129.

[evil generation] of Mt 12:45 certainly refers to those people who have been addressed in Mt 12:39."[10] Those who now stand condemned are the leaders; the crowds are merely warned. A similar pattern with a double audience may be discerned in Matthew 23.

The last pericope of the chapter, the identification of Jesus' true family, supports Tilborg's narrowing of the direct referent in 12:45. Here the crowds neither reject Jesus nor are they rejected by him. While their full acceptance is not explicitly stated, it is hinted at in the opening remarks of chapter 13: "Great crowds (ὄχλοι πολλοί) gathered about him...and the whole crowd (πᾶς ὁ ὄχλος) stood on the beach" (13:2).[11] Matthew 12:46-50 sums up the composition of these great crowds: those individuals manifesting faith through action receive the distinction of being called the members of Jesus' family. It is the family tree, Jesus' mother and brothers who remain out on a limb (12:46-50), and not the fruit-bearing tree. Again, Matthew contrasts a static group who could claim special leadership privileges because of their relationship to Jesus, the family members who "stood outside" (εἱστήκεισαν ἔξω) both symbolically and literally, with a spiritual family united by service to the deity. Equality within the church is particularly reinforced by the description of those who do the will of the Father. The members of the new family are identified as Jesus' "brother, sister, and mother," but no one is called "father." Thus Matthew anticipates the later injunction to the disciples: "call no one your father on earth, for you have one Father, who is in heaven" (23:9).[12] In the *Basileia*,

---

[10] *Jewish Leaders*, p. 33, citing Walker, *Heilsgeschichte*, pp. 35-38.

[11] But see Kingsbury, *Matthew*, p. 51.

[12] Fiorenza, *In Memory of Her*, pp. 146-48.

patriarchal structures are replaced by a community of equals.

Matthew 13:1-51

Those scholars who see a widening separation between Jesus and the Jewish community find confirmation of their view in Matthew 13. For this group, the fulfillment quotation in 13:14-15 indicates the persistent infidelity of Israel, the parable form withholds necessary information about the *Basileia* from the Jewish crowds, and the content of the parables themselves suggests a final judgment in which "Jews" will be separated from "Christians" (read "gentiles"). However, Matthew 13 reads smoothly as a continuation of the previous narrative section. While chapters 11-12 depict the division between Pharisees, disciples of the Baptist, and city-dwellers -- those who have institutional memberships and are characterized by stasis -- and the marginal, mobile crowds along with Jesus, the third teaching discourse spells out the implications of these affiliations. The parables therein teach that, like the Jewish characters in the gospel, the people in the new era will be distinguished not according to their group membership but according to their good works.

Matthew's explanation for Jesus' use of parables is the first datum cited by those who claim the discourse, chapter 13, is occasioned in part by Jewish perfidy. According to Mk 4:12 (Lk 8:10), Jesus speaks in parables "in order that" (ἵνα) the crowds will not understand; Matt 13:13 replaces ἵνα with ὅτι ("because"), and the critics explain that *because* the people have refused to understand "the parables will obscure the truth judgmentally." While Mark emphasizes the purpose behind the parables, Matthew stresses the reason and thereby intensifies the guilt of the Jews.[13] But the verse itself, the preface to a quotation from Isa 6:9-10, does not indicate that Jesus speaks in parables to punish Israel. Indeed, the Matthean conjunction could be indicative either of a softening of Mark's version -- "*because* the people were dull and insensitive, Jesus taught in parables in the hope that they would understand and repent" -- or of a causal connection -- Jesus uses parables because the secrets of the *Basileia* cannot be given to the crowd.[14]

When Matt 13:13 is read in conjunction with 13:35, the companion quotation which in several ancient manuscripts is assigned not just to "the prophet" but to "the prophet Isaiah" (the citation is actually to Psalm 78, and the prophet in question would be Asaph), the rationale for the parable form is partially explained: Jesus speaks in parables "to fulfill what was spoken by the prophet." Thus he indicates his conformity to biblical models and undercuts the suggestion that the parables are occasioned by Jewish guilt. Matthew 13:35 also states that Jesus utters "what has been hidden since the foundations of the world." Since his task therefore is to reveal the hidden, the parables cannot be completely obscure to the crowd. Thus the Pharisees understand the parable of the vineyard in 21:45, and Jesus plainly conveys his messages to

---

[13]Gundry, *Matthew*, p. 256; cf. Hare, *Jewish Persecution*, p. 149; Meier, *Vision of Matthew*, pp. 89-90; and J. Gnilka, *Die Verstockung Israels -- Isaias 6, 9-10 in der Theologie der Synoptiker* (Munich: Kösel, 1961), p. 103, on the parable form as punishment; Albright and Mann, *Matthew*, p. cxl; Fenton, *Saint Matthew*, p. 225; Hill, *The Gospel*, pp. 71, 226-28; Kingsbury, *Matthew*, p. 75. On the theory that the full citation is an early interpolation see Gnilka, *Die Verstockung*, pp. 103-5; Stendahl, *School of Saint Matthew*, pp. 129-31; and Cope, *Matthew, A Scribe*, pp. 17-19.

[14]See Dan O. Via, "Matthew on the Understanding of the Parables," *JBL* 84 (1965): 430-31; cf. Hill, *The Gospel*, p. 27.

the people in the rest of the text through healing and feeding miracles as well as by such teachings as 19:9 on divorce and 19:18-21 on the requirements for "eternal life." Given this pattern, the parables cannot be indicative of Jesus' withdrawal from or punishment of the Jewish people.

According to Matt 13:11, what remains hidden from the people is not the *Basileia* itself but its "secrets" (τὰ μυστήρια). Since throughout the gospel Jesus indicates the path to salvation (e.g., 19:16-22), the secrets cannot be the means by which one gains entry into eternal life. They are, instead, to be found in the special teachings which the disciples receive in 13:18-23, 37-50. These secrets or mysteries concern the composition of the *Basileia*: its unsurpassable worth, its separation of the evil from the righteous at the eschaton, the great joy it creates, etc. Only those who follow Jesus, the disciples, can "understand all this" (13:51); only they have the necessary connection to Jesus, the consistent witnessing of his activities, the full exchange of patriarchal patterns for a community of equality, and the "discipling" (μαθητευθείς, 13:52; RSV "trained") that permit them this knowledge. Until the crowds adopt the new ethos, they will never perceive the truths of the *Basileia*. Yet the crowds are not condemned, and they still have time to repent. Because the fulfillment quotations cannot be separated from the eschatological thrust of the seven parables[15] the crowds at this point cannot be irrevocably sentenced to damnation. Indeed, it will be the disciples' task "to disciple" them in the era of the church (28:19).

In the immediate context of the first fulfillment quotation, Jesus recognizes his special gift to those who can be called "disciples": "Many prophets and righteous ones longed

---

[15]See Cope, *Matthew, A Scribe*, p. 29.

to see what you see, and did not see it, and to hear what you hear, and did not hear it" (13:17; cf. Lk 10:23-24). The observation associates the disciples, and through them the crowds, not with the evil leaders but with the righteous people of their past. Matthew also notes that Jews continue to accept Jesus' message: not only does Joseph of Arimathea become a disciple (ἐμαθήτευσεν, 27:57), but because the gospel fails to specify the number of "disciples" who receive special instruction in chapter 13,[16] the term could easily refer to a substantial portion of the crowds who, together with gentiles, will comprise the abundant harvest of 13:23. By refusing to make explicit the number or composition of these "scribes" "discipled" for the *Basileia* of Heaven (13:52), Matthew leaves open the possibility that all the crowds might obtain salvation.

The most that can be concluded about the disciples in Matthew 13 is that they are Jews (cf. 10:5b-6) who willingly obey Jesus' commandments; they may falter, deny, and doubt, but they are still welcomed in the church. Yet in the new age, gentiles too will be divided into those who see and those who close their eyes; the resurrected Jesus commissions his Jewish followers to "make disciples" (μαθητύσατε, 28:19) of "all the gentiles." Since the parables have an eschatological emphasis, it is consequently appropriate to interpret them as including the gentiles in their allusions to the final judgment. It is inappropriate, however, to emphasize ethnic divisions within the new community, since these will be ended at the

---

[16]See U. Luz, "The Disciples in the Gospel According to Matthew," in Stanton, pp. 98-128. On those "with Jesus" -- Mary, tax collectors and sinners, Peter, a nameless follower (26:51), James and John, and the twelve -- see J. D. Kingsbury, "The Figure of Peter in Matthew's Gospel as a Theological Problem," *JBL* 98 (1979): 77-78, who suggests this restricted list indicates a distinction between the disciples and Israel.

resurrection. According to the eschatological parables, all are equal until the close of the age. Tilborg, for example, notes a difficulty in determining whether 13:38 and 13:49 refer to the church as a *corpus mixtum* or to the world which contains both good and bad.[17] The distinction is not needed: both the church and the world house Jew and gentile, good and bad, and Matthew indicates that neither ethnic descent nor institutional affiliation guarantees salvation. Like the Jewish community, which contains both those who follow Jesus and those who seek his death, in the new era both the church and the world will be comprised of ethnic Jews and ethnic gentiles, wheat and weeds.

The phrase "the birds of the air" (τὰ πετεινὰ τοῦ οὐρανοῦ, 13:32) in the parable of the mustard seed is occasionally identified as referring to the entry of gentiles into the church. While Dan 4:21; *Mid. Ps* 104 §13; I En 90:33; *T.B. A.Z.* 41a; JosAsen 15; etc., have been invoked to support this theory,[18] the content of the first gospel cannot be. The same expression appears in 6:26 where the equation of birds with gentiles is impossible and 8:20 where it is completely unnecessary. Even the parable itself concerns not the composition of the community but its growth from a small seed into a universal force. If a reference to the entry of gentiles into the *Basileia* is inherent in Matt 13:31-32, "this idea would, to say the least, be expressed only very obscurely by this metaphor."[19]

---

[17]*Jewish Leaders*, pp. 41, 44.

[18]Jeremias, *Jesus' Promise*, p. 69; Fenton, *Saint Matthew*, p. 222; Franzmann, *Discipleship*, pp. 119-20; Manson, *Sayings of Jesus*, p. 123; and *Teaching of Jesus*, p. 133 n. 1; Green, *The Gospel*, p. 135; Cox, *The Gospel*, p. 97; Schweizer, *Good News*, p. 305; Wilson, *Gentiles*, p. 6.

[19]Kümmel, *Promise and Fulfillment*, p. 131; cf. Hill, *The Gospel*, p. 233; Argyle, *The Gospel*, p. 105; Wilson, *Gentiles*, p.

Nor do those parables that depict eschatological universalism directly concern the mission to the gentiles. C. W. F. Smith suggests that the parable of the fishnet (13:47-50) may be related to the mission of the twelve to Israel and perhaps even to the gentile mission.[20] Similarly, Schaberg correctly observes that Matt 13:36-43, the explanation of the parable of the weeds in the field, is thematically connected to 24:14 and 28:16-20.[21] But these associations hold only to the extent that the final judgment and the Great Commission concern Jews and gentiles alike. The emphasis in Matthew 13 falls not on the approach to the gentiles, but on the unqualified universalism of both final judgment and *Basileia*.

This brief survey demonstrates that the responses of the Jews to Jesus do not fall into one monolithically constructed or even temporally bound category. Like the various gentiles who appear in the gospel, the Jews defy classification as consistently faithful or consistently faithless; they must be viewed as individuals. The only groups which display a consistently negative reaction to Jesus are those characterized by elite status and stasis: Herod, Pilate, and their respective cohorts, the Pharisees, and the scribes. The roles of both the disciples of John and the twelve as well as of the crowds are ambiguous: at times they display fidelity; at other times they manifest doubt and outright rejection. But any individual who demonstrates a willingness to follow Jesus

---

6.

[20]"The Mixed State of the Church in Matthew," *JBL* 82 (1963): 154; cf. Manson, *Sayings of Jesus*, p. 197. For the response see Jeremias, *Rediscovering the Parables*, p. 177; as well as Hill, *The Gospel*, p. 239; Albright and Mann, *Matthew*, p. cxliv; and cf. Tilborg, *Jewish Leaders*, p. 40.

[21]*The Father*, p. 285; cf. Trilling, *Das Wahre Israel*, p. 101; Manson, *Sayings of Jesus*, p. 194, on the field as the world.

literally and accept his message both spiritually and practically has a chance at salvation. Consequently, the distinction often drawn between the disciples and the Jews or between Jesus' followers and the Jewish people/Israel is inappropriate. While occasionally the "disciples" -- who are not always identified explicitly as the "twelve" -- receive special instruction withheld from the crowd, these "scribes for the *Basileia*" cannot be separated either from their Jewish background or from the members of Matthew's church: the readers who are privy to the same inside information. Therefore, because the Jews "as a corporate community" cannot be classified as rejected or rejecting, then Jesus' ministry to the lost sheep of Israel is not intended to prove their guilt, and the Great Commission is not a response to their rejection either of or by him.

Matthew 27:22-26

These several conclusions are also applicable to perhaps the most controversial verses in the first gospel: the condemnation of Jesus in 27:22-26. According to the majority of Matthean scholars, the various events surrounding the sentencing, which culminate in the cry of "crucify him, crucify him" by "all the people," indict the former people of God for Jesus' death.[22] In turn, the gentile world, represented

---

[22]Among others, Trilling, *Das Wahre Israel*, pp. 71-72; Strecker, *Der Weg*, p. 107; Senior, *Passion Narrative*, pp. 256-59; Fenton, *Saint Matthew*, p. 436; J. A. Fitzmyer, "Anti-Semitism," pp. 668-71; Davies, *Setting*, p. 290; Giblin, "Theological Perspective," p. 657; Brandon, *Jesus and the Zealots*, p. 302; Gibbs, "Purpose and Pattern," p. 451; Garland, *Intention*, pp. 40, 185; Gaston, "Messiah of Israel," p. 32; Meier, *Vision of Matthew*, p. 180. I have been unable to obtain a copy

primarily by Pontius Pilate and the Roman soldiers, is, like Barabbas, set free although guilty. For example, Tilborg proposes that "the anti-Jewish tendency in Matthew often goes hand in hand with an attempt to exonerate the non-Jews from guilt (27:11-14, 38-44)."[23] Each part of this statement is questionable. In Matthew's passion narrative, both Jewish and gentile characters span the spectrum from righteousness to total evil. Among the Jews, Jesus, the women from Galilee, and Joseph of Arimathea are positively depicted; the actions of the disciples in general and Peter in particular are ambiguous; and the chief priests and elders along with Judas are the villains of the account. In turn, while Pilate's role is ambiguous, that of his wife and the soldiers at the cross is primarily positive and that of his soldiers in the praetorium is negative. In the first gospel, there is no "anti-Jewish tendency" per se depicted during Jesus' ministry; there is only a rejection of certain groups within the Jewish community. Nor is "exonerate" appropriate. Even in passion predictions, particular groups of Jews and gentiles share responsibility for Jesus' crucifixion. Examination of these passion predictions along with contextual analysis of Matt 27:22-26, a survey of the various Matthean uses of "Jews" (Ἰουδαίοι), "crowd" and "crowds" (ὄχλοι), and "people" (λαός), and an investigation into the meaning of the peoples' statement "his blood be on our heads and on the heads of our children" (27:25) all argue against both Jewish corporate guilt and justification for the gentiles.

The cross-ethnic focus of the passion narrative is foreshadowed by the three predictions in 16:21; 17:22-23; and 20:18-19. Each emphasizes the responsibility of a different

---

of Vincent Mora, *Refus d'Israel* (Paris: Cerf, 1986).

[23]*Jewish Leaders*, p. 97.

group: Jesus first mentions his suffering at the hands of the "elders and chief priests and scribes" and that he will be killed. The beginning of the statement reveals that the entire Jewish leadership in Jerusalem is against Jesus, but the conclusion, with its passive verb "be killed" (ἀποκτανθῆναι), does not indicate the agents of the execution. In 17:22-23, this general notice is repeated: those who receive Jesus are called simply "people" (ἀνθρώποι), and so the emphasis shifts away from the Jewish leaders. According to the third prediction, while the Jewish leaders will deliver Jesus to the gentiles, these gentiles fully carry out their wishes. When juxtaposed, the predictions create a partial chiasm: Matt 16:21 begins with a reference to three groups of Jewish leaders; 17:22-23 is the neutral term indicating that all bear some responsibility for the passion; and 20:18-19 concludes with a reference to three tortures engineered by the gentiles: mocking, scourging, and crucifixion. The chiastic structure highlights the equal responsibility of Jews and gentiles; the order of the arrangement places the final emphasis on the role of the gentiles. Comparing the grammatical pattern in Matt 20:18-19 -- the use of εἰς τό plus the infinitives "to mock, to scourge, and to crucify" -- to the simple future verbs in Mk 10:34, Tilborg proposes that Matthew's version indicates purpose or result and so places greater emphasis on the actions of the Jewish leaders.[24] However, the explicitly described action of the Romans indicates that they not only "continued" the action begun by the Jewish leaders, they intensified it. This intensification, particularly when it is compared to the actions of Pilate's wife, goes beyond the claim that the soldiers who tortured and executed the Jew were just following orders.

---

[24]*Jewish Leaders*, p. 75.

The fulfillment of the prediction made in 20:18-19 of torture by gentiles appears in 27:27-31. Jesus is humiliated not by just a few soldiers but in front of "the whole battalion" (27:27); he is stripped twice, once of his own clothes and once of the scarlet robe, and therefore literally made one of the naked "least ones" (27:28 only in Matthew; 27:31; cf. Mk 15:20); he is mocked with the trappings and exclamations of royalty by "the soldiers of the governor" (27:27) who rest secure in the might of the Roman empire; and he is, finally, led away to be crucified. Were Matthew simply interested in the fulfillment of the passion prediction, the substantial detail devoted to this incident is inexplicable. This entire episode, moreover, follows Pilate's own scourging of Jesus. Indeed, while the third passion prediction states that the chief priests and scribes "will deliver" (παραδοθήσεται, 20:18) Jesus into the hands of the gentiles, in Matt 27:26 it is the gentile Pilate who "delivered him" (παρέδωκεν) to be crucified." Although Pilate's actions in 27:24 attempt to establish his innocence, he remains the direct catalyst for Jesus' death.

Contrasted to the Roman ruler are Pilate's wife and the centurion at the cross. While all three testify to Jesus' innocence (27:23-24, 19, 54), each reacts differently to the knowledge. Pilate proclaims Jesus innocent but sets Barabbas free instead; he is thus comparable to those who refuse to act upon their convictions and merely pay lip service to the truth (7:21; 25:31-46). His wife, on the other hand, breaks with social convention and interrupts the governor "while he was sitting on the judgment seat" with her warning (27:19). That she is a woman and therefore marginal to the gospel's Roman population -- all of whom are military men -- is not accidental, nor should the associations her dream has to both Joseph and the Magi be ignored. Again, the marginal and the mobile manifest faith; Pilate just sits there. Finally, the soldiers at the cross represent potential church members: they acknowledge Jesus' connection with the divinity, but they are not depicted as acting upon it. Action is taken only by the Jews: Joseph of Arimathea claims the body, and the women attend the tomb.

The Jews too display various responses toward Jesus in the passion narrative. The crowds (ὄχλοι) first appear in 27:20-21 (cf. 27:15, 24) where they are persuaded by the chief priests and elders to ask for the release of Barabbas. Here the greater blame -- in accord with the passion prediction -- is placed on the Jewish leaders; the crowd is manipulated (ἔπεισαν ["persuaded"], 27:20) into an unfortunate response. The negative depiction of the leaders as opposed to the people is heightened when Matt 27:57 is compared to its Marcan (15:43) and Lucan (23:50) parallels. Unlike the other synoptics, the first gospel does *not* describe Joseph of Arimathea as a member of the Sanhedrin but as a rich man (27:57). This economic indicator does not bankrupt Matthew's social axis: Joseph's behavior conforms to Jesus' statements in chapter 25 about caring for the needy; and the possession of wealth implies neither social privilege nor automatic support for the status quo.

While the crowds, like Pilate, accede to the desire of the Jewish leaders, they, like the disciples and the Roman soldiers, display a variety of responses to Jesus. Throughout the gospel (9:33; 12:23; 21:9, 15; etc.) the crowds, like the disciples, follow Jesus, marvel at his teaching, and align themselves with him against the Pharisees. Indeed, the expression "the crowds" (οἱ ὄχλοι) is a Matthean commonplace for depicting the people in confrontation with their leadership (7:28; 9:8; 12:23; 21:9, 11, 46; 22:33; and perhaps even 27:20, where they must be coerced).[25] But ultimately their role is

---

[25]Tilborg, *Jewish Leaders*, p. 160; cf. Garland, *Intention*, pp.

ambiguous. In 27:15-26 they are implicated in Jesus' death; they fail him just as did the disciples who slept at Gethsemane (26:40-45) and deny him just as Peter did in the High Priest's courtyard (26:69-75). Like the disciples, the crowds are inconsistent.[26] There is in fact no development either positively or negatively in their roles: some may come to believe; others may continue to doubt (cf. 28:16); still others will come to deny Jesus. Matthew cannot state whether the crowds will eventually number among the disciples because the future era of the church is both new and open. Each Jew has the choice either of following Jesus' instructions or of denying them and becoming one of the Ἰουδαίοι of 28:15.

These observations substantially weaken the theory that Matthew replaces "crowd" (27:15, 20, 24) with "all the people" (πᾶς ὁ λαός) in 27:25 to have the words "spoken by the Jews as *the people* of God."[27] If the shift in vocabulary conveys any soteriological associations then the employ of "people" here is best compared with its first appearance in the gospel: the observation that Jesus will save "his people" from their sins (1:21). Because the term also appears in 4:23 and so frames the public ministry, it further indicates Jesus' fidelity to the temporal axis: his mission to the Jewish people continues. Gibbs proposes that "the people" -- as opposed to "the crowds" -- emphasizes the connection rather than the separation between the people and their leaders (2:4; 21:23; 26:3, 47; and 27:1).[28] In these examples, however, the "people" do not "do"

36-39.

[26]See A. Suhl, "Der Davidssohn im Matthäus-Evangelium," *ZNW* 59 (1968): 67-81; Tilborg, *Jewish Leaders*, p. 159.

[27]Fenton, *Saint Matthew*, p. 436; cf. Tilborg, *Jewish Leaders*, p. 149.

[28]"Purpose and Pattern," pp. 450-51; cf. Strecker, *Der Weg*, p. 107.

anything; they serve merely as a frame of reference: rulers must rule someone, and since the rulers are evil, these "people" are the lost sheep without a good shepherd. Moreover, in 26:5, the "people" are clearly on the side of Jesus and against the Jewish leaders. Finally, the link between the two terms is established by their adjectival modifiers in 27:22, 25. In the former instance, "all" (πάντες) call for Jesus' crucifixion, and the antecedent is "the crowd"; in the latter example, "all" (πᾶς) respond to Pilate, and the noun accompanying the term is "the people." Because the two terms are interchangeable, Gibbs's conclusion that one indicates separation from and one connection to the leaders is difficult to support.

Fitzmyer posits that λαός might be taken in an "ethnic sense" to indicate to the Jewish-Christians why the church is becoming mostly gentile.[29] This more positive description of the theory of Jewish guilt is undercut by his own observation that the term is not employed in a consistent manner: it appears in a "generic sense" in 4:23; 26:5; and 27:64. Were the evangelist intent on making an ethnic distinction in 27:25 -- such as that in 28:15 -- then "Jews" rather than "people" would be the more appropriate term. Further, neither the gospel as a whole nor the passion narrative in particular hints that the Matthean church is "mostly gentile." Finally, Suhl's claim that the change in terminology exonerates the "crowd" is also weak; just as the "people" confirm the verdict, so the "crowd" initially calls for the sentence.[30]

Although the vocabulary of "people" and "crowds" defies categorization, the geographical associations made in chapter

---

[29]"Anti-Semitism," pp. 669-71.

[30]"Der Davidssohn," p. 81; and for the response see Garland, *Intention*, p. 40.

27 do conform to a Matthean pattern. Against the theory that "the people" in 27:25 includes pilgrims from outside of Jerusalem as well as city dwellers[31] is the pattern throughout the gospel of urban residents, particularly the people of Jerusalem, displaying hostility to Jesus (cf. 2:2). While the crowd in Jerusalem ultimately agrees with the leaders, the women "from Galilee" (27:55), Joseph from Arimathea (27:57), and probably Simon the Cyrenian (Κυρηναῖον, 27:32) do not support the death sentence. Thus, although the "crowds" condemn Jesus and "all the people" accept responsibility for the verdict, the composition of these groups is immediately qualified by references to those among "the people" who do not support the crucifixion.

Like the identity of the respondents in 27:25, the response itself has also been seen as indicating the rejection of Jesus by the corporate community. The phrase "his blood be on us" is a technical expression (Lev 20:9; Josh 2:19; Ezek 18:13; II Sam 1:16; 3:29; Jer 28:35 [LXX]; Acts 18:6) for accepting responsibility for someone's death, and the inclusion of offspring in such curses also appears in the early sources (II Sam 14:9; I Kings 2:33).[32] Although the plain meaning of the verse is therefore not in doubt, its implications for Matthean salvation history remain debated. Several commentators offer the plausible suggestion that the mention of children refers to the problems occasioned by the War with Rome in 66-70 (cf. 22:7),[33] but the richness of the verse goes

[31] P. Gaechter, *Das Matthäus-Evangelium* (Innsbruck, 1963), p. 913, cited in Fitzmyer, "Anti-Semitism," p. 669.

[32] See esp. H. Reventlow, "Sein Blut komme über sein Haupt," *VT* 10 (1960): 311-27.

[33] Hare, "Rejection of the Jews," p. 38; and *Jewish Persecution*, p. 156; Albright and Mann, *Matthew*, p. 345. On the historical reading connecting 27:25 to the *Birchat ha-Minim* see J.

beyond the historical association.

Two principal literary connections to Matt 27:25 found elsewhere in the gospel offer possible interpretations. On the one hand, the verse may be connected with the institution of the Eucharist in 26:28; Jesus offers the cup to his followers and states, "this is my blood (αἷμα) of the covenant, which is poured out for many for the forgiveness of sins." Thus the promise made at the beginning of the gospel that Jesus would "save his people from their sins" (1:21) is recapitulated by these same people. The crowd has, in very ironic circumstances, bestowed a blessing upon itself and its offspring. On the other hand, Gundry connects the blood on the heads of the children (τὰ τέκνα) in Matt 27:25 to the slaughter of the sons by Herod's soldiers and to Rachel's weeping for her children (τὰ τέκνα; the MT and LXX read "sons") in 2:16-17.[34] In both chapters 2 and 27 the actions of the leadership have dire consequences for the Jewish children, and the crowds' comment has substantially negative implications. Either reading, or both, is plausible since Matthew does not indicate who among the crowds will ultimately enter the *Basileia* and who will not.

Taking an ecclesiologically oriented approach, Meier concludes that "the wider meaning of 'all our descendants forever' is probably meant" because the evangelist needs to identify the "true people of God."[35] The association of Matt

---

Parkes, *The Conflict of the Church and the Synagogue* (New York: Atheneum, 1969), p. 79; Kilpatrick, *Origins of the Gospel*, p. 109. Correctly against this connection see esp. Hummel, *Auseinandersetzung*, pp. 28-33; Meier, *Antioch and Rome*, p. 48.

[34] *Matthew*, p. 36.

[35] *Vision of Matthew*, p. 200 n. 240; cf. Crossan, "Anti-Semitism and the Gospel," *TS* 26 (1965): 189-214; Fitzmyer, "Anti-Semitism," p. 667 (commenting on Crossan's article); G.

27:25 with the question of the "true people of God" is not uncommon in New Testament scholarship: if the church is the "true Israel," then, so the presupposition goes, some indication that the Jews have forfeited this designation is needed. The definitive treatment of this position is Trilling's *Das Wahre Israel*. He concludes that the Christian community continues in the role of the chosen people, a role forfeited by the Jews, and thus the church is the true, but not a new Israel.[36] Fenton, similarly, proposes that the church is the "new Israel" which replaced the old.[37] And Walker is the most prominent among those who see the church as a new, distinct entity, neither the "new" nor the "true" Israel.[38]

Because the evangelist never explicitly refers to the church as either the "new Israel" or the "true Israel" these classifications may be inappropriate at the outset. Nor have lexical analyses been helpful. If "Israel" is defined as an ethnic group (8:10; 10:6; 15:24; 19:28[?]) or a geographic location (2:20; 9:33; 10:23), then the church is not Israel but a new

---

G. O'Collins, "Anti-Semitism in the Gospel," *TS* 26 (1965): 663-66.

[36]Trilling, *Das Wahre Israel*, passim; followed by Tagawa, "People and Community," p. 159. Frankemölle's view in *Jahwebund*, that the church is the replacement of Israel -- and separated from the Jews -- is comparable.

[37]*Saint Matthew*, p. 193; cf. Dodd, "Matthew and Paul," p. 294; Tilborg, *Jewish Leaders*, pp. 71-73; Davies, *Setting*, p. 200; Hummel, *Auseinandersetzung*, pp. 157-60 (describing Christians as a new entity with Judaism but espousing different interpretations of Torah and a disinterest in nationalism).

[38]*Heilsgeschichte*, esp. pp. 81-83; cf. Hare, *Jewish Persecution*, pp. 156-62 (p. 158 responds directly to Trilling); Gaston, "Messiah of Israel," p. 33; Meier, *Vision of Matthew*, pp. 17, 55 n. 19.

entity comprised of Jews and gentiles with distinct religious practices (baptism). If, however, "Israel" is the group to which the promises of the Hebrew scriptures have been given and to whom Jesus has come (2:6; 15:31[?]; 27:42[?]), then the church is Israel (cf. Gal 6:16). In the first gospel, the only terms consistently applied to specific groups are: "the Jews" -- employed in the gospel four times by gentiles and once by the narrator to indicate a community distinct from the church (28:15); "the church" (εκκλησια), which indicates the community of the new era (16:18) and which is distinguished from the pagans or gentiles (εθνικος) in 18:17; and the εθνικοι themselves (5:47; 6:7; 18:17). The operative categories for Matthew are therefore Jews, the church, and gentile-pagans.

The question to ask the first gospel is consequently not whether the Christian community is the "new" or "true" Israel, but rather, whether "old Israel" -- the Jewish people -- has a place within it. According to Matthew, the church is formed on a Jewish base: the Great Commission is pronounced by a Jew, addressed to a group of Jews, and includes Jews in its scope. Further, Matthew highlights the church's retention not only of the written Torah but also of many Pharisaic interpretations. Finally, according to the gospel's soteriological perspective, God has not rejected the Jews as a corporate community nor have the Jews rejected God. Rather, the evangelist has condemned the elite of both Jewish and gentile religious and political organizations who exploit or ignore others on the social, economic, and spatial peripheries. With the end of the temporal axis and so the soteriological priority of the Jews or "Israel," the classification itself within the church is surpassed and is, therefore, meaningless.

IX

Summary and Conclusions

The Gospel of Matthew presents a program of salvation history constructed along two axes: a temporal axis that incorporates ethnic categories and a social axis that transcends the division between Jew and gentile. Soteriological divisions between ethnic groups are operative only for the era of Israel, the period inaugurated with Abraham (Matt 1:1) and brought to a close with the crucifixion of Jesus. During this era the Jews retain their privileged position in salvation history: the Law and the Prophets are theirs; the mission of Jesus and the twelve is directed only to them.

The shift in the temporal axis, the beginning of the era of the church, is signaled by the Great Commission (Matt 28:16-20). In this reformulation of the mission discourse, the disciples' evangelistic course obtains a universal extension. Because the promises to Israel have been fulfilled in Jesus' mission, the message of the *Basileia* can now be proclaimed to all the gentiles. But this extension does not entail a loss of the Jews' soteriological benefits: they have lost only their unique position. During the era of the church, from the resurrection until the eschaton, the disciples will preach the good news both to "the lost sheep of the house of Israel" and to "all the gentiles." Both will be judged according to the same criterion of faith in God demonstrated by action. Neither ethnic origin nor confessional affiliation will influence the final judgment.

This criterion of faith is also in effect during the era of Israel: the ethnic division that falls along the temporal axis is subsumed under and transcended by distinctions based on social position. On one end of the social axis are those who place their faith in personal authority and who use that authority to exploit or oppress others. Leaders, characterized by status and stasis, include not only the Pharisees and Pilate but also any member of a group with elitist possibilities or pretensions. Thus the disciples of John the Baptist are compared to rather than contrasted with the Pharisees, and the disciples of Jesus must be exhorted often to act as servants, not masters. The other end of the social axis is home to those disenfranchised from or marginal to official society as it is conceived by the dominant groups. Jesus' message is therefore directed particularly to prostitutes, sinners, tax collectors, women, lepers, and, given the contingencies of the temporal axis, (non-elite) gentiles, who are characterized by mobility and who live on the periphery of the status quo. Because they neither know their place nor have one, they threaten the legitimacy of the existing social structure and have the potential to replace its patriarchal ethos with an egalitarian community.

By directing his mission towards all those excluded from full participation in the religious and political structures, the Matthean Jesus indicates the structure the church is to take. Replacing the Temple with his own abiding presence within the community, he eliminates the formation of a new spatial center which would, necessarily, require peripheries. In the church the leaders are to be servants, and equality will be insured through the continuing critique of centers.

These conclusions call into question the reigning interpretation of both Matthean salvation history in general and of the exclusivity logion in particular. Studies of the first gospel are frequently carried out under the reductive rubrics of ethnic categories and categorizations. Practitioners of the historical-critical method have popularized the labels "Jewish Christian" and "gentile Christian." Further, they have described the *Sitz im Leben* of each group: gentile Christians live in freedom from the yoke of the Law and preach a universal gospel; Jewish Christians, on the other hand, are insular, exclusivistic, legalistic, and anti-gentile. Those interested in the thematic composition of the gospels also base their studies on either the explicit or, more often, implicit presupposition of ethnic divisions. Much exegesis presents a maximalist interpretation of Jewish groups and individuals who do not follow Jesus. The Pharisees, the population of Nazareth, the people who call for his crucifixion -- are described by this exegesis as "the Jews"; they retain their ethnic identity. Conversely, characters of Jewish descent -- the disciples, the women from Galilee, the prostitutes and sinners, the crowds who follow Jesus, even Jesus himself -- somehow lose their ethnic background: they become (prototypical) Christians. This approach appears even more striking when gentile characters are added to the equation. Unlike the Pharisees or the people in Jesus' hometown, the gentiles who display hostility toward Jesus in the gospel narratives (e.g., Pilate and his soldiers) are not portrayed as emblematic of the gentile nations, the gentile "corporate community." On the other hand, only those gentiles who follow Jesus (e.g., the Magi, the centurion, the Canaanite woman) receive the maximalist interpretation and so retain their ethnic identity.

These presuppositions are particularly prominent in treatments of Matt 10:5b-6. The problematic verse is frequently placed on the shelf of remnants left over from the early years of Jewish-Christian ethnic exclusivity. There the logion sits with other material no longer fashionable in the universalistic and increasingly gentile church: the proclamation of the Law's enduring validity (5:17-20); the exhortation to heed the scribes and Pharisees (23:2-3); and the advice to treat recalcitrant church members as gentiles and tax collectors (18:17). This "Jewish" material, judged antithetic to the gospel's universalistic outlook, is viewed as old lace: still valued by the community that preserved them, but no longer of practical use.

The deconstruction of this viewpoint begins with the presuppositions that the gospel is a literary whole, that the evangelist is both creative and competent, and that the early church was not a monolithic structure: each Christian community had its own concerns, its own theological and social proclivities and problems. Therefore, only if particular verses are incomprehensible within their narrative context is the appeal to pre-Matthean tradition necessary. These presuppositions in turn question the necessity of postulating a hypothetical (M) document as the source of 10:5b-6 and 15:24, preserve the credibility of the evangelist, and remove the temptation to harmonize the first gospel with material presented in the other canonical documents.

The prevailng interpretations of Matthew's exclusivity logion need to be reconsidered. The verse neither sets the scene for the rejection of the Jews, nor does it indicate any prejudice against gentiles and Samaritans. Rather, Matt 10:5b-6 is best regarded as the first step in the gospel's soteriological program: the mission begins with the Jews, and only at the Great Commission does it extend to the gentiles. Contextual analysis also indicates that the exclusivity logion is not modified by its juxtaposition to either 10:17-18 or 10:23. The former preserves the distinctions along the temporal axis by its strategic use of the future tense; the latter is, in the context of the first gospel, a reference to the resurrection appearance in 28:16-20 and not an unfulfilled prophecy or an indication that the disciples' mission is always to be limited to Israel.

The temporal and social axes in fact intersect at Matt 10:5b-6. The elimination of all non-Jews from the disciples' missionary focus makes explicit the soteriological privilege of those of Jewish descent. The emphasis on the "lost sheep" is a component of the social axis: not only is Israel distinguished from the gentiles and Samaritans, the sheep are distinguished from their faithless shepherds, the elite. Thus Matt 10:5b-6, along with its corollary in 15:24, is a determinate element in the gospel's program of salvation history.

To introduce this well-crafted program, the gospel begins with the unexpected mention of four women in Jesus' genealogy. Their symbolic import derives neither from their (at times questionable) gentile ancestry nor from their unexpected sexual activities. Tamar, Rahab, Ruth, and Bathsheba/Uriah were all socioeconomically, politically, or cultically powerless, and all fulfilled their role in Israel's salvation history by overcoming obstacles created by people in authority unwilling to fulfill their own responsibilities. Matthew 2 continues the theme of cross-ethnic social divisions. The gentile Magi and the Jewish Holy Family, each characterized by faith in God and the willingness to act upon this faith, are positively compared with the static elite of Jewish society: Herod the Great, the chief priests, the scribes, and the residents of Jerusalem. This second chapter also introduces a subtheme of the social axis: the critique of centers in general and cities in particular. Thus the center of the world, Jerusalem, is personified as faithless, and humble Bethlehem, gentile Egypt, and the otherwise unknown Galilean town of Nazareth provide homes for Joseph and his family.

Divisions that transcend ethnic categories are made explicit in Jesus' own contact with gentile supplicants. The accounts of the centurion in 8:5-13 and of the Canaanite woman in 15:21-28 illustrate that faith rather than ethnic origin separates those who will attain salvation and those who will be denied at the last judgment. In these pericopes, too, social categories of elites and marginals are depicted in conversation and reinforced by context. The centurion demonstrates his worthiness by subordinating his authority to that of Jesus; his social marginality is highlighted by his contextual association with two other individuals representative of the periphery of the religious establishment, particularly as based in the Temple cultus: a leper and a woman. The Canaanite woman demonstrates faith by accepting her inferior social position while concurrently arguing that even those most marginal to the establishment, the "dogs," are entitled to mercy.

These healings of gentiles do not, however, deviate from the temporal axis; they are portrayed as exceptions in Jesus' mission, and Jesus himself displays an adamant unwillingness to bestow the blessings of the *Basileia* proleptically upon the gentiles. The limitation of the mission is ended only at the Great Commission. And here again, challenges to certain branches of Matthean scholarship must be made. While the phrase πάντα τὰ ἔθνη in Matt 28:19 is best translated "all the gentiles," the verse does not imply that the mission to the Jews enjoined in the second discourse has ended. Rather, the mission to the Jews must continue, since the deity has not rejected the Jews, and since the corporate community of Israel has not rejected either its tradition or its God.

BIBLIOGRAPHY

Abel, Ernest L. "The Genealogies of Jesus O XPICTOC." *New Testament Studies* 20 (1973/74): 203-10.

_______. "Who Wrote Matthew?" *New Testament Studies* 17 (1971): 138-52.

Abrahams, I. *Studies in Pharisaism and the Gospels.* 2 vols. 1917. Reprint. 1st and 2d ser. Library of Biblical Studies. New York: KTAV, 1967.

Abramowski, L. "Die Entstehung der dreigliedrigen Taufformel -- ein Versuch," *Zeitschrift für Theologie und Kirche* 81 (1984): 417-46.

Albright, W. F., and C. S. Mann. *Matthew.* Anchor Bible 26. Garden City, NY: Doubleday and Co., 1971.

Allen, W. C. *A Critical and Exegetical Commentary on the Gospel According to St. Matthew.* 3d ed. International Critical Commentaries. Edinburgh: T. and T. Clark, 1912.

Allison, Dale C., Jr. "Matt. 23:39 = Luke 13:35b as a Conditional Prophecy." *Journal for the Study of the New Testament* 18 (1983): 75-84.

Alon, G. *Jews, Judaism and the Classical World.* Translated by Israel Abrahams. Jerusalem: Magnes Press, Hebrew University, 1977.

Anderson, J. C. "Matthew: Gender and Reading." In *The Bible and Feminist Hermeneutics*, edited by Mary Ann Tolbert, 3-28 (= *Semeia* 28 [1983]).

Argyle, A. W. *The Gospel According to Matthew.* Cambridge Bible Commentary. Cambridge: The University Press, 1963.

Bacon, B. W. *Studies in Matthew.* New York: Henry Holt and Co., 1930.

Baeck, L. *The Essence of Judaism.* Edited by Irving Howe. New York: Schocken Books, 1961.

Baird, J. Arthur. *Audience Criticism and the Historical Jesus.* Philadelphia: Westminster Press, 1969.

Bamberger, B. J. "Conversion to Judaism: Theologically Speaking." In *Conversion to Judaism: A History and Analysis*, edited by D. M. Eichhorn, 176-88. New York: KTAV, 1968.

________. *Proselytism in the Talmudic Period.* Rev. ed. New York: KTAV, 1965.

Banks, R. *Jesus and the Law in the Synoptic Tradition.* Society for New Testament Studies Monograph Series 28. Cambridge: The University Press, 1975.

________. "Matthew's Understanding of the Law: Authenticity and Interpretation in Matthew." *Journal of Biblical Literature* 93 (1974): 226-42.

Barrett, C. K. *Jesus and the Gospel Tradition.* London: S.P.C.K., 1967.

Barth, G. "Matthew's Understanding of the Law." In G. Bornkamm, G. Barth, and H. J. Held, *Tradition and Interpretation in Matthew*, 58-164. Translated by Perry Scott. Philadelphia: Westminster Press, 1963.

Barth, K. "An Exegetical Study of Matthew 28:16-20." In K. Barth, *The Theology of the Christian Mission*, 55-71. Edited by Gerald H. Anderson. Translated by T. Weiser. New York: McGraw-Hill, 1961.

Baskin, Judith R. *Pharoah's Counsellors: Job, Jethro, and Balaam in Rabbinic and Patristic Tradition.* Brown Judaic Studies 47. Chico, CA: Scholars Press, 1983.

Bauer, Walter. *A Greek-English Lexicon of the New Testament and Other Early Christian Literature.* 4th rev. ed. Translated and adapted by William F. Arndt and F. Wilbur Gingrich. Chicago: The University of Chicago Press, 1952.

Baum, G. *Is the New Testament Anti-Semitic?* Rev. ed. Glen Rock, NJ: Paulist Press, 1965. (Originally published as *The Jews and the Gospel.* Westminster, MD: Newman Press, 1961.)

Bavinck, J. H. *An Introduction to the Science of Missions.* Translated by D. H. Freeman. Philadelphia: The Presbyterian and Reformed Publishing Co., 1960.

Beare, F. W. "The Mission of the Disciples and the Mission Charge: Matthew 10 and Parallels." *Journal of Biblical Literature* 89 (1970): 1-13.

_______. "The Sayings of Jesus in the Gospel According to St. Matthew," in *Studia Evangelica* 4, edited by F. L. Cross, 146-57. Texte und Untersuchungen zur Geschichte des altchristlichen Literatur 102. Berlin: Akademie-Verlag, 1968.

_______. "The Sayings of the Risen Jesus in the Gospel Tradition: An Inquiry into Their Origin and Significance." In *Christian History and Interpretation: Studies Presented to John Knox,* edited by W. F. Farmer, C. F. D. Moule, and R. R. Niebuhr, 161-81. Cambridge: The University Press, 1967.

Bishop, K. M. "St. Matthew and the Gentiles." *Expository Times* 59 (1947/48): 249.

Blair, Edward P. "Jesus and Salvation in the Gospel of Matthew." *McCormick Quarterly* 20 (1967): 301-8.

_______. *Jesus in the Gospel of Matthew.* New York and Nashville, TN: Abingdon Press, 1960.

Blauw, J. *The Missionary Nature of the Church.* New York: McGraw-Hill, 1962.

Bloch, Joseph S. *Israel and the Nations.* Translated by Leon Kellner. Translation revised by H. Schneiderman. Berlin and Vienna: Benjamin Harz Verlag, 1927.

Bloch, R. "Juda engendra Pharès et Zara, de Thamar, Matt 1,3." In *Mélanges bibliques redigés en l'honneur de A. Robert,* 381-89. Travaux de l'institut Catholique de Paris 4. Paris: Bloud and Gay, 1957.

Bornkamm, Günther. "End-Expectation and Church in Matthew." In G. Bornkamm, G. Barth, and H. J. Held, *Tradition and Interpretation in Matthew,* 15-51. Translated by Perry Scott. Philadelphia: Westminster Press, 1963.

_______. "The Risen Lord and the Earthly Jesus: Matthew 28:16-20." In *The Future of Our Religious Past*, edited by J. M. Robinson, 203-29. London: SCM Press, 1971.

Bourke, Myles M. "The Literary Genus of Matthew 1-2." *Catholic Biblical Quarterly* 22 (1960): 160-75.

Brandon, S. F. G. *Jesus and the Zealots*. Manchester, G. B.: Manchester University Press, 1967.

Braude, William G. *Jewish Proselytizing in the First Five Centuries of the Common Era*. Brown University Studies 6. Providence, RI: Brown University Press, 1940.

Brown, F., S. R. Driver, and C. A. Briggs. *Hebrew and English Lexicon of the Old Testament*. Oxford: Clarendon Press, 1975.

Brown, J. P. "The Form of 'Q' Known to Matthew." *New Testament Studies* 8 (1961/62): 27-42.

Brown, Raymond E. *The Birth of the Messiah*. New York: Doubleday and Co., Image Books, 1977.

_______. "Not Jewish Christianity and Gentile Christianity but Types of Jewish Gentile Christianity." *Catholic Biblical Quarterly* 45 (1983): 74-79.

Brown, Raymond E., and John P. Meier. *Antioch and Rome*. New York and Ramsey, NJ: Paulist Press, 1983.

Brown, Raymond, et al. *Mary in the New Testament*. Philadelphia: Fortress Press; New York: Paulist Press, 1978.

Brown, Schuyler. "The Matthean Community and the Gentile Mission." *Novum Testamentum* 22 (1980): 193-221.

________. "The Mission to Israel in Matthew's Central Section (MT 9:35-11:1)." *Zeitschrift für die neutestamentliche Wissenschaft* 69 (1978): 73-90.

________. "The Two-Fold Representation of the Mission in Matthew's Gospel." *Studia Theologica* 31 (1977): 21-32.

Bruns, J. E. "The Magi Episode in Matthew 2." *Catholic Biblical Quarterly* 23 (1961): 51-54.

Bultmann, Rudolf. *The History of the Synoptic Tradition.* Translated by John Marsh. Oxford: Basil Blackwell, 1963.

Carlston, Charles E. "Interpreting the Gospel of Matthew." *Interpretation* 29 (1975): 3-12.

________. "The Things That Defile (Mark vii.14) and the Law in Matthew and Mark." *New Testament Studies* 15 (1968): 75-96.

Cave, C. H. "St. Matthew's Infancy Narrative." *New Testament Studies* 9 (1962/63): 382-90.

Charlesworth, James H. "Christian and Jewish Self-Definition in Light of the Christian Additions to the Apocryphal Writings." In *Jewish and Christian Self-Definition.* Vol. 2, *Aspects of Judaism in the Greco-Roman Period,* edited by E. P. Sanders, with A. I. Baumgarten and A. Mendelson, 27-55. Philadelphia: Fortress Press, 1981.

Clark, Kenneth W. "The Gentile Bias in Matthew." *Journal of Biblical Literature* 66 (1947): 165-72.

Comber, Joseph A. "The Composition and Literary Characteristics of Matt 11:20-24." *Catholic Biblical Quarterly* 39 (1977): 497-504.

Conybeare, F. C. "Matthäus 28,9: The Eusebian Form of the Text." *Zeitschrift für die neutestamentliche Wissenschaft* 2 (1901): 275-88.

Conzelmann, H. *The Theology of Saint Luke.* Translated by Geoffrey Buswell. New York: Harper and Row, 1960.

Cope, O. Lamar. *Matthew, A Scribe Trained for the Kingdom of Heaven.* Catholic Biblical Quarterly Monograph Series 5. Washington, D.C.: Catholic Biblical Association of America, 1976.

________. "Matthew xxv: 31-46, 'The Sheep and the Goats' Reinterpreted." *Novum Testamentum* 11 (1969): 32-44.

Cox, G. E. P. *The Gospel According to Matthew: A Commentary.* Torch Bible Commentaries. London: SCM Press, 1952.

Crossan, D. M. "Anti-Semitism and the Gospel." *Theological Studies* 26 (1965): 189-214.

Dahl, N. A. "The Passion Narrative in Matthew." In *The Interpretation of Matthew*, edited by G. Stanton, 42-55. Issues in Religion and Theology 3. Philadelphia: Fortress Press; London: S.P.C.K., 1983. (First published in *Jesus in the Memory of the Early Church*, 37-51. Minneapolis, MN: Augsburg Publishing House, 1976. Translation of "Die Passionsgeschichte bei Matthäus." *New Testament Studies* 2 (1955/56): 17-32.)

Dalman, G. *The Words of Jesus.* Translated by D. M. Kay. Edinburgh: T. and T. Clark, 1902.

Daniélou, J. *The Infancy Narratives.* Translated by Rosemary Sheed. New York: Herder and Herder, 1968.

Daube, David. *The New Testament and Rabbinic Judaism.* London: The Athlone Press, University of London, 1956.

Davies, Alan T. "The Jews and the Death of Jesus." *Interpretation* 23 (1969): 207-17.

Davies, W. D. Review of *Das Matthäusevangelium. Ein judenchristliches Evangelium*, by P. Nepper-Christiansen. *Journal of Biblical Literature* 79 (1960): 88-91.

________. *The Setting of the Sermon on the Mount.* Cambridge: The University Press, 1964.

Davis, C. T. "Tradition and Redaction in Matthew 1:18-2:23." *Journal of Biblical Literature* 90 (1971): 404-21.

Denis, A. M. "L'Adoration des mages vue par S. Matthieu." *Nouvelle Revue Theologique* 82 (1960): 32-39.

De Ridder, R. R. *The Dispersion of the People of God: The Covenant Basis of Matthew 28:18-20 against the Background of Jewish, Pre-Christian Proselytizing and Diaspora, and the Apostleship of Jesus Christ.* Kampen, Neth.: J. H. Kok Co., 1971.

Derrett, J. Duncan M. "Further Light on the Narratives of the Nativity." *Novum Testamentum* 17 (1975): 81-108.

Dibelius, M. *From Tradition to Gospel.* Translated by B. L Woolf. New York: Scribner's Sons, 1935.

Dobschütz, Ernst von. "Matthäus als Rabbi und Katechet." *Zeitschrift für die neutestamentliche Wissenschaft* 27 (1928): 338-48.

Dodd, C. H. "Matthew and Paul." *Expository Times* 58 (1946/47): 293-98.

_______. *The Parables of the Kingdom.* New York: Charles Scribner's Sons, 1961.

_______. "The Portrait of Jesus in John and in the Synoptics." In *Christian History and Interpretation: Studies Presented to John Knox*, edited by W. F. Farmer, C. F. D. Moule, and R. R. Niebuhr, 183-98. Cambridge: The University Press, 1967.

Donaldson, Terence L. *Jesus on the Mountain: A Study in Matthean Theology.* Sheffield: JSOT Press, 1986.

Donfried, Karl Paul. "The Allegory of the Ten Virgins (Matt 25:1-13) as a Summary of Matthean Theology." *Journal of Biblical Literature* 93 (1974): 415-28.

Dupont, Jacques. "L'Arrière-fond biblique du récit des tentations de Jésus." *New Testament Studies* 3 (1956/57): 287-304.

Eliade, Mircea. *The Sacred and the Profane.* Translated by Willard Trask. New York: Harcourt, Brace, and World, 1959.

Fenton, J. C. *Saint Matthew.* Westminster Pelican Commentaries. Philadelphia: Westminster Press, 1963.

Feuillet, André. "Les Origines et la signification de Mt 10, 23b." *Catholic Biblical Quarterly* 23 (1961): 182-98.

Filson, Floyd V. "Broken Patterns in the Gospel of Matthew." *Journal of Biblical Literature* 75 (1956): 227-31.

_______. *A Commentary on the Gospel According to St. Matthew.* Harper's New Testament Commentaries. New York: Harper and Brothers, 1960.

Fiorenza, Elisabeth Schüssler. *In Memory of Her: A Feminist Theological Reconstruction of Christian Origins.* New York: Crossroad Press, 1983.

Fitzmyer, J. A. "Anti-Semitism and the Cry of 'All the People' (Mt 27:25)." *Theological Studies* 26 (1965): 667-71.

Frankemölle, H. *Jahwebund und Kirche Jesu. Studien zur Form- und Traditionsgeschichte des Evangeliums nach Matthäus.*

Neutestamentliche Abhandlungen, n. F., bd. 10. Münster: Aschendorff, 1974.

Franzmann, Martin H. *Follow Me: Discipleship According to St. Matthew.* St. Louis: Concordia Publishing House, 1961.

Gager, John G. *The Origins of Anti-Semitism: Attitudes toward Judaism in Pagan and Christian Antiquity.* New York and Oxford: Oxford University Press, 1983.

Garland, D. E. *The Intention of Matthew 23.* Supplements to *Novum Testamentum* 52. Leiden: E. J. Brill, 1979.

Gaston, Lloyd. "The Messiah of Israel as Teacher of the Gentiles: The Setting of Matthew's Christology." *Interpretation* 29 (1975): 24-40.

Gerhardsson, Birger. "The Parable of the Sower and Its Interpretation." *New Testament Studies* 14 (1968): 165-93.

_______. *The Testing of God's Son (Matt 4:1-11 and par): An Analysis of an Early Christian Midrash.* Lund, Swed.: CWK Gleerup, 1966.

Gibbs, J. M. "Purpose and Pattern in Matthew's Use of the Title 'Son of David'." *New Testament Studies* 10 (1963/64): 446-64.

Giblin, Charles H. "Theological Perspective and Matthew 10:23b." *Theological Studies* 29 (1968): 637-61.

Gnilka, J. *Die Verstockung Israels -- Isaias 6,9-10 in der Theologie der Synoptiker.* Studien zum Alten und Neuen Testament 3. Munich: Kosel-Verlag, 1961.

Goldstein, Jonathan A. "Jewish Acceptance and Rejection of Hellenism." In *Jewish and Christian Self-Definition.* Vol. 2, *Aspects of Judaism in the Greco-Roman Period,* edited by E. P. Sanders, with A. I. Baumgarten and A. Mendelson, 64-87, 310-26. Philadelphia: Fortress Press, 1981.

Goldstein, Morris. *Jesus in the Jewish Tradition.* New York: The Macmillan Co., 1950.

Green, H. B. *The Gospel According to Matthew.* New Clarendon Bible. London: Oxford University Press, 1975.

Grindel, John. "Matthew 12, 18-21." *Catholic Biblical Quarterly* 29 (1967): 110-15.

Guelich, Robert A. "Not to Annul the Law Rather to Fulfill the Law and the Prophets: An Exegetical Study of Jesus and the Law in Matthew with Emphasis on 5:17-48." Ph.D. diss., University of Hamburg, 1967.

Gundry, Robert Horton. *Matthew: A Commentary on His Literary and Theological Art.* Grand Rapids, MI: Eerdmans, 1982.

__________. *The Use of the Old Testament in St. Matthew's Gospel.* Supplements to *Novum Testamentum* 18. Leiden: E. J. Brill, 1967.

Güttgemans, Erhard T. *Candid Questions Concerning Gospel Form Criticism: A Methodological Sketch of Fundamental Problematics of Form and Redaction Criticism.* 2d ed. Translated by William G. Doty. Pittsburgh Theological Monographs 26. Allison Park, PA: Pickwick Press, 1979.

Haenchen, E. "Matthäus 23." *Zeitschrift für Theologie und Kirche* 48 (1951): 38-62.

Hahn, F. *Mission in the New Testament.* Studies in Biblical Theology 47. London: Alec R. Allenson, 1965.

Hare, Douglas R. A. "The Rejection of the Jews in the Synoptic Gospels and Acts." In *Antisemitism and the Foundations of Christianity*, edited by Alan Davies, 27-47. New York: Paulist Press, 1979.

_______. *The Theme of Jewish Persecution of Christians in the Gospel According to St. Matthew.* Society for New Testament Studies Monograph Series 6. Cambridge; The University Press, 1967.

Hare, Douglas R. A., and Daniel J. Harrington. "'Make Disciples of All the Gentiles' (Mt 28:19)." *Catholic Biblical Quarterly* 37 (1975): 359-69.

Heffern, Andrew D. "The Four Women in St. Matthew's Genealogy of Christ." *Journal of Biblical Literature* 31 (1912): 69-81.

Held, Heinz Joachim. "Matthew as Interpreter of the Miracle Stories." In G. Bornkamm, G. Barth, and H. J. Held,

Tradition and Interpretation in Matthew, 165-299. Translated by Perry Scott. Philadelphia: Westminster Press, 1963.

Higgins, A. J. B. "The Sign of the Son of Man (Mt xxiv,30)." *New Testament Studies* 9 (1962/63): 380-82.

Hill, David. *The Gospel of Matthew.* New Century Bible. London: Oliphants, 1972.

Hooke, S. H. "Jesus and the Centurion: Matthew vii.5-10." *Expository Times* 69 (1957/58): 79-80.

Hooker, Morna D. "Christology and Methodology." *New Testament Studies* 17 (1971): 480-87.

_______. "Uncomfortable Words X: The Prohibition of Foreign Missions (Matt 10:5-6)." *Expository Times* 82 (1971): 361-65.

Howton, J. "The Sign of Jonah." *Scottish Journal of Theology* 15 (1962): 288-304.

Hubbard, Benjamin J. *The Matthean Redaction of a Primitive Apostolic Commissioning: An Exegesis of Mt 28:16-20.* Society of Biblical Literature Dissertation Series 19. Missoula, MT: Scholars Press, 1974.

Hummel, Reinhart. *Die Auseinandersetzung zwischen Kirche und Judentum im Matthäusevangelium.* Beiträge zur evangelischen Theologie 22. Munich: Kaiser-Verlag, 1966.

Jeremias, J. "The Gentile World in the Thought of Jesus." *Studiorum Novi Testamenti Societas Bulletin* 3 (1952): 18-28.

_______. *Jesus' Promise to the Nations.* Translated by S. H. Hooke. Studies in Biblical Theology 24. London: SCM Press, 1967.

_______. *The Parables of Jesus.* Rev. ed. Translated by S. H. Hooke (from the 6th German ed.). New York: Charles Scribner's Sons, 1963.

_______. *Rediscovering the Parables.* New York: Scribner's, 1966.

Johnson, M. D. *The Purpose of the Biblical Genealogies with Special Reference to the Setting of the Genealogies of*

Jesus. Society for New Testament Studies Monograph Series 8. Cambridge: The University Press, 1969.

Käsemann, E. "The Problem of the Historical Jesus." In *Essays on New Testament Themes*. Translated by W. J. Montague. Napierville, Il: Allenson, 1964.

Kasting, H. *Die Anfänge der urchristlichen Mission*. Munich: Kaiser-Verlag, 1969.

Kennard, J. Spencer, Jr. "The Place of Origin of Matthew's Gospel." *Anglican Theological Review* 31 (1949): 243-46.

_______. "The Reconciliation Tendenz in Matthew." *Anglican Theological Review* 28 (1946): 159-63.

Kiddle, M. "The Death of Jesus and the Admission of the Gentiles in St. Mark." *Journal of Theological Studies* 35 (1934): 45-50.

Kilpatrick, G. D. "The Gentile Mission in Mark and Mark 13:9-11." In *Studies in the Gospels. Essays in Memory of R. H. Lightfoot*, edited by D. E. Nineham, 145-58. Oxford: Basil Blackwell, 1955.

_______. *The Origins of the Gospel According to St. Matthew*. Oxford: Clarendon Press, 1946.

Kingsbury, Jack Dean. "The Composition and Christology of Matt 28:16-20." *Journal of Biblical Literature* 93 (1974): 573-84.

_______. "The Figure of Peter in Matthew's Gospel as a Theological Problem." *Journal of Biblical Literature* 98 (1979): 67-83.

_______. "Form and Message of Matthew." *Interpretation* 29 (1975): 13-23.

_______. *Matthew*. Proclamation Commentaries. Philadelphia: Fortress Press, 1977.

_______. *Matthew: Structure, Christology, Kingdom*. Philadelphia: Fortress Press, 1975.

_______. "The Structure of Matthew's Gospel and His Concept of Salvation History." *Catholic Biblical Quarterly* 35 (1973): 451-74.

Knox, John. "Romans 15:14-33 and Paul's Conception of His Apostolic Mission." *Journal of Biblical Literature* 83 (1964): 1-11.

Kraabel, A. T. "The Roman Diaspora: Six Questionable Assumptions." In *Essays in Honour of Yigael Yadin*, edited by G. Vermes and J. Neusner, 445-64 (= *Journal of Judaic Studies* 33 [1982]).

Krentz, E. "The Extent of Matthew's Prologue. Towards the Structure of the First Gospel." *Journal of Biblical Studies* 83 (1964): 409-14.

Kümmel, W. G. *Promise and Fulfillment.* 2d English ed. Translated by D. M. Barton. Studies in Biblical Theology 23. London: SCM Press, 1961.

La Piana, G. "Foreign Groups in Rome during the First Centuries of the Empire." *Harvard Theological Review* 20 (1927): 183-403.

Leany, R. "The Birth Narratives in St. Luke and St. Matthew." *New Testament Studies* 8 (1961/62): 158-66.

Linton, O. "The Demand for a Sign from Heaven." *Studia Theologica* 19 (1965): 112-29.

Lohmeyer, Ernst. "Das Abendmahl in der Urgemeinde." *Journal of Biblical Literature* 56 (1937): 217-52.

_________. "'Mir ist gegeben alle Gewalt!' Eine Exegese von Mt 28.16-20." In *In Memoriam Ernst Lohmeyer*, edited by W. Schmauch, 22-49. Stuttgart: Evangelisches Verlagswerk, 1951.

Lohr, C. H. "Oral Techniques in the Gospel of Matthew." *Catholic Biblical Quarterly* 23 (1961): 403-35.

Luz, U. "The Disciples in the Gospel According to Matthew." In *The Interpretation of Matthew*, edited by G. Stanton, 98-128. Issues in Religion and Theology 3. Philadelphia: Fortress Press; London: S.P.C.K., 1983. (Originally published as "Die Jünger im Matthäusevangelium," *Zeitschrift für die neutestamentliche Wissenschaft* 62 [1971]: 141-71.)

McCasland, S. V. "Matthew Twists the Scriptures." *Journal of Biblical Literature* 80 (1961): 143-48.

McNeile, Alan Hugh. *The Gospel According to St. Matthew.* London: Macmillan and Co., 1915.

Malina, B. "The Literary Structure and Form of Matt. xxviii.16-20." *New Testament Studies* 17 (1970): 87-103.

Mann, C. S. "Epiphany -- Wise Men or Charlatans?" *Theology* 61 (1958): 495-500.

Manson, T. W. *Jesus and the Non-Jews.* London: Athlone Press, University of London, 1955.

_______. *The Sayings of Jesus.* London: SCM Press, 1971.

_______. *The Teaching of Jesus.* Cambridge: The University Press, 1945.

Martin, Ralph P. "St. Matthew's Gospel in Recent Study." *Expository Times* 80 (1969): 132-36.

Meier, John P. *Antioch and Rome* (= Brown, Raymond E., and J. P. Meier, *Antioch and Rome*).

_______. *Law and History in Matthew's Gospel. A Redactional Study of Mt 5:17-48.* Analecta Biblica 71. Rome: Biblical Institute Press, 1976.

_______. "Nations or Gentiles in Matthew 28:19?" *Catholic Biblical Quarterly* 39 (1977): 94-102.

_______. "Salvation-History in Matthew: In Search of a Starting Point." *Catholic Biblical Quarterly* 37 (1975): 203-15.

_______. "Two Disputed Questions in Matt. 28:16-20." *Journal of Biblical Literature* 96 (1977): 407-24.

_______. *The Vision of Matthew: Christ, Church and Morality in the First Gospel.* Theological Inquiries. New York: Paulist Press, 1979.

Meyer, Ben F. "Jesus and the Remnant of Israel." *Journal of Biblical Literature* 84 (1965): 123-30.

Meyer, Paul D. "The Gentile Mission in Q." *Journal of Biblical Literature* 89 (1970): 405-17.

Michaels, J. Ramsey. "Apostolic Hardships and Righteous Gentiles: A Study of Matthew 25:31-46." *Journal of Biblical Literature* 84 (1965): 27-37.

Michel, O. "Der Abschluss des Matthäusevangeliums." *Evangelische Theologie* 10 (1950/51): 16-26.

Milton, Helen. "The Structure of the Prologue to St. Matthew's Gospel." *Journal of Biblical Literature* 81 (1962): 175-81.

Moo, Douglas J. "Jesus and the Authority of the Mosaic Law." *Journal for the Study of the New Testament* 20 (1984): 23-28.

Munck, Johannes. "Israel and the Gentiles in the New Testament." *Studiorum Novi Testamenti Societas Bulletin* 1 (1950): 26-38.

_______. "Jewish Christianity in Post-Apostolic Times." *New Testament Studies* 6 (1960): 103-16.

_______. *Paul and the Salvation of Mankind.* Richmond, VA: John Knox Press, 1959.

Murray, Robert. "Jews, Hebrews, and Christians: Some Needed Distinctions." *Novum Testamentum* 24 (1982): 194-208.

O'Collins, G. G. "Anti-Semitism in the Gospel." *Theological Studies* 26 (1965): 663-66.

Parkes, J. *The Conflict of the Church and the Synagogue.* New York: Atheneum, 1969.

Perrin, Norman. "The Evangelist as Author: Reflections on Method in the Study and Interpretation of the Synoptic Gospels and Acts." *Biblical Research* 17 (1972): 5-18.

_______. Review of *Die Heidenmission in der Zukunftssschau Jesu* by D. Bosch. *Journal of Biblical Literature* 79 (1960): 188-89.

Plummer, Alfred. *An Exegetical Commentary on the Gospel According to St. Matthew.* 3d ed. London: Robert Scott, 1911.

Pokorny, P. "The Temptation Stories and Their Intention." *New Testament Studies* 20 (1974): 115-27.

Raisin, Jacob S. *Gentile Reactions to Jewish Ideals with Special Reference to Proselytes.* New York: Philosophical Library, 1953.

Reumann, John. Review of *Das Wahre Israel* by W. Trilling. *Journal of Biblical Literature* 79 (1960): 376-79.

Reventlow, H. "Sein Blut komme über sein Haupt." *Vetus Testamentum* 10 (1960): 311-27.

Robinson, J. A. T. "The 'Parable' of the Sheep and the Goats." *New Testament Studies* 2 (1955/56): 225-37.

_______. Review of *Jesu Verheissung für die Völker* (*Jesus' Promise to the Nations*) by J. Jeremias. *Journal of Biblical Literature* 68 (1959): 101-4.

Rohde, Joachim. *Rediscovering the Teachings of the Evangelists*. New Testament Library. Philadelphia: Westminster Press, 1968.

Sanders, E. P. *Jesus and Judaism*. Philadelphia: Fortress Press, 1985.

Schaberg, Jane. *The Father, the Son and the Holy Spirit: The Triadic Phrase in Matthew 28:19b*. Society of Biblical Literature Dissertation Series 61. Chico, CA: Scholars Press, 1982.

Schille, G. "Bemerkungen zur Formgeschichte des Evangeliums II. Das Evangelium des Matthäus als Katechismus." *New Testament Studies* 4 (1957/58): 101-14.

Schweizer, Eduard. *The Good News According to Matthew*. Atlanta: John Knox Press, 1975.

_______. "Matthew's Church." Translated by R. Morgan. In *The Interpretation of Matthew*, edited by G. Stanton, 129-55. Issues in Religion and Theology 3. Philadelphia: Fortress Press; London: S.P.C.K., 1983. (Originally published in E. Schweizer, *Matthäus und seine Gemeinde* [Stuttgart: Verlag Katholisches Bibelwerk, 1974], pp. 138-70.)

_______. "Observance of the Law and Charismatic Activity in Matthew." *New Testament Studies* 16 (1970): 213-30.

Senior, Donald P. "The Death of Jesus and the Resurrection of the Holy Ones (Mt 27:51-53)." *Catholic Biblical Quarterly* 38 (1976): 312-29.

_______. *Invitation to Matthew*. Garden City, NY: Doubleday and Co., Image Books, 1977.

_______. *The Passion Narrative According to Matthew: A Redactional Study.* Bibliotheca Ephemeridum Theologicarum Lovaniensium 39. Louvain: Leuven University Press, 1975.

Sevenster, J. N. *The Roots of Pagan Anti-Semitism in the Ancient World.* Supplements to *Novum Testamentum* 41. Leiden: E. J. Brill, 1975.

Smith, C. W. F. "The Mixed State of the Church in Matthew's Gospel." *Journal of Biblical Literature* 82 (1963) 149-68.

Smith, J. Z. "Earth and Gods." Chapter 5 in *Map Is Not Territory.* Leiden: E. J. Brill, 1978.

Spitta, F. "Die Frauen in der Genealogie des Matthäus." *Zeitschrift für wissenschaftliche Theologie* 54 (1912): 1-8

Stegemann, H. "'Die des Uria': Zur Bedetung der Frauennamen in der Genealogie von Matthäus 1,11-17." In *Tradition und Glaube: Festgabe für K. G. Kuhn*, edited by G. Jeremias et al., 246-76. Göttingen: Vandenhoeck and Ruprecht, 1972.

Stendhal, K. "The First Gospel and the Authority of Jesus." (Review of *Jesus in the Gospel of Matthew* by E. P. Blair.) *Interpretation* 16 (1962): 461-64.

_______. "Quis et Unde? An Analysis of Mt 1-2." In *The Interpretation of Matthew*, edited by G. Stanton, 56-66. Issues in Religion and Theology 3. Philadelphia: Fortress Press; London: S.P.C.K., 1983. (Originally published in *Judentum, Urchristentum, Kirche,* edited by W. Eltester, 94-105. Berlin: Töpelmann, 1960.)

_______. *The School of St. Matthew.* 2d ed. Philadelphia: Fortress Press, 1968.

Stoevesandt, H. Summary of "Jesus und die Heidenmission." Ph.D. diss., University of Göttingen. *Theologische Literaturzeitung* 74 (1949): 242.

Strecker, G. "The Concept of History in Matthew." In *The Interpretation of Matthew*, edited by G. Stanton, 67-84. Issues in Religion and Theology 3. Philadelphia: Fortress

Press; London: S.P.C.K., 1983. (Originally published in German in *Evangelische Theologie* 26 [1966]: 57-74; in part translated and reprinted in *Journal of the American Academy of Religion* 35 [1967]: 219-30.)

_______. *Der Weg der Gerechtigkeit.* Forschungen zur Religion und Literatur des Alten und Neuen Testaments 82. Göttingen: Vandenhoeck and Ruprecht, 1966.

Streeter, B. H. *The Four Gospels.* London: Macmillan and Co., 1956.

Suggs, M. J. *Wisdom, Christology, and Law in Matthew's Gospel.* Cambridge: Harvard University Press, 1970.

Suhl, A. "Der Davidssohn im Matthäus-Evangelium." *Zeitschrift für die neutestamentliche Wissenchaft* 59 (1968): 67-81.

Tagawa, K. "People and Community in the Gospel of Matthew." *New Testament Studies* 16 (1970): 149-62.

Tatum, W. Barnes. "The Origin of Jesus Messiah (Matt 1:1,18a): Matthew's Use of the Infancy Traditions." *Journal of Biblical Literature* 96 (1977): 523-35.

Theissen, Gerd. *Sociology of Early Palestinian Christianity.* Translated by John Bowden. Philadelphia: Fortress Press, 1977.

Thompson, W. G. "An Historical Perspective in the Gospel of Matthew." *Journal of Biblical Literature* 93 (1974): 243-62.

_______. *Matthew's Advice to a Divided Community: Mt. 17,22-18,35.* Analecta Biblica 44. Rome: Biblical Institute Press, 1970.

Tilborg, S. van. *The Jewish Leaders in Matthew.* Leiden: E. J. Brill, 1972.

Trilling, Wolfgang. *Das Wahre Israel.* 3d ed. Studien zum Alten und Neuen Testament 10. Munich: Kösel-Verlag, 1964.

Via, D. O. "Matthew on the Understanding of the Parables." *Journal of Biblical Literature* 84 (1965): 430-32.

Vogelstein, Hermann. "The Development of the Apostolate in Judaism and Its Transformation in Christianity." *Hebrew Union College Annual* 2 (1925): 99-123.

Vögtle, A. "Die matthäische Kindheitsgeschichte," in *L'Evangile selon Matthieu: Rédaction et théologie*, edited by M. Didier, 153-83. Gembloux: Duculot, 1972.

Waetjen, H. C. "The Genealogy as the Key to the Gospel According to Matthew." *Journal of Biblical Literature* 95 (1976): 205-30.

Walker, Norman. "The Alleged Matthean Errata." *New Testament Studies* 9 (1962/63): 391-94.

Walker, R. *Die Heilsgeschichte im ersten Evangelium*. Göttingen: Vandenhoeck and Ruprecht, 1967.

Walker, William O., Jr. "A Method for Identifying Redactional Passages in Matthew On Functional and Linguistic Grounds." *Catholic Biblical Quarterly* 39 (1977): 76-93.

Weir, T. H. "Mt x.23." *Expository Times* 37 (1925/26): 237.

Wilkinson, J. "Apologetic Aspects of the Virgin Birth of Jesus Christ." *Scottish Journal of Theology* 17 (1964): 159-81.

Wilson, Stephen G. *The Gentiles and the Gentile Mission in Luke-Acts*. Society for New Testament Studies Monograph Series 23. Cambridge: The University Press, 1973.

Index of Subjects

Index of Scriptural Passages

STUDIES IN THE BIBLE AND EARLY CHRISTIANITY

1. Hugh M. Humphrey, **A Bibliography for the Gospel of Mark, 1954-1980**
2. Rolland Wolfe, **The Twelve Religions of the Bible**
3. Jean LaPorte, *Eucharistia* **in Philo**
4. Peter Gorday, **Principles of Patristic Exegesis: Romans 9-11 in Origen, John Chrysostom, and Augustine**
5. Marcus J. Borg, **Conflict, Holiness & Politics in the Teachings of Jesus**
6. Watson E. Mills, **Glossolalia: A Bibliography**
7. Matthew Baasten, **Pride According to Gregory the Great: A Study of the Moralia**
8. Douglas Oakman, **Jesus and The Economic Questions of His Day**
9. John McGuckin, **The Transfiguration of Christ in Scripture and Tradition**
10. Raymond A. Martin, **Syntax Criticism of the Synoptic Gospels**
11. Tom Robinson, **The Bauer Thesis Examined: The Geography of Heresy in the Early Christian Church**
12. John Chrysostom (translated by Duane A. Garrett), **Commentary on Isaiah 1-8**
13. John Chrysostom (translated by David G. Hunter), **A Comparison Between A King and A Monk/Against the Opponents of the Monastic Life**
14. Amy-Jill Levine, **The Social and Ethnic Dimensions of Matthean Salvation History: "Go nowhere among the Gentiles..." (Matt. 10.5b)**
15. Allan Fitzgerald, O.S.A., **Conversion Through Penance in the Italian Church of the Fourth and Fifth Centuries: New Approaches to the Experience of Conversion from Sin**
16. William Craig, **Assessing the New Testament Evidence for the Historicity of the Resurrection of Jesus**